Nicolas Schwalbe

Living wayside(s)
The Unheard Intercultural Philosophy of François Jullien

De-coincidence press

*To the memory of my grandfather(s),
great lover(s) of books and civilization(s).*

CONTENTS

CHAPTER IX
Truly living or "life truly lived."

CHAPTER X
Re-opening possibilities: de-coincidence, an *ars operandi*.

CODA
De-coincidence, (a)live transmission(s): encounter(s)

Foreword
The Story of an Encounter.

I first encountered François Jullien's writing when I returned home to Paris at the outset of the Covid-19 pandemic after living in the US for ten years. At the time, I was beginning my doctoral research program at Université Sorbonne Paris Nord and was discovering that my French colleagues did not always welcome my ideas and presence with enthusiasm.

Hell-bent upon making sense of the clinical experiences I had had working as a psychiatric social worker for a large publicly funded mental-health provider in Los Angeles, I was determined to investigate why my own personal obsession with Early China and its medical treatises seemed to somehow elicit interest and therapeutic effects with some of the patients I had worked with over the past two years, many of whom suffered either from chronic homelessness, psychosis, drug addiction or a combination of the above.

As I left California's sunny and yet dystopian New Age shores and penetrated Paris' sublime gothic gloom once more, I realized that I would need to rekindle with the dense language of freudo-lacanian psychoanalysis to make my voice heard in the Parisian academic and clinical milieu.[1] The psychotherapeutic practice combining talk-therapy with traditional breathing and visualization techniques associated with "Eastern spirituality" that I was developing in LA and that had warranted that I receive the "Lilian Hawthorne Award for Innovation in the Field of Social Work" at the University of Southern California provoked, at best puzzlement, and at worst scorn, from more than a few Parisian colleagues who remained committed to an irreducible, characteristically French, and undeniably Cartesian form of methodological doubt when it comes to all matters "Eastern" and "spiritual."[2] One university professor stated that she would be willing to accept me as one of her doctoral students only on the condition that I let go of the "integrative" aspect of my research proposal[3]; my passion for Ancient China's medical treatises was of "absolutely no interest" to her. Another aging analyst evaluating my admissibility in a psychoanalytic society told me from behind her gold-minted desk: "What does Ancient Chinese medicine have to do with psychoanalysis? Don't you think you're making a bit of a stretch there? You don't want to be a jack of all trades and a master of none, now do you? My advice for you: forget about Ancient China, focus on psychoanalysis."

Through a fortunate twist of fate, I found early on in the figure of my doctoral advisor a sincere supporter who welcomed the singularity of my itinerary, the unorthodoxy of my proposal, and the value of the clinical experience I was bringing to the table. He encouraged me to pursue the philosophical and epistemological questions that my research brought about; and yet, he also cautioned me and strongly suggested that I avoid any form of analysis that would merely content itself with a comparison of Ancient Chinese medicine and psychoanalysis and simply enumerate the "resemblances and differences" separating and uniting the two clinical practices. Heeding his advice, I (re)read a great deal of Freud, discovered the sinophilic works of Jacques Lacan,[4] and thus began to penetrate the notoriously demanding academic field of sinology in order to approach Ancient Chinese medical treatises from a philological, historical, and philosophical perspective.[5] As I was browsing about in a large bookstore of the Latin Quarter, seeking inspiration and mulling over the difficulty of the task that I had set up for myself, I stumbled upon a used copy of François Jullien's Conference on Efficacy.[6] *His name sounded familiar and the fourth-cover indicated that the book was about Ancient Chinese strategy; it was an inexpensive used copy so I made an "impulse purchase." I justified this impulse-buy with some form of rationalization along the lines of "strategy and efficacy get people hooked; this could be useful somewhere down the line." I walked back home from the bookstore, sat down on the couch, and opened the book: as soon as I began reading, I knew there and then that I had found precisely what*

I had been looking for ever since I had returned to Paris.

*

It was not only François Jullien's sinological erudition which captivated my attention; above all else, it was his philosophical acumen coupled with his engaging and stylized prose. I had finally found a voice that eloquently justified the utility and importance of an interdisciplinary and methodological recourse to Early Chinese thought in strong, well-written, and convincing terms. As a student of French philosophy, Ancient Greek, German, and Comparative Literature, I was delighted to find an author and specialist of Ancient China whose analyses were also grounded in this distinctly "continental" heritage.[7] When I found out that he had also written a book about the usage of Early Chinese thought in psychoanalysis and that his work had been widely received in the Francophone psychoanalytic world,[8] I knew that I had no other choice but to dive deep into the rivetingly dense work of this author who had written more than forty books over the course of the past 30 years.

After having read about ten of them, I reached out to him over email to tell him about my clinical practice and research; he very cordially responded within a couple of hours and expressed his interest in my work, suggesting that we talk over the phone. Following our first phone conversation, he invited me to meet him in-person in his office during the peak of the second wave of Covid-19 lockdowns in Paris. The following book is the result of this encounter and of the working relationship that developed from it.

***

The aim of this book is to provide a synthetic overview of the entirety of François Jullien's published works for the academic and non-academic anglophone public: it is not so much a "critical introduction" as it is a "reader."[9] The book offers pedagogical syntheses of many of Jullien's already translated works, as well as supplement-

ed translations of select passages of some of his most important books which have yet to be published in English.[10] For the past ten years, Jullien has taken a "turn" as a philosopher: he has developed a singular philosophy of living *that is not as explicitly grounded in sinology and in the intercultural "comparatist" work that he is most known for in the anglophone (academic) world.*[11] *One of the core purposes of this book is to promote this* living *aspect of his philosophy, as it is arguably the most important one – not just for academics, but for* all *readers.*

*

In an effort to maintain a coherent style of writing throughout the book, I have chosen to not write any commentary along the lines of "François Jullien writes that..." or "for François Jullien..." and I do not mention his name outside of this introduction and few notes. Readers that wish to develop their own critical perspective of his philosophical project can refer back to Jullien's books and to the bibliography at this end of this volume. The bibliography offers a complete list of available English translations of Jullien's books, as well as a comprehensive overview of existing English-language publications on his work.

This book's core purpose is not to situate François Jullien's work within the contemporary academic fields of philosophy, sinology, and/or "cultural studies." Rather to offer readers a comprehensive and immediate point of entry into his illuminating and yet, as he puts it himself, distinctly French *and unapologetically* demanding *style of writing and thinking. This book is not meant to be read in a rapturous, quantifiable frenzy and should instead be savored over the course of an extendable and qualitative* philosophical moment *that moves alongside the rhythm of the seasons, at its own unhurried pace.*

*

Before going any further, it makes sense to offer a brief explanation of the concept suggested by the title of this book: the wayside(s).

François Jullien has explicitly stated that his concept of the way-side(s) can essentially be thought of as his alternative to the over-played concept of difference:

> "The concepts of difference and of the *wayside* both mark a separation; difference marks this separation under the auspice of (a) *distinction*, while the wayside does so under the auspice of (a) *distance*.
>
> As it makes its distinctions, difference determines a specificity that leads to a definition. [...] Difference is classificatory [...], it allows us to compartmentalize knowledge, its primary function is to identify and classify. Difference fixates itself upon a specificity or an identifiable feature; in doing so, it casts aside what it has not identified: once I have defined A in relationship to its difference with B, I cast aside B and only keep A and its perceived identity.
>
> The wayside, on the other hand, *opens up* a distance. It does not involve (an) *identification*; instead, it suggests (an) *exploration*. [...] It leads us out of the normed, of the expected, and of the convened: when we explore uncharted territories, we wander *on the wayside* of conventions, be they linguistic or behavioral."[12]

As a concept, the wayside functions both on an analytical and existential level. On an analytical level, it allows the "exploration" of a potentially infinite number of (cultural) patterns that cease to be automatically assigned to immutable positions of dissimilarity and/or resemblance, "difference" and/or "identity." Much of the contents of this book will be devoted to exploring how the concept of the wayside allows us to circulate in between European and Chinese literary and philosophical traditions, without having to resort to the enclosures of "cultural identity."[13]

On an existential level, the concept of the wayside acts like a foundational, inter-cultural metaphor that allows us to find the "distance" we need to stand outside the identifiable confines of the world. As I explore waysides, I step out of the well-trodden (and yet inert) pathways of commonplace knowledge; I begin to stand outside my habitual tendencies, my "values," my "relationships," and "myself" altogether. On the wayside, *I can experience exhilaration as I venture out into the unknown; I can also find an* intimate shelter *that protects me from the noisy storms of life. The exploration of a wayside (re) opens an* in between. *The* operative (no)place *of the wayside lies in between the road and its limit,* in between *You and I, in between Us and Them. When we explore waysides together, we tap into a constant and ceaseless capacity that allows all of us, not "to be," but rather to (co)operate, pass through, and, finally, live.*

*

Although the existential dimension of philosophy which touches upon death, intimacy, and sexual pleasure appeals (in theory) to all of us, its technical features as a geographically and historically determined academic field of inquiry and its embeddedness in contingent processes of translation and intercultural exchange require both patience and caution. Anyone who wishes to find "one-size-fits-all" answers to life's great questions about God, Death, and Sex in this book will inevitably be disappointed by its contents. My desire is to instead encourage readers to wander on the wayside *of the boring, boorish, and insidious* ideologies *which color the innumerable "recipes for living" that inundate doctrinal approaches to religion, self-help literature, and social media discourse.*

The (scholarly) resources *that this book offers readers are* demanding: *they* challenge *a desire for instant satisfaction that is only becoming more and more ubiquitous with the proliferation of digital technology. "Rome was not built in a day" as the saying goes and one does not become well-versed in the foundational texts that have shaped human civilizations across Time and Space over the course of an afternoon. The process of learning Classical languages like Ancient Greek, Latin, Sanskrit, and Classical Chinese is in many ways the polar opposite of a process of instant gratification.*

*

Most of the works cited in this book- aside from François Jul-

lien's own writings and a few scholarly tomes and articles- can be freely accessed, both in translation and in their original language, on the World Wide Web. This book aims to be a democratic work of scholarship that seeks to make available, not only the works of François Jullien, but also the timeless resources of Ancient and Classical literature available for students, scholars, and lay-folk around the globe. My hope is that by introducing a wider audience to the "extreme importance, newness, and fecundity" of François Jullien's "diagonal research,"[14] I can also contribute to the transmission, diffusion, and promotion of some of the foundational texts that have enriched human existence throughout History. These reference(d) texts continuously circulate in between cultures, places, and eras: the process of their exchange and translation throughout Time and Space highlights a universalizing common ground(s) of intelligence. Ancient and Classical philosophical writings indeed still hold the capacity to transform our daily lives; not in an instance of immediate gratification, but rather one sentence and "one day at a time," as the infamous and yet potent truism goes...

***

The book is structured in a series of ten chapters and two annexes composed of multiple sections and sub-sections intended to help readers navigate throughout its contents according to their personal interests. The endnotes provide references for Jullien's source texts as well as further bibliographical indications and commentaries for the scholarly (or simply curious) reader. The principal themes of each chapter are outlined below:

Chapter I, "Philosophy in between Cultures," provides a justification for the strategic usage of Classical Chinese literature in a philosophical context; in order to do so, it offers a pedagogical overview of the two pivotal Ancient Greek concepts or "philosophemes" that structure Western thought -Being and logos. This quick overview lays the foundation for the reader to understand the intercultural philosophy developed by François Jullien and its relationship to the practice of translation.

The second chapter, "Yang Sheng or Nourishing Living," continues to questions constitutive categories of Western thought like the "body" and "soul" by turning towards the Zhuangzi, *the* Laozi *and the* Mengzi, *three of the most revered literary and philosophical texts of Ancient China.*[15] *The chapter is a useful introduction to Classical Chinese thought for readers that are not familiar with it as it offers a synthetic overview of its key notions like* Yin/Yang, Dao *and* Qi, *as well as insights into the lesser-known expression* Yang Sheng. *It should be of particular interest to students of Chinese Medicine, Martial Arts, and Zen Buddhism who wish to familiarize themselves with foundational Classical Chinese texts that continue to bear a decisive influence on their respective fields of study and practice.*

The third chapter, "Strategies of Efficacy," *approaches the question of strategy from an intercultural perspective and offers a synthetic overview of key elements of Ancient Chinese strategic literature (the famous* Art of War) *and Ancient Greek philosophy. It explores the ways in which notions like effortless action or* Wu Wei *and concepts like* modelization, maturation, *and* silent transformation *can be used across a wide range of strategic, political, and economic situations today.*

Chapter IV, "From "Being Here Now" to Living in/with the moment(s)," *approaches the philosophical question of temporality or of "Time" from a geo-historical, epistemological, and sinological perspective. Drawing readers into a complex web of reasoning that invites them to question the universality of the category of "Time," it etches out in that process the contours of an intercultural* philosophy of living *which lies* in between *cultures and* on the wayside of ideology.

The 5th chapter, "The Bland, the Nude, and the Beautiful," *provides an introductory overview of key notions of Classical Chinese and Western esthetic culture. It also calls into question the falsely universal concept of "the Beautiful" that the now globalized academic discipline of "esthetics" has promoted in both the East and the West over the course of the past two centuries.*

Chapter VI, "Resource(s) of the Intimate," *offers an intercultural perspective on the (neglected) European notion of the* intimate. *It draws upon St. Augustine and Rousseau's* Confessions *and a late 18th century Classical Chinese text (Shen Fu's* 6 Notes on Floating Living*) to promote a philosophical concept of the intimate as an* existential resource.

The seventh chapter, "When the Idea of God does not Unfold," *investigates the historical encounter that occurred between European Jesuit priests and Imperial Court scholars in 16th century China. By examining Early Chinese sources as well as Early Modern French sources, the chapter outlines the ways in which this* encounter *between East and West can be thought of as an opportunity to reflect upon our understanding of one of the (academic) world's most hotly debated philosophical concepts: the (metaphysical)* Other.

Chapter VIII, "The Incommensurable Unheard or the Metaphysical Minimal(s)," *offers the most extensive insight into François Jullien's "existential" turn as a philosopher. It draws upon not only a series of textual analyses but also upon singular experiences that rupture daily living from within; mundane and yet life-changing moments that compel us to come to terms with an ineradicable* metaphysical minimal: *an "Other" which colors our experience of orgasm, death, and the intimate.*

Chapter IX, "Truly Living or "Life Truly Lived," *offers a close-reading and translation of select passages of Proust's* In Search of Lost Time *and of the 12th century Song-dynasty era Chinese Buddhist text* Wu-men Guan, *or* Gateless Barrier, *alongside reflections on Plato and Theodor Adorno's* Minima Moralia. *By way of these close readings and meticulous translations, the chapter outlines how* marginal concepts *like* medi(t)ation, (en)light(e)ning, *and* (en)livening *can be turned into effective and efficient tools of intercultural* resistance *that allow us to* step outside *of oppression and alienation so that we can, finally,* access *"life truly lived."*

Chapter X, "Re-opening possibilities or De-coincidence, an art of operating," *explores François Jullien's concept of* de-coincidence *which was first developed at the Taiwan Biennale in 2016. It details how this concept encapsulates not only the esthetic and ethical dimensions of François Jullien's intercultural philosophy of living, but also its political vocation.*

Finally, the book concludes with a coda section which ties back the concept of de-coincidence *to my clinical experience working as a psychiatric social worker in Los Angeles and to my work as an academic in France.*

CHAPTER I
Philosophy *in between* cultures: singular itineraries of thought amidst a globalizing world surface

1/ Living, or the wayside of Being.

Westerners are in the habit of stating that they are the inheritors of the Greeks, but how can they understand this legacy without having ever left it? In other words, how can Westerners measure the significance of their intellectual heritage if they have no notion of what lies *outside* of it? If we are to measure the Greek inheritance in Western thought, it is necessary to devise a strategic approach that steps outside the learned, inherited reflexes of Western thinking. The written language of Ancient China, Classical Chinese, shakes the Western mind up and destabilizes it because the *literal* building block of Western civilization, the verb "to be" and the subsequent notion of "being," does not exist, as such, in this language which neither conjugates verbs nor declines nouns.

a. *"Being," a most Greek of words.*

The verb "to be" and the notion of "being" indeed form the historical and semantic foundation of the West's *ontological*, and subsequently epistemological and theological understanding of the world: science studies the physical, material properties of immanent or worldly "beings,"- whereas religion studies the spiritual or immaterial properties of transcendent, other-worldly "Being(s)" or God(s).[16] Ontological thinking or *ontology* constitutes the foundation of the Western "Arts and Sciences," it is the inherently *problematic* bedrock upon which they lie.

*

    Long before Shakespeare famously captured the angst which underlies the existential and ontological dilemma of Western thought ("to be or not to be"), the "Founding Father" of philosophy, Plato himself, questioned the very relevance of the ontological philosophy that his predecessors like the great pre-Socratic thinker Parmenides of Elea had held in such high esteem. Although little remains of Parmenides' written work, the fragments of his enigmatic *Poem* that we are left with make it clear that, from his perspective, what "is" matters a great deal more than what "is not":

> "Come now, and I will tell you, listen to my words and carry them along with you
>
> These are the only two paths that can be thought of when it comes to research:
>
> The first one, namely, is, and it cannot not be
>
> It is the road of Persuasion
>
> Truth is its companion
>
> The second one, is not, and, by virtue of necessity, it cannot be
>
> It is a most unknown passageway, I tell you
>
> Thus, what is not cannot be known- it cannot lead to any accomplishment
>
> It cannot even be said"[17]

Parmenides could not be clearer: non-being or "what is not" bears no relevance for philosophical research *(dizesis)*, it is a "most unknown passageway" *(panapeuthea emmen atarpon)*. The language that Parmenides uses leaves little doubt about his disregard for non-being: the pre-Socratic thinker forges a neologism *(panapeuthea)* which alludes both to the "unknown" and the "ignorant" to qualify the "narrow path" (another possible translation of *atarpon*) of "what *is not*."

*

Despite Parmenides' warnings, Plato was nonetheless forced to go down the "narrow" road of non-being and metaphorically "kill the Father" in one of his most important dialogues, the *Sophist*. In this crucial text, Plato attempts to hunt down Socrates' nemeses, the Ancient Greek literati class known as the "Sophists."[18] The Sophists were master rhetoricians and inventive thinkers who were famous for their disdain of truth. Athenian democracy was a very litigious society and citizens were in charge of their own defense when they stood trial: the Sophists often made fortunes writing defense speeches and legal arguments for citizens who wished to sway a jury in their favor, regardless of the truth or falsity of the accusations brought against them. From the perspective of the Sophists, it did not matter whether an argument was true or false, what mattered was whether an argument was *persuasive* or not.

In his quest to "pin down" the Sophists and demonstrate the unethical falsity of their ways, Plato was forced to recognize that they were masters in the art of trickery. Speaking through the voice of a mysterious "Visitor" who hails from Elea, the same region in Greece that Parmenides came from, Plato tries to resort to the philosophy of Being to prove that the Sophists "are" inherently wrong when they profess the value of falsity. And yet, the characters of his fictional dialogue cannot help but state the following when they are confronted with the vastness of the Sophist's ruse:

> "THEAETETUS: Maybe that which *is not* is *intertwined* with that which *is* in some way ; it's quite bizarre."
>
> VISITOR: Of course, it's bizarre. Anyway, you can see that the many headed Sophist is still using this *interweaving* to force us to agree unwillingly to the following: that which *is not,* in a way, *is.*"[19]

The "intertwinement" *(sumplokè)* and "interweaving" *(epallaxeos)* of "being" and "non-being," of "what is" with "what is not," of the true and of the false, constitutes the core fragility of ontology, and thus of Western thought on the whole. This crucial passage in Plato's dialogue highlights how the foundation of Western thought, namely the construction of a positive, *ontological representation* of reality as a *model form* of "what is," holds within itself the seeds of its own "deconstruction."[20] The dumbfounded-ness of Plato's fictional characters highlights the political and existential impossibilities associated with ontology: while the "study of Being" might be a privileged avenue to investigate the physical and the metaphysical, it falls short when it comes to addressing problems that arise in political situations, let alone *existential* ones.

b. What lies on the wayside of Being: Classical Chinese, the unthought and intercultural reflection.

Classical Chinese represents an *outside* for the traditional ontologies of Western philosophy. The *singularities* of this language reflect unquestioned dimensions within Western thought because they are formulated *on the wayside* of the great onto-logical language of Being. Nonetheless, this *exteriority* should not be confused with some kind of radical and insurmountable alterity or "Otherness." Classical Chinese writings should *not* be exoticized, nor should they serve as yet another lazy avatar of the problematic "Oriental Other."[21] Rather, the recourse to the exteriority of Classical Chinese literature should be understood in *geo-historical* terms.

Ancient China developed its civilization outside of the historical and linguistic community that tied together the Vedic world with the Hellenistic world. The languages and cultures of Ancient and Medieval China were essentially unbeknownst to the Greeks, the Romans, and later to the European Christians roughly until the Middle Ages (Marco Polo) and until the arrival of the Jesuits at the Ming court in the late 16th and early 17th century. Without entering into the details of such historical and linguistic data points, it is important to underscore the inherently *philosophical* nature of the recourse to the geo-historic exteriority of Ancient China. The philosophical recourse to Ancient China's exteriority within the traditional history of philosophy and ideas forms the basis of a *strategic* approach to philosophy that allows us to, if not discard, then assuredly *question* patterns of thought betrodden to philosophy's rootedness in Greek ontology.

*

The line of questioning brought forth in this book does not seek to destroy or even deconstruct philosophy or ontology. Rather, it is moved by a desire that seeks to wake up philosophy from its atavistic slumber and "shake it up and move, to get it in a groove" as the great rockabilly singer Derrell Felts once sang. In other words, the kind of philosophy discussed from here onwards supposes a capacity to lose one's footing and allow oneself to become stripped of certitudes and preconceptions. As we follow the twists and turns of a seminal philosophical desire that strips us down to an "aporetic" bedrock of *un-knowing*,[22] it becomes possible to catch glimpses of a thought that is neither "Eastern" nor "Western:" an *unheard* intercultural *philosophy of living*. The point of intercultural philosophy is not to lead to an identification with any given ethnic or national philosophical heritage; journeying back and forth between philosophical cultures instead enables the fabrication and development of conceptual tools and passageways that facilitate a genuine *intercultural dialog* turned towards the global complexities of the 21st century.

In such a dialog, the implicit and unbeknownst *biases* inherent to each way of thinking are brought to light without a shade of negative or positive *judgment*: they are simply *reflected upon*, thus fostering the *construction* of a *common understanding* of the *human* that highlights a shared *community of intelligence* which can only be accessed by probing the *unthought* bed that lies beneath any thought; that which has *not yet* been thought and which can therefore *still* be thought.

*

The unthought bed upon which thinking lies is first and foremost determined by language, both spoken and written. This basic fact eluded Descartes himself who, despite doubting the existence of everything, did not put into doubt the very language he used to construct his systematic and universalizing mode of rational thinking. From an intercultural perspective, the very universality of Cartesian subjectivity is embedded in a language, in Descartes' case an amalgamation of French and Latin. When Descartes writes *"cogito ergo sum," "je pense, donc je suis,"* or "I think, therefore I am," he does not once suspect that the verb "to be," which forms the foundation of his reasoning, might in fact be indissociable from the language he is using. In other words, Descartes is so embedded in his language that he does not realize that the kind of ontological reasoning he uses to found and find truth might not be as universal and rational as he thinks it is. This embeddedness of Cartesian thought in language does not render it invalid or irrelevant, rather it compels diligent and attuned readers to incessantly *question* their *modes of reading* so that they can begin to probe the *unthought* "linguistic bed" that they lie in, get themselves out of it, and begin to *wake up* their thinking.

c. Logos *and predication: ontological vs. accidental.*

In a sense, it is already possible to distance oneself from the thought and language of the Greeks within the confines of the Western tradition by investigating the Biblical tradition and the Hebrew language. Drawing out the tension that arises from the meeting of Athens and Jerusalem is a well-trodden trope in Western thought that was not unfamiliar to Hegel, Kierkegaard, Nietzsche, Heidegger, Levinas, and Derrida. Yet unlike Heideggerian existential philosophy, intercultural philosophy does not search for some fabled "origin" of Western thought, be it Hebraic or pre-Socratic. The philosophical usage of Classical Chinese literature offers instead an external point of reference which possesses its own fabled origin story and, most importantly, its own form of *writing* that bears no resemblance with any alphabetic system.[23]

Classical Chinese's ideographic structure constitutes a *de facto* departure from the alphabetic and, above all, *predicative* structure that characterizes the Greek language of Being- *logos*.[24] *Logos* is a vastly polysemic term that denotes reason, logic, discourse, and argumentation. It is arguably the most important of all Ancient Greek

28

terms as it continues to condition contemporary language, all the way down to "mixology" which is, in a literal translation, the "reasoned discourse" or "logic" of cocktail making…

*

The structure of *logos* is founded upon *ontological predication* as exemplified by a paradigmatic logical and analytical form: the syllogism. The syllogism's three distinct steps illustrate how a predicative, analytical sentence -a sentence in which the predicate or attribute is contained within the subject, like "Socrates is a man"- can form the basis for a *repeatable method* which can then serve as a solid *ground* for logically sound, and above all else, *true* reasoning: "If Socrates *is* a man and all men *are* mortal, then Socrates *must be* mortal." We see here how associating an attribute or a predicate ("mortal") with a set of subjects ("Socrates" or "men") through a determinative usage of the verb "to be" constitutes the logical basis of an analytic form of reasoning that produces statements of *necessity* which "are true*"* by virtue of their predicative and attributive structure. These kinds of statements possess, in Western thought, a guaranteed *ontological value*: their logical, methodical, repeatable, and self-identical structure appears to transparently describe the nature of what "possesses being" or of what, irrevocably and necessarily, *is.*

*

The predicative and attributive structure of *logos* and its subsequent logical propensity for ontological reasoning finds no exact equivalent in the Classical Chinese writing system.[25] Classical Chinese of course has its share of predicative statements, yet from the point of view of Western ontology, these predicative statements correspond to "accidental predication," as opposed to "ontological predication." An example of "accidental predication" is a statement like "I am sick today." If I say that I am sick today, I am stating that "being sick" is an accidental predicate, it is not in my *essence* to be sick. "Sickness" in this case is a descriptive, "accidental" attribute, it is not an ontological one insofar as it does not refer to a permanent or essential feature of my "being."

A less technical, and thus less accurate, way to describe this subtle linguistic distinction between accidental vs. ontological predication as it relates to Classical Chinese writing and Ancient Greek *logos* could lead one to make the following, overly general, but pedagogically valuable generalization: Classical Chinese writing focuses on *how things work* whereas Ancient Greek *logos* focuses on *what things are*.[26] In Classical Chinese, thought weaves in and out of dense and compact allusions, rarely threading a systematic and enclosed discourse in the style of philosophers like Aristotle or Kant. Unlike the Sanskrit language studied from a structuralist perspective in France by the historian George Dumézil and the linguist Emile Benveniste,[27] Classical Chinese does not bring us back to the common, albeit hypothetical, substrate of Indo-European: its lack of ontological predication leads its (Western) readers *out* of the *logos* of Being. The language of Ancient China instead draws readers into an allusive way of thinking shaped by parataxis and parallelisms; it combines formulaic linguistic structures with inscriptive *breath-gestures* designed to reflect the cosmic alternating polarities of the *Yin* and the *Yang*, the *breath(ing)* of *Qi,* and the hexagram figures of the *Yi Jing*.[28]

Classical Chinese thus offers a concrete "way out" of the ontological predication which characterizes the *logos* of Being. It forces any reader to recognize the following: in order to depart from the language of Being, it is necessary to *learn* another one. Even philosophers Levinas and Derrida, who argued with each other about their respective capacity to leave behind metaphysics and the language of Being, never fully took this step *outside* of Being: they never learned a language that could take them there. In many regards, Ancient China, and East Asian thought more broadly, constitute a blind spot for Western philosophy which has been all too content to *imagine* East Asian languages as some "Oriental Other." Indeed, another language is not imagined, it is learned through careful and patient study up until the point where that which was once foreign and uncanny becomes familiar and understandable. Learning another language, especially a language wholly unrelated to one's own, allows one to reflect on the *conditions of possibility* of human thought's singular capacity to *think outside* of its habitual terms and customs.[29] Such a deep reflection on the conditionings and possibilities that simultaneously delimit, contain, and at once *open* the parameters of human thought requires a *strategic* approach to thinking, one capable of addressing the adversities that arise when faced with confusion and incomprehension.

Understanding philosophy through the lens of language and interculturality compels philosophers to devise a coy, oblique, and indirect approach to their discipline that recuses both easy universalism and lazy culturalism. In the intercultural approach to Ancient China and Ancient Greece, the tensions which oppose the two languages are neither glossed over nor hypostatized but rather *translated*.

2/ Translation, strategy, and interculturality: recusing ethnocentric universalism and comparatist multiculturalism, building an intercultural common(s) of human intelligence.

a. Translation as exchange vs translation as "treason."

In intercultural philosophy, translation is not approached from the perspective of truth, treason, and fidelity. Instead, we seek to emphasize the complexities and opportunities that arise within any given *exchange process*. The notion of strategy thus becomes effective and operative insofar as the intercultural philosopher must necessarily devise ruses and side-steps that allow him to skirt around the difficulties that surface in the exchange process of translation. The ruses and asides of the translator-philosopher convey and transmit, if not the true substance of a translated text, then assuredly an *effective significance*. Strategic translation thus seeks to highlight the *processual tensions* and *literal reflections* that arise when two languages gaze into each other's embedded reflexes and conditionings. The translation process exposes the presuppositions and predeterminations that bind together language and thought, it produces a *prism of significance* that *reflects* a comprehensive approach to language where *meaning is made and not found*.

In the intercultural approach to language and translation, meaning bears no connection to an original significance attributable to a mythical Author; instead, meaning becomes *a resource,* subject to cycles of generation and depletion. The working processes of intercultural philosophy are therefore not methodical but rather *operative*. They do not seek to systematically delimit tangible, unequivocal, *a priori* dimensions of Knowledge and Truth; they offer instead *conceptual tools* that enable and assist the *realization* of *spontaneous intercultural exchange*. Intercultural exchange processes occur within the *interstices* and *liminal zones* that lie *in between* the translated and the translating languages; they weave together compact threads of *language-thought*. The complexity of these threads of language-thought *resists* any form of *assimilation*. The strategic translator-philosopher-scholar should avoid "comparing and contrasting" Ancient China and Ancient Greece, East and West, Classical and Modern. The point is not to enumerate differences and similarities; doing so tends to further isolate each culture, Place, and Era into a lifeless and predetermined silo.

b. Intercultural reflection, dialog and the "philosophy of difference": neither universalist nor (multi)culturalist.

In this regard, intercultural philosophy stands in stark contrast with the French "philosophy of difference" (Deleuze, Derrida) where the concept of difference itself continues to operate as a primal metaphysical substrate.[30] Positing the primacy of difference or "*différance*" reduces the examination of the historical, cultural, and philosophical field to a classificatory enterprise where thought is compartmentalized into different and differing "schools" and thus rarely *utilized*. Comparing and contrasting the language-thought of Ancient Greece -Ancient Greek- with the language-thought of Ancient China -Classical Chinese- or comparing "Eastern" and "Western" thoughts or "philosophies" under the auspice of some metaphysical "difference" pulls the rug from underneath them, it neatly draws them into a corner and *covers up* the *unheard possibilities* that lie *in between* the two. The language-thought that lies in between Greece and China, in between East and West, in between Classical Chinese and Ancient Greek, does not result from a comparison and even less so from a confrontation; nor does it result from a differentiation of what is authentically Eastern or "Chinese" from what is authentically Western or "Greek." On the contrary, the strategic meeting of China and Greece, of East and West, and the *dialog* that results from it, generates a newfound *operativity* of thought which highlights, not only unthought pre-conceptions, but also unthought *inventions*.

*

The term *dialog* itself is of critical importance here and it must be referred to the Greek prefix *dia* in both its acceptance as a signifier referring to *division* and in its acceptance as a signifier related to a means of action which *threads* a sense of continuity. In other words, the strategic *dia-log* between Ancient Greece and Ancient China, between "East and West," that intercultural philosophy orchestrates allows us to: 1) take the measure of the *distance* that separates the two; 2) invent *conceptual tools* that *weave together* the continuous threads of *language-thought* that emerge *in between* them.

Intercultural philosophy thus relies on the careful construction of a vantage point of *dia-log* which stresses a shared *common soil* of *intelligence*; it also honors the *singularity* of each protagonist, of each culture. Rather than promoting the (pre)existence of some supposed universal "perennial philosophy" of "difference" or of "sameness" that lies beneath or beyond all cultures, the dia-logs of intercultural philosophy remain *rooted* and *grounded* in the *problems* of translation. Intercultural philosophy promotes the effective cultural *resources* of operative notions like the Greek *logos* or the Chinese *Dao*: these ubiquitous notions can be used to address the *concrete difficulties* that come up not only in translation but also in *living* itself.

The concepts of intercultural philosophy therefore do not discover or unearth a universal "truth of life." Instead, they *reflect* and *construct* the *universalizing* weaves of language-thought that operate *in between* the dividing lines separating cultures and languages. The *effective* universalizing dimension of intercultural philosophy resides in its capacity to efficiently bridge these dividing lines without dissolving them. The concepts produced by intercultural philosophy are generated through a simultaneously *reflexive* and *constructive* process in which cultural, material, and existential difficulties are not erased, but rather *addressed.*

*

Interculturality and multiculturalism are *not* equatable. Multiculturalism is an ideology born out of the reversal or "overthrowing" of Platonist metaphysics that the French "philosophy of difference" championed following Nietzsche's suit.[31] In this "ideology of difference," the Multiple or the Different is substituted to the One or the Identical. In other words, multiculturalism posits a primal *difference* between cultures. From a multicultural standpoint, the shared value of human cultures becomes a mere sum of the parts.

In this regard, multiculturalism is of course at the opposite ends of its ideological counterpart, universalism. Universalism posits a primal *unity* which supposedly lies behind or beyond cultures. Yet from an intercultural perspective both universalism and multiculturalism are equally ideological. Instead of positing the difference or sameness of cultures, intercultural philosophy prefers to stress their *plurality*. Unlike difference or unity, plurality does not act as a bedrock concept: it is a simple assessment, a statement of fact. Having stressed the observable plurality of cultures, intercultural philosophy does not seek to outline some great universality of "human nature." Instead, it highlights how the *encounter* of cultures generates interstitial *spaces of exchange.*

An intercultural approach to cultural plurality bears no ressemblance with an overplayed multiculturalist ideological discourse where the diverse is touted as a boon. Rather, it constitutes the starting point of any serious philosophical reflection, the *common soil* that can be plowed in order to generate intercultural *concepts* that can help us navigate *in between* cultures. Whereas multiculturalism seeks to silo cultures in their respective units, the intercultural approach to plurality aims to take the measure of the *distances* which separate cultures in an effort to find novel ways to *travel across* these distances. A philosophical approach to cultural plurality therefore isn't multicultural but rather intercultural: it does not "mix and match" notions formed on the basis of some arbitrary or methodic appreciation of cultural differences, nor does it attempt to unveil some universal substrate of "human nature." The task of intercultural philosophy is thus to weave itself *in between* cultures: it constructs *passageways* that allow us to *circulate* throughout the diverse cultural parameters of language-thought that have shaped human experience across Time and Space.

c. Tools for living or "standing out" vs. Way(s) of Being: interculturality and the "existential."

Much like intercultural philosophy gives us tools to address problems of translation, it also gives us tools to approach the problems of *existence*. An intercultural approach to the existential thus isn't an attempt at outlining, yet again, the foundations of some universal human subjectivity rooted in transcendent or immanent Being. Instead, the intercultural *dia-log* offers us conceptual *tools for living*. These tools for living are designed to help us "exist" or *stand out*. The word "existence" should be understood here as referring directly to the Latin verb *ex-istere,* which means to "stand out" or to "arise."[32]

*

What could existence mean outside of the language of Being? What dimensions of existence have been covered up by the great history of Being?

Probing underneath the unthought bedrock of Being allows us to *un-cover* an existential notion that has been obfuscated by Western thought: *living.* Whereas Ancient China developed a subtle approach to living centered around the life-generating practices and processes of *Yang Sheng* (養生) that will be examined in greater detail in Chapter II, Western philosophy developed an understanding of existence as a finite resource destined to be ultimately depleted. As we shall see, the intercultural space that lies *in between* Western "existential" and "spiritual" philosophies of "body and soul" and Chinese *Yang Sheng* practices delineates an *unheard* dimension of *existing*: a dimension where the question of *what to be* transforms itself into the question of *how to (not) live*. By way of a close reading of select passages of some of the most famous texts of the Classical Chinese tradition (the *Zhuangzi,* the *Laozi,* and the *Mengzi*), Chapter II will strategically put into question and historically situate some of the greatest philosophical concepts of the Western tradition -the "mind-body-soul" trinity first and foremost- in order to outline a newfound intercultural understanding of what it means to "nourish life," *on the wayside* of happiness.

CHAPTER II

Yang Sheng 養生, or "nurturing-nourishing living," on the wayside of happiness

1/ "Nurturing-nourishing living," on the wayside of body, mind and soul: a pedagogical overview of an epistemological dissociation.

The question of nourishment marks a primal point of reflection where, once put face to face, the thought traditions born in Ancient Greece and Ancient China can gaze into each other's fertile *unthought*. Throughout the ages, the Western philosophical tradition has often stressed the separateness of the "nourishment of the body" from the "nourishment of the soul." The Classical Chinese characters *Yang Sheng* (養生), on the other hand, reflect a contrasting understanding of the *correlation* that binds nourishing, supporting, and rearing, 養 or *yang*, to birthing, living, and growing, 生 or *sheng*. These characters, which can be translated as "nourishing living" or "nurturing living," allude to Classical Chinese texts written as far back as the Warring States Period (5th to 3rd century BCE) and as recently as the Qing Dynasty (17th to 20th century CE). These texts discuss a wide array of techniques and behavioral dispositions – controlled breathing, seated or standing meditation, gymnastics, sexual practices, acupuncture, massage, herbal medicine and dietetics- that are said to foster the "nourishment" or "nurturance" (養) of "life" or of "living" (生).

Yang Sheng texts often assume the form of dense, disparate, and yet methodically structured "laundry-lists;" they are filled with practicable insights and prescriptions couched in an ancient cosmological worldview. Even though these technical "laundry-lists" require thorough historical contextualization and patient philological study, they continue to hold immense relevance not just for practitioners of traditional Chinese healing "arts and sciences" today, but for care workers more generally.[33] The Classical Chinese *Yang Sheng* literary corpus and the techniques it describes do not distinguish the "nourishment of the soul" from the "nourishment of the body" in the same way that the English language does. It is obvious that the *differentiation* of "body" (*soma*) and "soul" (*psychè*) inherited from Ancient Greece is hard-wired into the English language: this *unthought* Greek hard-wiring of our common language becomes most apparent when we contrast "feeding," reserved only for primal bodily needs, with "nourishing," where the experience of eating is elevated, spiritualized, and *dissociated* from its bodily corollaries.

The term "nourishment" in the English language is thus already caught in a *dissociative process* of *differentiation* where "body" and "soul" become isolated and later categorized as distinct, identifiable, separable, and, above all, *(un)knowable* entities. Examining the *Yang Sheng* texts and techniques of Ancient China allows us to measure the extent of how the epistemological dissociation separating "body," "soul," and (later) "mind" imbues the history of the spiritually and intellectually inflected concept of "nourishment" in the English language. Such an analysis can help us shed light on a refreshed intercultural appreciation of Early Chinese notions like "nourishing-nurturing"(養) and "living-life" (生). For pedagogical purposes, we will begin this investigation with a brief historical overview that will bring into focus the two following questions:

a) How did the dissociative separation of "body," "mind," and "soul," into distinct *(un)knowable entities* emerge as a paradigmatic feature of Western philosophy which then fostered the conception and development of Modern Science?

b) In what ways do the "laundry-lists" and narratives of *Yang Sheng* literature *wander on the wayside* of such epistemological and philosophical preoccupations?

a. The tragic loss of a beloved Master or how the early childhood trauma of Western philosophy led to the moral injunction to nourish the soul, not the body.

From a psychoanalytic standpoint, dissociation can be understood as a *defensive response* to early childhood trauma.[34] Without veering too far into a questionable psychoanalytic (over)interpretation of History, it seems fair to say that the trial of Socrates in 399 BCE and his subsequent death sentence constitute the early childhood trauma of Western philosophy; the philosophical dissociation of body and soul would thus constitute a response to this trauma, psychoanalytically speaking... The first staunch theoretical separation of body and soul, of *psychè* and *soma,* can indeed be found in Plato's dialogue *Phaedo,* the one which narrates Socrates' last living moments and his ultimate discussions with his beloved disciples as he prepares to drink the poison that will end his life:

— Socrates: [...] do we believe that there is such a thing as death?"

— Simmias: "Certainly."

— Socrates: "And is this anything but the separation of psychè and body (*somaton*)? And being dead is the attainment of this separation; when the psychè exists in itself, and is parted from the body and the body is parted from the psychè—that is death?"

— Simiais: "Exactly: that and nothing else."

— Socrates: "And what do you say of another question, my friend, about which I should like to have your opinion, and the answer to which will probably throw light on our present inquiry: do you think that the philosopher ought to care about the pleasures—if they are to be called pleasures—of eating and drinking (*sition kai poton*)?"

— Simmias: "Certainly not."[35]

Plato's text is remarkably clear when it comes to the question of nourishment: nourishing the mortal body by way of "the pleasures of eating and drinking" has nothing to do with the philosophical quest to nourish the immortal soul. Philosophy thus bears little concern for the question of physical or material nutrition and is instead wholly turned towards the instance wherein the soul separates itself from the body at the moment of death. In this regard, it is obvious that nourishing the soul has everything to do with the spiritual "art of dying" and with the metaphysical theory of "metempsychosis" (the Ancient Greek equivalent to Buddhist re-incarnation). The soul's immortality precludes it from bearing any relationship to organic, physical forms of *living*. If "the safest general characterization of the European philosophical tradition is that it consists of a series of footnotes to Plato" as the British philosopher A.N. Whitehead famously and brilliantly put it,[36] then it is also safe to say that later, less deprecative, and more "holistic" Western conceptions of nourishment as it relates to the philosophical question of body and soul can only be thought of in relationship to Plato's dissociated response to the loss of his beloved Master.

b. Mending broken pieces: Aristotle's material-formal approach to nourishment, animation, and intellection.

The first and most substantial "footnote" to Plato's dissociated and "dualistic" understanding of the body, of the soul and of their respective modes of nourishment can of course be found in Aristotle's text "On the Soul" or *Peri Psychè,* later translated as *De Anima* in Latin.[37] Aristotle indeed *departs* from Plato, particularly when it comes to the question of nourishment: he insists on the intimate relationship that ties the soul to physical, material processes, particularly nutrition and respiration. Aristotle's understanding of *psychè* refers to an *animating principle*; this principle *(archè)* is bound to the materiality of respiration, *pneuma,*[38] and to nutrition, *trophè;* and yet, it nonetheless *exceeds* them. Breathing and eating represent elementary, material, and "nutritive" physical "figures" (*morphai*) whose movements illustrates the immaterial, intelligible "forms" (*eidoi*) of the soul of plants. Desire (*orexis*), self-impulsed motion (*auto-kinesis*), and individual sensibility (*aisthesis*) represent the singular characteristics of the souls of animals. The various figures (*morphai*) of "logical" (*logistikon*) intellection (*noesis*) characterize the human and the Divine soul. For Aristotelians, the organic or instrumental "nutritive function" of breathing and eating does not represent the soul or the spirit's true finality, its true *telos* or realization. Even though *psy-*

40

chè, pneuma, and *trophè* are tied together, *psychè* is pulled upwards towards the ethereality of *noesis* or "intellection" whereas *pneuma* and *trophè* gravitate downwards towards *phusis* or "natural matter"; *psychè*'s spiritualizing essence, its *ousía,* instills the spiritual within the physical, imprinting the ideality of figure and form, *morphè* and *eidos,* upon the concreteness of matter, *hylè.*[39]

The Ancient Greek philosopher's "hylomorphic" or "material-formal" understanding of the soul as an intelligible animating principle turned towards the ideality of *nous* fosters the materialization of a disembodied, and yet *spiritualized* form of knowledge or science (*episteme*); the significance of Aristotle's epistemological and "noetic" understanding of the soul as an intelligible "knowing-activity-principle," and his consequent assessment of breathing and eating as a significant, nutritive, and yet ultimately material i.e., *passive* organic processes cannot be understated when accounting for the historical emergence of the Early Modern epistemic paradigm of the "body as a machine"; a paradigm which continues to influence the contemporary "food as fuel" discourse that floods the market of "health, wellness, and fitness" lifestyle products.

c. The body-machine and the unthought legacy of Descartes' "Animal Spirits."

The Early Modern thinker most easily associated with the characterization of nutrition and breathing as passive mechanical "fueling" processes that service the (self)cognizing activity of the soul and mind is, without a doubt (pun intended), René Descartes. Famous for his hard epistemological dualism, Descartes turns the logical supposition of the tripartite separation of body (*corps*), soul (*âme*), and mind (*esprit*) into the *indubitable* metaphysical foundation upon which true scientific knowledge can be founded.

In a strange Latin text of theoretical fiction, the posthumously edited and incomplete *Treatise of Man,*[40] Descartes paints the portrait of an imaginary species of human beings who, much "like us," are "composed of a Soul (*Âme*) and a Body (*Corps*)." The body of these fictional beings is "nothing more than a statue or a machine made of earth." Organic processes like "walking, eating, and breathing" are mere physical features of the machine. Just as "clocks, artificial fountains, windmills, and other similar machines" are moved by a set of physical, self-propelling, natural forces (wind, gravity, flux), the body-machine is moved by the self-propelling forces of "animal Spirits (*Esprits animaux*)." These "spirits" move alongside blood within the arteries and travel through the nervous system; their activity is likened to "a certain very subtle wind, or rather to a very vivid and pure flame" which impulses and animates the command-center of the body-machine- the brain. The "ordinary and natural actions" of the body-machine like "respiration," and by extension eating, are "dependent on the flow of the spirits (*cours des esprits*)." Just like "the movements of clocks and mills" can be regulated and "made continuous" by the propulsive activity of "the ordinary flow of water (*cours ordinaire de l'eau*)," the propulsive activity of the ordinary flow of "animal spirits" throughout the arterial and nervous system regulates the nutritive organic processes of the body-machine and guarantees its sustenance. According to Descartes, when the "reasonable soul (*l'âme raisonnable*)" will be ready to inhabit the body-machine, it "will be seated primarily in the brain" and will act like a "fountaineer" or, in (even) more modern terms, like a hydraulic technician…

For the French philosopher and polymath, the soul is thus capable of "exciting, preventing or changing in any manner the movements" of the "animal spirits" of the body-machine in the same way that the "fountaineer" *controls* the flow and distribution of water in a waterworks system. The Cartesian soul, much like the Aristotelian soul, acts like an intellecting, governing, and regulating epistemic principle: its scientific verification and justification resides in the mind's (*esprit*) self-conscious capacity to *know* that it is thinking even as it doubts the veracity of its own existence -the infamous *cogito ergo sum* or "I think therefore I am" thought experiment first expounded in French in 1637 the *Discourse on Method*, and later in Latin in the *Metaphysical Meditations* in 1641.

*

Descartes' evocative description of the body-machine in *The Treatise of Man* prefigures in many ways the neuroscientific understanding of the brain: the "animal spirits" can easily be understood as the electric current that runs through neural pathways and/or as the chemical exchange processes that govern and regulate hormonal activity. Nonetheless, the strangeness of the text's language should not be hastily brushed aside as some kind of quaint historical artifact. Despite the advances of Modern Science -which confirmed and contradicted many of Descartes' fundamental intuitions- there are elements of this text which remain largely *unthought*: what *spiritual* significance do these curious "animal spirits" hold? If the "reasonable soul" indeed acts like a hydraulic technician, then what does the actual *technique* of "spiritual rearing" look like? Does the spiritual dimension of the body-machine need to be so strongly dissociated from the soul if they are engaged in a mutual process of *co-operation*? In what ways does Descartes' text suggest an approach to nourishment and *living* which extends beyond the perspective of knowledge and *control*?

*

Intercultural philosophy can, if not answer, then assuredly *explore* the ramifications of such questions. It can also reveal novel perspectives and terms which can then help us approach the nutritional, spiritual, and even *existential* problems they raise with a newfound sense of clarity and focus. The intercultural investigation of Classical Chinese *Yang Sheng* literature offers in this regard a fertile soil to plow: the idiosyncratic approach to "nurturing-nourishing" (養) and "living" (生) that it developed does not require the strong differentiation, let alone dissociation, of mind, body, and soul that characterizes the history of Western (anti)metaphysics and of its *epistemes*. While some might hastily categorize, and thus easily misconstrue, *Yang Sheng* literature as a form of mystical and pre-scientific thought, that is to say as a cultural variation of the universalizing "One is All and All is One" logic which precedes the development of Modern Science's fractured, entangled, dissociated, and yet intentionally *universal* vision of the World and of its Laws, we will demonstrate that it continues to offer an intriguing and, above all, *operative* approach to "nurturing-nourishing" as it relates to the existential problem(s) of *living*.

The Classical Chinese texts that will be explored moving forward *wander on the wayside* of the tired tropes and debates of Western philosophy (holism vs. dualism, spiritual intellection vs. embodied cognition, Science vs. Faith). The language-thought that ties them together revolves around a vast semantic pool of graphemes that eludes the apparent univocity of terms like "body, "mind," and "soul." Key notions in *Yang Sheng* literature- vastly polysemic terms like *Qi* (氣), *Jing* (精), and *Shen* (神)- carry along with them a wealth of significations that refuses any kind of definitive translation. Exploring possible translations of these sinograms and approaching them by way of one of Ancient China's most revered texts, the *Zhuangzi*, can indeed offer us, if not scientific knowledge, then assuredly *philosophical clarification* when it comes to what we name, in Latin-English, the *spiritual*.

2/ Introducing the *Zhuangzi*: seminal mortal spirit(s) (精), immortal invisible spirit(s) (神), and aimless wandering (遊) along the Way(s) (道) or what *Yang Sheng* doesn't need to (not)know about the soul.

If there ever was such a thing as a masterpiece of "world literature,"[41] then the *Zhuangzi* would surely qualify. Written in a highly idiosyncratic and irreverent style, its cryptic, playful, and, above all, *singular* expressions have befuddled and bewildered commentators and translators across cultures and throughout history. The *Zhuangzi* was diffused across the world alongside other major works of Classical Chinese literature, first in Korea, Vietnam, and Japan in the Ancient and Medieval Eras, and then later in Europe and in the West in the Modern and Industrial Eras. Since then, it has become an exceptional literary object of fascination, the fetish-text *par excellence* for many a scholar and thinker attuned to the *subtlety* of its poetic, argumentative, and narrative formulations.[42] Thought to be the written legacy of Master Zhuang or *Zhuang Zi* (莊子), philological consensus deems that the first seven "inner chapters" of the text are indeed attributable to an individual named Zhuang Zhou (莊周) who lived in the Kingdom of Song during the Warring States Period in the 3rd century BCE. The remaining 26 "outer chapters" first compiled by Guo Xiang (郭象) in the late 3rd and early 4th century CE are thought to be the byproduct of posterior admirers and of self-styled disciples who supplemented the Master's original text with their own renditions of his blazing poetics. The *Zhuangzi* is perhaps most famous for its searing wit and for their sardonic pieces of "philosophical fictions," elliptic and enigmatic anecdotes that paint vivid portraits not only of Emperors and Sages, as many works of Classical Chinese literature do, but also of wise-cracking butchers, carpenters, cripples, hermits, and fools.[43]

a. Yang Sheng *in the* Zhuangzi*: the poetic and operative (de) constructions of correlative cosmology.*

The most literal reference to *Yang Sheng* in the *Zhuangzi* is undoubtedly the piece of philosophical fiction featuring a Butcher and a Prince found in the third chapter of the book entitled *Yang Sheng Zhu (*養生主*)* or "What Matters in the Nurture of Life" as A.C. Graham translates it. Before analyzing this quaint, surprising, and crucial story, it will prove useful to *enter* the *Zhuangzi* by way of another, less obvious, and yet equally relevant gate: the anecdote of the Yellow Emperor seeking guidance from the Wayward Sage of the Mountain found in the 11th chapter.

This story indeed provides a more global overview than the tale of the Butcher when it comes to grasping some of the key structural notions that underlie the mythical cosmology of Early China. It serves as a valuable point of entry into the *Zhuangzi* because it shows how the literary form of the text itself- its ironic narration, its subtle word-play, and its ambiguous meaning- offers an understanding of *nurturance-nourishment* (養) that recuses the kind of thirst for univocal and universal *knowledge* which underlies the Western paradigm of nourishment. The anecdote offers a hyperbolic portrait that illustrates the intricate and complex relationships which bind the Early Chinese notion of *nurturing-nourishing* (養-食) to political, ethical, technical, cosmological, and mythical dimensions; although it touches upon key elements of the cosmology and mythology of Early China, the story's singular poetic form destabilizes the integrity of these established "systems" of *(un)knowing*.

If we keep in mind the Western concepts and notions discussed previously (the body, the soul, the mind; passive nutrition vs. active intellection; knowledge vs. ignorance), a series of clear *philosophical insights* emerges when combing through the text's dense webs of signifiers and significations: the *seminal spirit* (精) of the "utmost Way" or "perfected *Dao*" (至道)[44] of *nurturing-nourishing* (養) has nothing to do with an immortal and transcendent soul dissociated from the body (Plato), nor is it equatable with some kind of transcendent(al) "noetic" knowing-activity of the spirit-mind (Aristotle); it is not even reducible the hypothetical impulsions of "animal spirits" (Descartes). Instead, the "seminal spirits" of the "Utmost Way" are tied to the *aimless wandering* (遊) of strange *invisible-spirits* (神) and to the *fictional figure* of a powerful and mythical Sage endowed with an imperishable *bodily form* (形):

When the Yellow Emperor had reigned as Son of Heaven for nineteen years, and his writ ran throughout the empire, he heard that Guangchengzi was living on Mount Kongtong, so he went to visit him.

'Sir, I hear that you have attained the Utmost Way (道)*, and venture to ask about the Utmost Way's **seminal spirit(s)*** (精)*. I wish to pick out the seminal spirits of heaven* (天) *and earth* (地) *and use them to assist the Five Grains and **nurture-nourish*** (養) *the people. I wish too to put the* Yin *and* Yang *to service in order to perfect the growth of everything that lives* (生)*. What would you advise?'*

'What you wish to ask about', said Guangchengzi, 'is the substance of things, but it is the ruins you have made of them that you are trying to put to service. Ever since you have been rul-

*ing the empire, it has rained before the **vapor-breath** (氣) of the clouds has even gathered, the plants and trees have shed their leaves before they were even yellow, the light of sun and moon has got dimmer and dimmer. You, of the shallow fawner's heart, why should you deserve to be told about the utmost Way?'*

When the Yellow Emperor withdrew, he relinquished the Empire, built a special house, matted it with white reeds, and lived in retirement for three months.

*He went again to request an audience. Guangchengzi was asleep with his face turned south. The Yellow Emperor approached on his knees, northward like a subject before the throne, kowtowed twice and asked 'Sir, I hear you have attained the Utmost Way, and venture a question. How shall I rule **my body** (身) to make it **long-lasting** (長久)?'*

Guangchengzi rose with a start. 'A good question! Come, I shall tell you about the Utmost Way. The seminal spirits of the Utmost Way are dark, dark, secret, secret: the apex of the Utmost Way is mystery, mystery, silence, silence.

*Look at nothing, listen to nothing, cling to the **invisible spirit(s)** (神) and be still, the **bodily form** (形) will correct itself. Always be still, always be pure, don't put your bodily form under strain, don't let your seminal spirits waver, and then it will be possible to live on and on. When the eye has nothing that it sees, the ear nothing that it hears, the **heart-mind** (心) nothing that it knows (知), your invisible spirit will abide in the bodily form, and then the bodily form lives on and on (長生).*

Take care of the inside of you, shut up the outside of you, to know too much is to decay. For you, I shall ascend above the supremely bright, as far as the source of the utmost Yang; for you, I shall enter the gate of the dark and secret, as far as the *source of the utmost Yin. Heaven and Earth have their own offices, The Yin and Yang their own treasuries. Take care to abide **in your own body** (身), and other things will flourish of themselves. I abide where they are one, in order to settle where they harmonize, and so I have been training myself for 1,200 years and my bodily form has never decayed.'*

*The Yellow Emperor kowtowed twice. 'It is Guangchengzi whom I declare my "Heaven".' 'Come,' said Guangchengzi, 'I shall tell you. The things which belong to That are boundless, but all men think they have an end; the things which belong to That are immeasurable, but all men think they have a limit. Whoever grasps my Way is of the Emperors that were and the Kings that shall be, whoever misses my Way begins in the light of day and afterwards is earthen soil (土). Now everything that springs forth is born from earthen soil and returns to earthen soil. Therefore, I shall leave you to enter the gate of the boundless and **wander aimlessly** (遊) in the fields of the limitless. I shall be a third luminary with the sun and moon, I shall share the constancy of heaven and earth. Close up to me, a blur! Far away from me, a blank! Yes, the rest of men die, every one of them, and I alone remain!'*[45]

The core area of focus of the Sage's teachings thus isn't tending to the immortality of the soul but rather *Chang Sheng* (長生), the *lengthening of living*. Lengthening living thus represents a nutritive and *gubernatorial* process of *plowing through* the obstructions that get in the way of the very source of vitality, the transformative "seminal spirit" (精)[46] that stirs the Yellow Emperor's thirst for knowledge (知).[47] Nurturing-nourishing (養) the people and ruling one own's own body thus does not reflect a body/soul dualism nor even mind/body/soul trinitarianism, it describes instead the continuous transitions wherein nurturing-nourishing enables the transformation of the seminal-perishable *jing* spirit (精) into the invisible-immortal *shen* spirit (神).[48]

The transformative process at the heart of this transition consists in a refining of the crude seminal *jing* spirit, born in the loins which proceed from the earth *di* (地), into the subtle immaterial *shen* spirit which in turn emanates from the "heart-mind," *xin* (心)[49], and ascends towards the sky or Heaven, *tian* (天). This continuous transition from one plane to another, from the plane of *jing* towards the plane of *shen*, from the plane of the Earth below to the plane of the Sky above, represents an elevation of the seminal-perishable spirit into the immortal-invisible spirit that in no way suggests a *separation* between these two planes but rather the *subtle processes* detailing their *mutual implication*.

Whereas the transition from being a mortal body to becoming an immortal soul is marked by a disjunctive separation in the Western tradition, the spiritual transitions (mortal to immortal, earthly to heavenly) of nourishing-nurturing are on the contrary defined by continuous processes of *intertwinement* and *entanglement*. The transition of *jing* into *shen* therefore does not describe a process of individuation wherein a soul, separating itself from its body, ascends towards the Divine; instead, it describes a *decanting* process akin to the one wherein the sediment and the "spirit" of a wine transform themselves into a diffusion of subtle, invisible effusions.

b. Aimless wandering along the Way: leaving aside goals, nurturing viability instead.

The *Yang Sheng* techniques that the Emperor seeks to glean from the Sage are anchored in the *experience* of living, they do not represent an end in itself, a goal. They capture instead a capacity to engage in a process already at play, without setting a finality to the process itself. The aimless engagement that characteristizes the nourishing process is best captured by the character *you* (遊) which can be translated as "aimless wandering" or "roaming." The aimlessness and direction-lessness of *Yang Sheng* lie at the heart of the nourishing-nurturing practices that extend living. Although the lengthening of living might appear to be a goal, it is a mere consequence of nurturing-nourishing life, a beneficial side-effect of walking along the Way or Dao (道). Long life therefore represents in no way the reaching a desired outcome, it cannot be conceived of as an arrival to a predetermined destination.

Another less dramatic and more pastoral anecdote found in the *Zhuangzi* can help us better understand this paradoxical dynamic where the nourishing of life is rendered as an aimless yet life-extending process.[50] In this bucolic scene, "those who skillfully nourish their life" are said to be like "shepherds" who "whip up their sheep from behind" to maintain them in movement, thus spontaneously accomplishing the process of transhumance without ever acting as a guides or leaders. Whereas the pastor is traditionally viewed in the West as a guide and as a leader figure positioned at the head of the flock, the "whipping of the sheep" from behind described in the *Zhuangzi* induces a self-accomplishing process of shepherdship where a flock of sheep moves from pasture to pasture, from one landscape to another, following the continuous flow of the seasons.

Nurturing-nourishing life thus constitutes a fighting of immobility, it requires no set destination. The Way or *Dao* of the shepherd, thus is the Way of circulation, not destination. Whereas the theme of the pathway has often been equated with the notions of objectives and goals in the West,[51] the Way of the *Dao* deals with the question of the *viable*. Viability in this regard joins the notion of sustainability insofar as the viable Way is the one which sustains the lengthiest wandering. The viable Way is therefore never rushed nor hurried; it is never a pathway where predefined goals justify rabid means. Instead, the viable Way makes possible the experience of *you* (遊), an experience where aimless wandering along the *Dao* becomes the life nurturing-nourishing process of *Yang Sheng* itself.

3/ Do I (need to) have a body? From the spirit/matter and body/soul opposition to the *Yin* and *Yang* continuum of living.

The story goes that when Michel Foucault was the examiner at the famous Ecole Normale Supérieure, he asked the twenty-year-old contestants to write a 6 hours dissertation on the following topic: "Do I have a soul?" One can sense here the philosopher's keen interest in the question of the soul as a mere explicative construct. From an intercultural perspective, it nonetheless seems as though the question "Do I have a body" would have been at least as preoccupying and difficult for the young contestants: it challenges even further the relevance of our seemingly "natural" categories of thought. As we've seen, *Yang Sheng* puts into question the relevance of the body/soul duality, thus putting into the question the very relevance of the concept of "body" itself. Does one even have a *single* body in the *Yang Sheng* paradigm? Indeed, if there no is no need for a unified soul principle, *psychè,* then is there still a need for a unified *soma* or body?

*

a. Multiple vs. single bodies, or the lackluster uniformity of globalized translation.

The dissociative opposition of *psychè* and *soma* first found in Plato's *Phaedo* traverses Western thought to the point where the idea of not having a body becomes difficult to grasp in any European language. Even the German distinction between *körper*, the base, inanimate body, and *Lieb*, the living body, connected to life, das Leben, does not fully encompass the wealth of semantic options used to designate "the body" in the *Zhuangzi*.[52] Whereas the notion of the body understood as soma possesses a massive form of univocity, the *Zhuangzi* proposes a variety of equivocal terms whose significations neighbor soma without ever being equatable with it. In the *Zhuangzi* the following terms offer a far less univocal understanding of corporeity: *xing* (形), the actualized (bodily) form -i.e. the body as a circumstantial form in motion-, *shen* (身), the personal entity -i.e one's *own* body-, and *ti* (體), the constitutive body -i.e. the components that constitute a body or the body as an assemblage of parts. These terms are then coupled with the ones we've already seen, polysemic notions like *xin* (心), the heart-mind or *shen* (神), the invisible-spirit.

None of these terms are equivalent or substitutable with one another; they describe opposing polarities that aren't dissociated and relationships of coupling where there is no hierarchical dominance of one term over the other. The contrast between the actualized bodily form(s), *xing* (形), and the invisible spirit(s), *shen* (神), does not constitute an opposition but rather a mutual inclusion. In other words, *xing* acts as a vehicle for *shen*, one cannot live without the other. The equivocal terms used to designate the body in the *Zhuangzi* are markers of intensity: lying in between the physical and the spiritual, they stress the vital tensions that move through the polarities of living. These words become barely distinct from each other, their meaning is unstable and wholly dependent on context: they bring to light the fundamental indeterminacy that governs the Classical Chinese understanding of what the West has regrouped under the single, univocal term of "body."

*

It is interesting to note that the Western term of "body" has been translated in modern Chinese as *shenti* (身體), which as we have seen, refers to the idea of the body as an individuated material substance composed of distinct parts. This translation exemplifies a conjunction where the convergence of two terms is used to approximate an understanding of the body that is initially foreign to Classical Chinese's ideographic logic. *Shen* (身) the body as propriety, and *ti* (體), the body as an assemblage of components, can indeed be joined together to designate what we refer to as the "physical body" yet in doing so the translation subsumes the invisible spiritual dimension contained in terms like *shen* (神) which play a critical role in the Early Chinese understanding of corporeity.[53]

The *shenti* (身體) conjunction thus loses the fertile *bipolar continuum* that stressed the mutual *interdependence* of the *opposing yet complementary* polarities of *xing* (形) and *shen* (神) for example. In this regard the *shenti* conjunction exemplifies the uniformization of thought tied to the process of globalization where the singularities of languages and thought-traditions become subsumed under the weight of an imperious desire to accelerate the ceaseless exchanges of the global market economy; we see here how the technological modernity forged within the language of Being effaces the subtle shadings *correlative thinking* articulated so poetically in Classical Chinese language-thought.

b. Yin-Yang: *opposing and complementary.*

In an effort to stress the effective resources offered by the correlative thinking of Ancient China, it seems appropriate and pedagogical to return to the correlative binome that is perhaps most constitutive of Ancient Chinese thought, the famous *Yin* (陰) and *Yang* (陽). Any student of Chinese medicine, martial arts, or East Asian art history has of course come across these characters in a transliterated form at some point or another of their studies. The very notion of *Yin* and *Yang* has permeated mass culture through the *Taijitu* (太極圖) image: a ubiquitous illustration depicting two swerving hues of black and white forms enlacing and interpenetrating each other that dates back to the Song Dynasty (11th century CE). To which degree this widely diffused image articulates the mutual implication of the two poles of *Yin/Yang* is a matter of philosophical and historical debate; the varying representations over time of this image have stressed diverging aspects of their opposition and mutual implication. Yet across time, the core idea that the *Yin* and the *Yang* forms symbolize an *opposing yet complementary* relationship persists, offering a striking contrast to the Western body and soul opposition where the two substances are, if not opposed, then assuredly *separate*.

*

The Ancient Chinese understanding of health as a *balancing of opposing forces* which also *complement each other* fosters an understanding of illness that isn't causative but rather *correlative*: sickening and healing are never attributable to a single pathogenic agent, these processes are instead tied to an interrelating web of correlations shaped by *Yin* and *Yang* polarities. Thus the great vehicle of illness in the Ancient Chinese medical texts is the wind, *feng* (風)[54]: the wind is never, as such, the single attributable cause of an illness and yet it always carries with it the subtle shiftings of one *Yin* or *Yang* pattern merging into another *Yin* or *Yang* pattern. Wind acts as a *vehicle* for the *transformation* of cold into heat, it accompanies the *shifting* of dampness into dryness, and the *transitioning* of darkness into light-one of the earliest known significations of *Yin* and *Yang*.[55] The *Yin* and *Yang* continuum *governs* a series of processes of concretion and emanation wherein the spiritual emanates from *within* the material: it precludes the idea of a "body" understood as a solely material substance separated from the spiritual substance of the soul, or from the cognizing substance of the mind.

The ubiquitousness of the *Yin* and *Yang* continuum in Classical Chinese language-thought unties the reductive conjunction that limits and reduces the corporeal to *shenti* (身體), all the while expanding the understanding of what the English language can designate as bodily processes of sickening and healing. In this regard, the language of Ancient China offers us an opportunity to wander on the wayside of the presuppositions carried by the language of Being gone global: the uniform and intercontinental "Globish" of the capitalist franchises that unwittingly leverage advertising technologies to spread an ideology of the body which coerces individuals into conforming with logics of consumption, comparison, and exploitation.

Thinking of ourselves as *Yin* and *Yang* polarities, as opposed to physical bodies and spiritual souls, allows us to return to an understanding of *living* that lies *on the wayside* of consumption or exhaustion; it gives us the possibility to describe ourselves as metaphorical "processes at play." These processes entail a complex *intertwining* of bindings and un-bindings, complementary cycles of generation and depletion, and even simultaneous *actuations* of living and dying. Living thus becomes a *process* wherein the *Yin* and *Yang* motions of concretion and emanation, of clarification and opacification, of lightening and darkening, merge in and out of the nutritive *vapor-breath* that lies at the source of life itself, the famous *Qi* (氣) of the acupuncturists.

4/ *Qi* (氣) as source, or the fertilizing motion(s) of voiding(s).

a. "Vapor-breath" vs. "energy" or the hazards of (mis)translating Qi.

As we trace the ancestral and constitutive semantic *Yin* and *Yang* knots around which the Classical Chinese medical language revolves, we are compelled to discuss the term *Qi* (氣) which, as Paul Unschuld rightly pointed out, cannot be reduced to the Western concept of "energy" or *energeia* in Ancient Greek.[56] Whereas *energeia-* the actualized force in motion- is contrasted with *dynamis-* the potential non-actualized force- in Aristotelian physics, the character *Qi* (氣) itself refers to nourishment and nutrition insofar as it is a "phono-semantic compound" derived from the character *mi* (米) which refers to rice and the radical *qì* (气) which refers to air. The character *Qi* can therefore be understood as referring to the *vapor-breath* which *emanates* from a pot of cooked rice. It is easy to reduce this "emanating of vapor-breath" into the Aristotelian understanding of a physical force in action, in this case heat, and thus to translate *Qi* (氣) as "energy," thus making the sinogram an avatar of *energeia;* yet doing so overshadows both the *nutritive image* at the heart of the character's significance as well as the cosmological connotations carried along by the idea of "vapor-breath."

*

Once freed from the energetic understanding of *Qi*, it becomes possible to envision with greater clarity the subtle *generative* processes that bind together nurturing-nourishing (養), living (生), and vapor-breath to the *Yin* and *Yang* continuum found across the poetic and scientific texts of Early China. *Qi* indeed bears a close relationship to *Yin* and *Yang* as suggested by the second sentence of the 42nd paragraph of the *Laozi:*

萬 物 負 陰 而 抱 陽， 沖 氣 以 為 和

Wan wu fu yin er bao yang, chong qi yi wei de

55

"All things carry *Yin* and hold onto *Yang*, thus harmonizing the outpouring(s) of *Qi*."

This understanding of *Qi* as a harmonizing (和) *vector of living* instills the notion that *Qi* refers to a primal moment of outpouring and emptying (沖) where, as Lacan put it, "language eats the real."[57] That is to say that the linguistic character *Qi* (氣), with its anchoring in the nutritive image of the grain of rice, designates an elementary process wherein nourishing is both the source and the product of living. This linguistic *equation* of nourishing and living, of input and output, underlies the logic of *Qi*. Talking about *Qi* instead of bodies, souls, or even spirits allows us to (re)connect with a level of existing that *precedes* the instillation of language.

Qi is indeed both beneath and beyond human language; not only does it instill "animate beings" with life, *Qi* also *(en)livens* so called "inanimate beings" like rocks, buildings, and literary texts. *Qi* traverses both the human and non-human realms; it deploys its motions both at the source and at the limit of anything that can be expressed within the confines of language. In the fifth century CE literary treatise *Wen Xin Diao Long* (文心雕龍), which could be translated into "writing feeling and dragon carving," there is a marvelous poetic description in a chapter entitled *Feng Gu* (風骨) or "wind(s)-bone(s)" where a literary text is likened to a bony structure, *Gu* (骨), traversed by wind(s) (風).[58] For the author of this theoretical treatise, the Buddhist monk and scholar Liu Xie (劉勰), the *Qi* of a literary text thus emanates from the amalgamation of "wind and bone" that composes it. *Qi* thus permeates language itself to the point where the very term, much like the Greek "Being," constitutes a semantic point of origin within the Classical Chinese language that acts as a primal unifier, lying *beneath* even the *Yin* and *Yang* continuum.

b. Qi as a semantic voiding impulse or the Zen master's bathroom.

In both a literal and a figurative sense, the term *Qi* acts as primal and unifying-semantic void, as a vacancy or vacating of language that can be filled with endless significations; *Qi* is never dissociated from the primary filling gesture of nourishing that its image designates; and yet, it also never seizes the voiding impulse that enables the filling in the first place.

*

It is therefore not a coincidence that the notion of *Qi* found in Early Chinese texts like *Zhuangzi, Laozi* or *Huangdi Neijing* bears a close affinity with the Zen or *Chan* (禪)[59] Buddhist notion of vacating, *kong* (空)[60]. Channeling Qi encapsulates the *operative* voiding and emptying that characterizes meditative activity: meditators (re)connect with a primary state of *indetermination*, a primal *moment of voiding* where they transform themselves into an *empty vessel*. A Zen master was once asked what the most Zen moment of his day was, he replied laughing: "When I go to the bathroom!"[61]

*

The operation of *Qi* works both on the "metabolic" or "material" level of emptying the bowels and on the "existential" or "spiritual" level of emptying awareness. The spiritual emptying process is correlated to the basal defecation process, both are tied to the *(im)pulsating motions* of *Qi*, both are wholly dependent upon its ceaseless impetus. (Re)connecting with this primal input/impulse of *Qi* is what allows the meditator to tune into the *emptying operation* that enables the release of suffering and the welcoming of "enlightening" or "satori" (悟) which could also be translated playfully as *(en)light(e)ning*.[62] Meditation thus becomes a vehicle for the *dejection of obstruction*, while also serving as a primal nurturing-nourishing *activity*. Ancient Greece and its resolute attachment to the ideality of the theoretical model form (*eidos*), appear to lie, once again, thousands of miles away from the effortless nurturing-nourishing and the carefree emptying of the laughing Zen Master attuned to the *flowing(s)* of *Qi* as it moves in and out of his bowels and his urethra.

c. Landscape(s) and the ethics of Qi.

In this regard, it is clear how the language of Ancient China neatly ties the ethical plane to the vital plane. Ethics in this context consists in the unthawing of *Qi* in an effort to deploy its animating function. Ethical living thus isn't the embodiment of some transcendent ideal, it becomes instead a process of natural elevation and deployment wherein humanity (re)connects itself to the base motion of *Qi* which moves both within us and without us. Practicing ethical living thus (re)connects us with this elemental and foundational dimension of *Qi*: ethical living is therefore neither an idealistic nor a materialistic pursuit, it is instead a process of perpetual *refining* and perpetual *attuning* where the connection to the source of flux is both *enlivened* and *sustained*.

Classical Chinese thought offers a particularly wide-ranging and ecological understanding of ethical conduct that envisions not only our relationships with the human realm but also our relationship with the non-human realm. In a dense, complex and critical passage of the *Mengzi*, Master Meng details how the nourishment of the heart-mind's (心) proclivity towards humaneness (仁) can be likened to the nourishment of the trees that cover a mountainous landscape.[63] Much like trees need to be nurtured and nourished by the "rain and dew" carried along by "the peaceful morning *Qi*" in order to grow and thrive, the human heart-mind also needs to be nourished by the peaceful *Qi* of morning and replenished by night time *Qi* in order to "live its best life." Proper nurturance and nourishment allow the heart-mind to thrive and to realize its inherent moral propensity: they are what prevents it from veering into abject inhumaneness. Thus, the emotional disposition of the heart-mind and its natural moral propensity need to be nourished like trees: "If it receives proper nurturance nourishment, there is nothing that will not grow; if it loses its nurturance-nourishment, there is nothing that will not vanish."[64]

This analogic equation of a physical *landscape* with an *emotion-*

al disposition shows that the notions of *Qi* and nurturing-nourishing (養) extend both *beyond and beneath* the human realm. The ethics of *Qi* and nurturance-nourishment are both natural and civilizational; they lie *on the wayside* of a nature/culture distinction where ethics would consist in either separating ourselves from a predetermined "natural order" or in a capacity to model our action on this supposed "natural order." Nourishing and nurturing life, when understood as an ethical path, therefore has little to do with conforming to a metaphysical ideal and much more to do with a subtle capacity of *attunement*.

d. The Way(s) of living nurturance or the aimless wandering of the Butcher's Knife.

One of the most famous passages of the *Zhuangzi* is without a doubt the tale of Butcher Ding. This remarkable story offers both an enigmatic meditation on the theme of *Yang Sheng* as well as a striking portrait of a joyous laborer who is unafraid to talk back to a Prince, an offence that could have easily been punished by death in Early China. There is no better way to introduce the story of Butcher Ding than to restitute it in its entirety.

*

Butcher Ding's Way(s)

Butcher Ding was carving an ox for Lord Wenhui.

His hand slapped, his shoulder lunged, his foot stamped, his knee bent;

with a hiss! With a thud!

The brandished blade as it sliced never missed the rhythm,

now in time with the Mulberry Forest dance,

now with an orchestra playing the Jingshou tune.

'Oh, excellent!' said Lord Wenhui.

'That skill (技) should attain such heights!'

*'What your servant cares about is **the Way(s)** (道), I have left skill behind me.*

When I first began to carve oxen,

I saw nothing but oxen wherever I looked.

Three years more and I never saw an ox as a whole.

*Nowadays, I am in touch through the **invisible spirit** (神) in me, and do not look with the eye.*

With the senses I know where to stop, the invisible spirit I desire runs its course.

I rely on Heaven's structuring (天理),

cleave along the main seams,

let myself be guided by the main cavities,

go by what is inherently so.

A ligament or tendon I never touch, not to mention solid bone.

A good cook changes his chopper once a year, because he hacks.

A common cook changes it once a month, because he smashes.

Now I have had this chopper for nineteen years, and have taken apart several thousand oxen,

And yet the edge is as though it were fresh from the grindstone.

*At that joint **there is an interval** (有間),*

and the chopper's edge has no thickness;

if you insert what has no thickness where there is an interval, then,

what more could you ask, of course:

*there is ample room to **wander** (遊) and move the edge around.*

That's why after nineteen years the edge of my chopper is as though it were fresh from the grindstone.

'However, whenever I come to something intricate,

I see where it will be hard to handle and cautiously prepare
myself,

my gaze settles on it;

action slows down for it,

you scarcely see the flick of the chopper–

and at one stroke the tangle has been unraveled,

like a clod crumbling to the ground.

I stand chopper in hand,

look proudly round at everyone,

dawdle to enjoy the triumph until I'm quite satisfied,

then clean the chopper and put it away.'

'Excellent!' said Lord Wen Hui.

'Listening to the words of Butcher Ding,

I have learned from them how **to nurture-nourish living** *(養*
生).[65] '

e. When two butchers from Antiquity meet: theory and practice vs. rhythm and activity.

As hinted at earlier, the *Yang Sheng* described in the *Zhuangzi* bears little resemblance to the nourishment of the soul found in the Western tradition. The distance separating the *Yang Sheng* paradigm from the mind/body/soul paradigm is made most apparent when considering a contemporaneous example from Antiquity which involves a butcher: the one found in Plato's *Phaedrus*.[66] Whereas the butcher in Plato's text is valued for his capacity to neatly separate the parts (*stoicheion*) from the whole, proving himself to be a master of division (*diairesis*), Butcher Ding is praised for his capacity to thread his knife through the *interstices* that lie *in between* (間) the joints of the ox. In Plato's text, butchering is an art of division: its true action consists in stressing the existence of a dividable, greater bodily whole. In the *Zhuangzi*, Butcher Ding's knife becomes a surface of fine tuning, the expression of his ability to nourish life as he roams along the Way (道).

As the Butcher becomes more acquainted with his craft of butchering throughout the years, he does not develop an anatomical knowledge of the different parts of the ox. Instead, he cultivates a *sensitivity* that allows the knife to glide and *aimlessly wander* (遊) alongside the void, interstitial spaces that lie *in between* the joints of the beast. Butcher Ding's knife thus never loses its sharpened edge, it embodies the admirable perfecting of his sensitivity throughout his life. It isn't Butcher Ding's capacity to divide the ox into neatly separated parts which causes the marveling of the Prince of Wen Hui and which leads the sovereign to become *absorbed* by the *rhythmical musicality* of the chopping gestures; instead, it is the butcher's capacity to thread his knife *in between* the ox's joints in an effortless, fluid, and harmonious manner and to thus aimlessly *make possible* the nurturing-nourishing of life which makes him so worthy of praise and admiration.

*

Butcher Ding's story thus exemplifies the materiality of the Way or the *Dao* in which the spiritual decanting process of *Yang Sheng* can be performed by way of an activity as elementary as butchering. Butchering isn't a metaphor for a capacity to join a separate, ideal Way understood to be the model for all Ways; it is instead a vital activity which results from the execution of the effortless activities of threading, cutting and chopping. The butcher's precision, his capacity to be *efficient*, results from the *ease* with which he wields his knife, not from his knowledge of the anatomical parts that compose the ox. In other words, unlike Plato's butcher who derives a universal knowledge of the ox by dividing it into distinct parts, Butcher Ding does not acquire any other knowledge than the one derived from his activity.

The term knowledge is in fact inadequate to describe his activity since the perfecting of his craft (技) is but a pure result of his ability to *fine tune* his gestures, a consequence of his capacity to lean into the Way of the knife as it cuts through the void spaces lying in between the joints of the ox. The Butcher's gestures therefore do not represent his capacity to integrate an ideal, pre-existing understanding of the ox's anatomy; he does not acquire knowledge per se as he slices through the ox, he doesn't learn anything about the essence of the ox's anatomy or about the essence of what it means to be a good butcher. He instead learns how to *lean into* the Way of his knife, moving through a series of effortless movements, weaving them together into a musical, rhythmical, and patterned sequence where the crafter becomes indistinguishable from the crafting; a *rhythm* where effortless activity becomes a vehicle for the nurturing-nourishing of life itself.

The story of the butcher thus portrays *Yang Sheng* as a worldly Way that cannot be dissociated from simple quotidian activities. Butcher Ding's activity involves a circulatory process where activity allows one to move with ease both along and across the *Dao*. Activity thus becomes an educative process of learning where the experience of passing with ease through the interstitial voids threaded by the cutting of the knife is more important than learning or formulating a theoretical base of knowledge designed to be applied by all practitioners of the craft. The execution of a rhythmical activity therefore induces a connection to the vital proceedings of nourishment and living that is indistinguishable from these proceedings themselves. In Butcher Ding's story, the notions of theory and practice, procedures and outcomes, ideals and goals are rendered, if not useless, then surely irrelevant; it is instead effortless and aimless *(in)activity* which becomes the primal, *operative* vector of nurturance, nourishment, and vitality. There is nothing "aspirational" about the Butcher's story, he does not represent a set path of living that can be formulaically idealized or replicated, he instead channels and demonstrates a propensity towards rhythmicity and attunement that renders his fluid and easeful approach to living admirable on both an esthetic and ethical level.

*

Evoking the story of Butcher Ding alongside Plato's butcher does not necessarily amount to a comparison, the point isn't to "compare and contrast" the different representations of butchering found across cultures at a given point in time, in this case the 5th and 4th century BCE. Instead, the intercultural approach to philosophy seeks to offer a strategic *point of viewing* where the *fertile unthought* lying *in between* the cultures of Ancient Greece and Ancient China can be *probed* in order to *address* the challenges we face in today's globalized context. The construction of this strategic point of viewing allows us to reflect, not upon the differences separating cultures, but rather upon the *resources* that they can *share* with each other once put face to face. In this regard, intercultural philosophy does not adhere to an astringent, self-loathing critique of Western thought nor is it complacent when it comes to the rabid commercialization of a fantasized image of East Asian culture. The understanding of *Yang Sheng* developed through an intercultural reading of the *Zhuangzi* alongside Plato does not represent an overturning or a deconstruction of Western *logos,* simply a desire to *wander along its wayside.*

Any analysis of this meeting between two contemporaneous texts of Antiquity as somehow reflecting or illustrating the positivity, negativity, let alone superiority, of one civilization over the other would be wholly misguided; any enterprise that seeks to merely enumerate the *differences* separating these texts and thus silo them into cultural niches would be counterproductive and unstimulating. The understanding of *Yang Sheng* derived from the face to face with the butcher of the *Phaedrus* and Butcher Ding reflects instead what can *still* be thought today, *in between* the dividing lines which separate cultures.

One could say that such a strategic, intercultural approach to *Yang Sheng* remains steeped in a euro-centric perspective. Indeed, it does not engage in an overt denunciation of Western thought's perceived ills, even though it categorically refuses a facile and marketplace-ready caricature of Ancient Chinese thought. This kind of criticism of the strategic ans intercultural approach to *Yang Sheng* appears to be wholly ideological in nature, it betrays a dogmatic adherence to the proliferation of contemporary discourses which blame Western civilization and the technological capitalism it produced for all the ills of the world. The ideological worldview wherein the West is exclusively responsible for the diffusion of atrocity further neglects the vast history of abjection, oppression, misogyny, and violence that characterizes not only Western civilization but arguably all other civilizations as well. It is particularly important when discussing the topic of *Yang Sheng* to dispel any fantasized appreciation of East Asian culture while also stressing the critical junctures that eluded Western thought in its quest to define a teleological understanding of morality and politics; that is to say, in its quest to define an understanding of morality and politics wholly turned towards a single, ultimate goal: *happiness*.

5/ Wandering, or the wayside of happiness.

a. The (impossible) search for happiness, or the story of a (Western) neurotic fixation.

If there is one concept which, from a psychoanalytic perspective, constitutes the neurotic point fixation of Western thought, it is assuredly happiness. The idea of happiness as being the final goal that every human being aspires to is indeed so deeply embedded in Western thought that it traverses its history from Aristotle all the way into the 20th century.

*

At the beginning and at the end of his *Nicomachean Ethics* (books I and IX), Aristotle posits that happiness is the supreme finality towards which all human beings tend, as suggested by the usage of the verb *epiesthai* followed by the genitive which opens and closes the treatise. Happiness thus serves as a theoretical end that in turn generates a model for ethical conduct. For Aristotle, happiness represents the goal of ethical conduct, the ultimate self-realization of the human being.

Following Aristotle's lead while also adopting a decidedly more pessimistic outlook, Sigmund Freud remains tributary to this idea of the ultimate goal of happiness in the second paragraph of his famous essay *Unbehagen in der Kultur*, translated as "Civilization and its discontents" in the English Standard Edition. In the 1930 text, Freud argues that the neurotic nature of the civilizational process condemns the human being to frustration because it represses the satisfaction of his libidinal drives in order to foster social cohesion, thus precluding the human being from ever reaching happiness. Nonetheless the human being desires happiness because of his attachment to the pleasure principle, *eros*; and yet the bondage of this pleasure principle with a destructive principle, *thanatos*, renders it impossible for him to ever reach his final goal: happiness[67].

The goal of happiness thus represents from a psychoanalytic standpoint an impossible and unattainable destination, a source of misery and discontent. Even though the psychoanalytic perspective avoids in many ways the common tropes of Western thought and sheds a hitherto *unbeknownst* light upon them,[68] it is striking to see Freud struggling to break free from the conceptual framework of happiness inherited from Aristotle. Despite his best effort to argue that the desire for destruction, *thanatos*, exists *within* the desire for construction, *eros,* Freud remains unable to dispel the idea that somehow the civilizational process is correlated to a real, and therefore impossible as Lacan would say,[69] quest to find happiness.

*

The pursuit of happiness thus acts as a foundational ground of Western thought while also constituting one of its greatest limitations. Investigating the intercultural potential of the *Yang Sheng* paradigm does not correspond to an overturning of the notion of happiness; rather, it invites us to foster a capacity to *distance* ourselves from the very *ideal* of happiness so that we can *wander on its wayside*. Happiness must not be overturned in favor of nurturing-nourishing living, nor should it be thought that happiness understood as "good fortune" does not constitute an important, if not constitutive, facet of Ancient Chinese culture. There is indeed a commonality between the Early Chinese understanding of good fortune, the commonplace term *Fu* (福) found as early as the ancient *Classic of Poetry*, and the ancient Greek concept of *eudaimonia* found in the pre-Socratic texts of Democritus and Heraclitus which alludes to a "good demon" who bears fortuitous tidings.[70] Nonetheless, the understanding of *Yang Sheng* found in the *Zhuangzi* represents a *departure* from idea of good fortune as it is found not only in Ancient Greece- the Greek understanding of the *daimon* relies upon the *psychè* and *soma* duality- but also in earlier conceptions of *Fu*. Instead of offering an understanding of happiness, blessings, or good fortune understood as a destination or a finality, the *Zhuangzi* describes instead a process of progressive attunement to the flowing of living itself, a process of continuous transformation that bears no resemblance with the reaching of a final goal.[71]

b. The Way(s) of the viable or the wayside of the marketplace of (un)happiness.

The approach to living found in the *Zhuangzi* exemplifies the Way(s) of the *viable*, the Way(s) encapsulated in the common question/answer: "how goes it? It *goes*." This pathway of "just going," which lies *on the wayside* of "going good" or "going bad," exemplifies a fluidification of existence where the simple act of living places one both *beneath and beyond* the oppositions that constitute happiness and its corollary, unhappiness. The Sages who practice *Yang Sheng*, the ones who fine tunes their capacity to nurture and nourish life, learn to move like the fish in water: they flow alongside the stream, match its intensity, and cycle through motions of transformation, as they float in and out of the void spaces that tie inspiration to expiration. Nourishing and nurturing living, *on the wayside* of happiness, thus requires both a capacity to prevent stagnation and an ability to *stand outside* a logic of pre-conceived values and goals. In this regard, the understanding of health that is found when "nourishing and nurturing living" bears little resemblance with a marketplace-ready conception of "wellness."

Such a predetermined understanding of "health and wellness" understood as the absence of disease would only point towards an idealized representation of these concepts as perfected states of being destined to be attained through the application of a rigorous practice derived from a theoretical model. *Yang Sheng* fosters instead an understanding of living where vitality is nurtured and nourished, as opposed to sought out. The simultaneous simplicity and subtlety of *Yang Sheng* endows the bare, quotidian motions of breathing, walking, and eating with a deep capacity to nurture and nourish life on a spiritual, material, and existential level.

Yang Sheng therefore bears in this regard a far greater resemblance with land management and with governance than it does with a surgical and interventionist understanding of medicine. Western thought stresses a seemingly tragic opposition where hard, fast, and intense living becomes opposed to slow, lengthy, and boring living; a *chiaroscuro* portrait akin to a Caravaggio painting where the sharp brightness of flickering light stands in stark contrast with the dimmed tones of dying ember. Thousands of miles away from these tragic theatrics and dramatic portraits, *Yang Sheng* literature encourages us to understand living as a plot of land destined to be managed and cultivated. Nourishing and nurturing living thus becomes the result of a *regulatory activity* where the *resources* generated by the very processes of living are channeled by and within a set of technical frameworks that promote growth and prevent depletion. [72]

*

It is therefore *Yang Sheng*'s very propensity towards economic thinking that makes it the big business that it is today. The 4.2 trillion-dollar global wellness industry has indeed specialized itself in the commodification and commercialization of Instagram-ready "wellness routines" that invoke connections to ancestral knowledge and healing, often citing East Asian *Yang Sheng* practices as quintessential "alternatives" to Western medicine. While one can admire, deride, or ignore these hucksters who profit off *Yang Sheng* in the global (un)happiness market, it is nonetheless critical to stress the rich possibility that the *Yang Sheng* paradigm holds for the care workers of the globalized world. *Yang Sheng* can indeed foster an approach to care work that emphasizes not just the worry of caring but also the joyful vitality that goes alongside nourishing and nurturing living.

*

Although the *Yang Sheng* paradigm fosters an extraordinarily subtle understanding of attunement to living, it fails to offer us a meaningful understanding of *the political*. The story of Xi Kang, a 3rd century CE man of letters who authored a "Discourse on *Yang Sheng*," seems to exemplify the political limitations of the ethics of *Yang Sheng*.[73] Having cultivated his entire life a desire to remain *on the wayside* of politics, Xi Kang could nonetheless not escape being born into the ruling class: he ended up being caught up in the whirlwind of court intrigue despite his best intentions and was sentenced to death by the tyrant that he refused to serve. The story goes that even as he was preparing himself to be sentenced to death, Xi Kang continued on with his *Yang Sheng* activities, playing one last "Ode to Harmony" on his *Guqin* lute before his execution.

Xi Kang's story thus exemplifies a terrible state of political *alienation* and powerlessness; the absolute *lack of ideal* found in the *Yang Sheng* activities he had devoted his life to seemed to have precluded him from ever developing an effective capacity of *resistance*: the imperialistic and militaristic style of government that he despised and sought to avoid at all costs had no difficulty crushing him and imposing itself for the long haul over the course of Chinese history. It is safe to say that, to this very day, the figure of Xi Kang remains the image *par excellence* of what could be called a "marginal character." As we shall see in the following chapter, a character that was much more central in Early Chinese political life was the Strategist. Drawing from oft commented texts like the famous *Art of War,* we will investigate the ways in which the Early Chinese and Ancient Greek cultural contexts produced various representations of *efficacy* which continue to bear a decisive influence on management, politics, and culture today.

CHAPTER III
Strategies of efficacy

1/ Modelization and ideality, or the confines of the theory/ practice dichotomy.

The question of strategy appears to be an efficacious one to address issues arising in the world of management and on the geopolitical level. It constitutes one of those prime vantage points where the distance separating the geo-historic worlds of Ancient China and Ancient Greece is both apparent and operative. What this means is that it is possible to envision novel approaches to the question of strategy by probing the fertile *unthought* that lies *in between* Ancient Greek and Early Chinese conceptions of strategy. While the Ancient Greek approach to strategy emphasizes *modelization*, the Ancient Chinese understanding of strategy emphasizes *xing shi* (形勢) or the *situation's potential*.

In the final sections of this chapter, we will demonstrate how an intercultural and a philosophical appreciation of notions derived from Ancient Greek and Early Chinese texts can give us powerful conceptual tools that can help us make sense of the most troubling trends in 21st century politics: the erosion of democracy and the re-birth of totalitarianism.

a. The Greek passion for the eidos or the model form.

Before delving into the specificities of the Early Chinese approach to strategy exemplified by the notion of the *situation's potential*, it is critical to approach with greater detail the Ancient Greek understanding of strategy characterized by the practice of *modeliza-*

tion. The Greek understanding of strategy is first and foremost based on the apprehension of an ideal *model form*, the *eidos*, and on the strategist' capacity to bring this model form forth into the world. The Greek strategist seeks the best plan in advance; he implements this plan according to his will and *forces* the ideality of the *eidos* into the world. His heroic approach is best summarized by the adage "where there's a will, there's a way."

Modelization, and its corollary, implementation, represent the paradigmatic components of the Greek and therefore Western conception of strategy. These two concepts permeate the Western understanding of military, political, and economic issues; more than ever, the couple of modelization and implementation continues to guide decision-making processes in domains where elaborate mathematical "projective modeling" informs key strategic plans and actions.

b. Phronesis *vs. metis,* theory *vs. practice.*

The Greek emphasis on modelization continues to this day to shape an understanding of strategy which relies heavily on the Theory/Practice distinction. Theory of course corresponds to the model while Practice consists in the implementation or application of the model. Although modelization came to dominate the Greek approach to strategy, it was not always so. Aristotle theorized the importance of *phronesis*, which has been translated as "prudence" or "practical wisdom" in the 6th book of his *Nichomachean Ethics*. For Aristotle, *phronesis* constitutes an "intellectual virtue" capable of addressing the gap separating the modelized ideality of the *eidos* and its practical finality, the *telos*. The strategic action of *phronesis* focuses on the transition wherein a model becomes enacted; it pertains to the decision-making processes that are inherent to political governance. Whereas the mathematician Thales can understand reality on the basis of pure *eidos*, that is to say on the basis of the pristine model forms of geometry, the Athenian politician Pericles must approach reality on the basis of *phronesis*: it is mindful caution which allows him to alleviate the ideality of theory and facilitate its pragmatic implementation.

Another Greek term pertaining to strategy that is perhaps most distant from the modelizing theoretical regime of the *eidos* is the *metis* or the "cunning ruse" found in the *Odyssey*.[74] Odysseus embodies the values of *metis* because he exemplifies a capacity to profit from a given situation, and adapt his actions to circumstances. He is not a hero celebrated for his brazen actions but rather a survivor praised for his inventiveness. To use familiar terms, Odysseus is the one who manages to always "pull it off." Yet the significance of Odysseus' *metis* is short lived in Ancient Greek culture, the notion is quickly subsumed by the primacy of the *eidos*: Greek mythology even states that Zeus marries *metis* and then devours her![75] The development of post-Homeric Greek civilization indeed confirms that the thought of the *metis* was (literally) devoured by the *eidos*.

c. The situational, or the unthought within Western strategy.

The supremacy of the *eidos* and of its modelizations has led to a relative deficit of strategic thinking in the history of Western thought. While there are several tactical treatises and a plethora of war narratives dating back to the Greeks, the question of strategy is often merely approached under the angle of general considerations and few thinkers seek to investigate the notion itself. The great 19th century European theorist of war Carl von Clausewitz offers perhaps the most striking example of this tendency which dissociates the ideal plane of the *eidos* from the actual plane of the what he terms "circumstances" or "peculiarities" (*die Eigentümlich*).[76] Clausewitz indeed distingui-shes the model of war, its *eidos*, from real war. For Clausewitz, the reality of war encompasses what escapes from the model, what deviates from it. The very concept of war in Clausewitz' thought represents a deviation from the modelizing regime of the *eidos*, it forges a novel understanding of the "circumstantial" or of "circumstantiality" (*Eigentümlichkeit*).

From the perspective of the 19th century German strategist, the advent of the circumstantial therefore represents that point in time where the application of a project or the realization of a model deviate from their original set course as they become confronted with the absolute contingency of circumstances: literally the things "standing around" (*circum stare* in Latin, *peri stasis* in Greek) the model image of war. Clauswitz's idea of the circumstantial or of "circumstantiality" is nonetheless hampered by the limitations of its own cultural context and theoretical assumptions; it betrays the implicit perspective and gaze at the heart of an idealistic or formalistic worldview: the perspective of a desiring ego gazing at a defective world where the indeterminacy of circumstantiality prevents the linear unfolding of an ideal *model- form* or *eidos*.

d. Modelization and the birth of Modern Science.

It is not excessive to state that the development of Western science and technology is intertwined with the history of the modelization strategies first developed in Ancient Greece. Mathematics and geometry represent the ultimate form of modelization, the figures of Euclidean geometry and the universal theorems that they unearth constitute the basis of the Western scientific and technological method of *projective modeling*. The technological application of mathematics, geometry, and projective modeling is apparent when considering the (literally) projectile invention of the catapult attributed to Archimedes. The Ancient Greek military treatises which detail the geometric modeling that underlies the development of strategic infantry formations like the phalanx also showcase the importance of projective modeling in warfare strategies. And yet, as the seminal works of the British biochemist and sinologist Joseph Needham demonstrate, until the 15th century CE, the Chinese maintained technological superiority over the West, partially because their science did not presuppose such a radical division between an ideal theoretical plane and a circumstantial plane of action.[77] How is it then that European projective modeling came to dominate the technological sphere in the Modern Era despite its initial inefficacies?

It appears as though projective modeling left the confines of military strategy and found its fullest and most effective development in the scientific and technological domain with the advent of Galilean physics in the Renaissance. While traditional Aristotelian science emphasized the observational methods of the life-sciences, the study of pure mathematics remained confined to the more mystical teachings of Pythagoreanism and Neoplatonism during the Middle Ages. It is Galileo's affirmations that mathematics compose "the alphabet that God used to write the universe" and that "the book of nature is written in mathematics"[78] that set the course for a shift in the history of science and technology, a shift where projective modeling would offer us tools that allow us to become "like the masters and possessors of nature"[79] as Descartes famously stated. Although Galileo's world-view does not radically depart from Archimedes' understanding of the relationship binding the mathematical to the physical, he furthers the Archimedean paradigm of mathematical modelization by applying it not only to static bodies but also to rotating bodies. It is this furthering of Archimedean mathematical modelizations applied to physical phenomena set forth by Francis Bacon, Galileo, Descartes, and Newton which lead to the astounding development of technology of the Modern Era.

Modelization is a potent strategy that "explains the real by way of the impossible" as Alexander Koyré, and later Lacan, elegantly put it.[80] Bacon and Descartes were keenly aware of the powerful historical technological *shift in the possible* that Galilean projective modeling enabled. Despite its indubitable technological force, the political and gubernatorial efficacy of mathematical projective modeling remains lacking to this day. If anything, the COVID-19 crisis has demonstrated the impossible limits of governance strategies solely predicated on mathematical projective modeling: it has left us hungry for an *efficient* understanding of governing, managing, and leading founded upon a careful assessment of complex intertwining processes that bind together the social, the economic, and the scientific.

2/ Singularity of the Chinese *Bin Fa* (兵法) strategical treatises: correlativity and the situation's potential.

Thousands of miles away from Ancient Greece and its projective modeling strategies, Early Chinese culture developed a unique literature devoted to strategy and warfare that finds no equivalent in other civilizations. This literature of course finds its apex point in the famous *Art of War* by Sun Tzu or *Sunzi Bin Fa* (孫子兵法).[81] This widely referenced treatise is prominently featured in popular culture: high-powered characters in films like Oliver Stone's *Wall Street* or in the TV series *The Sopranos* seek inspiration in its aphoristic formulas. If we try to understand the factors that enabled the development of the singular approach to strategy and warfare found in the *Bin Fa* strategical treatises, it becomes clear that the development of these texts has nothing to do with a higher prevalence of warfare in Ancient China: the countless war narratives we find throughout the entirety of Antiquity, from Ramses II all the way to Caesar, amply suggest that the Mediterranean world was just as rife with constant warmongering!

After careful consideration, it appears as though the singularity of the Early Chinese approach to strategy finds its origin in the *correlative* thinking found most famously in the *Yin/Yang* paradigm discussed in the previous chapter.[82] While the Greeks developed an approach to strategy and technology focused on the unearthing of *causal relationships*, the Ancient Chinese developed an understanding of strategy focused on *interdependent processes*. The Ancient Chinese approach to strategy can, in essence, be summarized by the popular expression: "it takes two to tango."

a. Xing shi *(形勢) or the situation's potential.*

While the correlative *Yin/Yang* dichotomy of course plays a critical role in the Ancient Chinese approach to strategy, it is possible to unearth in the *Bin Fa treatises* a set of two terms which shed newfound light on the question of strategy: *xing* (形),[83] commonly translated as "form" or "bodily form," and which can also indicate "situation," and *shi* (勢),[84] which can be translated as "power," "tendency," or "potential." Together, these two terms form the basis of the intercultural concept of the *situation's potential: xing* (形) refers to the situation, the configuration, and the terrain, while *shi* (勢) refers to potential, potentiality, and potency. The concept of the situation's potential, *xing shi* (形勢), establishes strategy not as technique of modelization, but rather as an art of *maturation*.

Much like the Ancient Greeks, the Ancient Chinese looked at the physical world for inspiration; the image of water flowing down a hill came to define their strategic understanding of the situation's potential. The downstream effect of water flowing down a hill and the acceleration it induces form the basis of an understanding of *propensity* where the strategist leverages an existing terrain or situation to his advantage, just like water leverages the incline of the hill to accelerate its descending motion.[85] Leveraging the situation's potential or the terrain has little to do with projective modeling and much more to do with a meticulous *assessment* process. When assessing and reviewing the singularities of the strategic terrain of operation, the strategist detects and evaluates the various situations at play to guarantee the optimal efficiency of his military or political operation.

The Ancient Chinese strategist thus did not defeat his enemy because he possessed the best plan, he defeated his enemy because he had assessed the terrain more thoroughly than his opponent. Having probed and detected the various strengths, weaknesses, saturations, and aerations that the terrain presented, the strategist merely adjusted his actions so that they could lean more efficiently upon the propensity already *at play* in the given situation. He did not ask himself what model was best suited to apprehend the circumstance; instead he asked himself how he could correctly analyze the strategic *situation* and the forces at play in order to fully lean in or out of the *potentials* that they held. Much like the surfer who waits patiently for the wave that can sustain the longest and smoothest surf, the Ancient Chinese strategist remained on the lookout for those powerful situations that could sustain him in his effort to defeat his enemy in the most effortless fashion, miles away from the heroics of the Greek epics.

Although the *xing shi* binome only concerns two chapters of the *Sunzi Bin Fa* and could therefore be understood as an ancillary notion, the philosophical approach to sinology developed in this book seeks to emphasize the understanding of *efficacy* suggested by these terms. The *xing shi* binome can help us re-envision any situation's potential as a *resource* that can be detected and leveraged. The notion of *xing shi* allows us to bypass the Theory/Practice division, it gives us the means to detach ourselves from the pre-conception that associates concrete situations to bothersome hindrances.

b. Strategic vs. pragmatic.

Although we can find examples of strategists leveraging a situation's potential in the West (Napoleon casting aside the battle plan at Austerlitz to strategically leverage the fog to launch his attack), the recourse to Early Chinese strategical treatises gives us the means to further articulate a philosophy of strategy that isn't solely limited to a commonplace form of pragmatism. The approach to strategy found in the *Bin Fa* treatises is informed by a sensitivity to the barely perceptible. Unlike pragmatism, Early Chinese strategy does not limit its enquiry to the empirical realm of observable phenomena. Whereas pragmatism focuses its actions on what has already appeared -i.e. the empirical appearance of phenomena-, the strategic thought of the *Bin Fa* treatises aims to detect subterranean processual dynamics *prior* to their appearance in the realms of empirical perception and observation.

In this regard, Early Chinese medical practices and their approach to illness offers a striking example of Ancient Chinese strategic thinking at play in a field that is neither political nor military.[86] Early Chinese doctors did not limit themselves to a pragmatic course of treatment derived only from the observation of the illness as it appeared to them: their treatments were not solely destined to address the visible symptoms exhibited by the ill person. Their approach to medicine wasn't programmatic, they instead sought to assess and detect underlying processual patterns that were conducive to sickening or healing, thereby attempting to inhibit or leverage the processes of generation and depletion at play in illness and in healing.

Much like the strategist who detected a metaphorical propensive incline that allowed the effects of his strategy to effortlessly snowball towards victory, the Ancient Chinese doctor detected situational potentials that allowed him to curtail the depletive and destructive processes of illness and leverage instead the propensive processes that nurture and nourish both living and healing. Early Chinese approaches to strategy and medicine might resemble pragmatism insofar as they do not rely on theoretical models that are validated *a priori*, that is to say independently from experience, as in the idealist paradigm. Nonetheless, the attention and importance they grant to the pre-phenomenal, and thus the pre-empirical, distinguishes them from a philosophy where the observable constitutes the primary point of reference (pragmatism or empiricism). In other words, the strategic thinking of the *Bin Fa* treatises and of the Early Chinese medical texts developed an understanding of the *processual* where paying attention to the non-observable was just as important as correctly analyzing the observable.

3/ Effects without ends: goal vs. maturation.

a. Ends, means, models, and causes: the foundations of Greek strategy.

The paradigm of modelization is predicated upon the Means/Ends distinction. The Western thought of the *eidos* and of the model form is intrinsically tied to the concept of *telos*, the end or the goal. The best and most efficient model in this paradigm is the one that enables the fastest attainment of the goal. The concept of the *telos* structures Greek and therefore Western thought to a dazzling extent: the scientific understanding of causality itself, *aitia*, is determined by this preponderance of the *arche*, the commanding principle governing the strategic modelization, and the *telos*, the goal that the strategy seeks to achieve or accomplish. For the Greeks, actions detached from goals are devoid of value: they are vain, *mataios*. It is striking to observe how even the simple and seemingly purposeless activity of going for a walk can be subjugated to the teleological apprehension of reality that structures the Ancient Greek world. For Aristotle, one does not simply go for a walk to go for a walk, one goes on a walk in order to benefit one's health.[87] This attention to the "in order to," *epi* + genitive in Ancient Greek, permeates not only the Greek understanding of military strategy but also the realms of science and politics. To this day, the idea of the goal conditions our understanding of reality as evidenced by the now proverbial formula "#goals," which on Instagram alone comprises over 100 million posts. Escaping the Means/Ends paradigm and the idea of the goal that it carries along with it is a particularly complex affair: it is safe to say that our entire reality itself is now predicated on the teleological #goals worldview of the Greeks, as anyone who has ever worked in business can attest!

Even though we are moving away from teleological thinking as we become more and more critical of the idea of finality, we remain tributary to the idea of "the means." We are still hungry for methods and protocols that offer effective means for achieving results, if not a surefire pathway towards salvation. The advent of mindfulness meditation as a stress-relieving technique reflects a very Greek understanding of the intentionally *purposeless* approach to meditation exemplified by Zen or *Ch'an* practice. The Zen or *Ch'an* meditator does not meditate to reduce his stress or to achieve some kind of goal, he does not view his practice as a means to attain an end. Whereas the commodified and protocolized approach to mindfulness proclaims a "benefit" to the meditation practice, Zen meditation emphasizes the aimlessness of the practice, thus sharpening the meditator's attention to the *processual patterns* that characterize the meandering(s) of the mind.

b. Correlation, maturation, propensity and profit: the Chinese Way of strategy.

Once again, the attention to process so characteristic of the strategic literature of the Ancient Chinese civilization lies miles away from the teleological projective modeling of Ancient Greece. The strategic paradigms of the *Bin Fa* treatises are best understood as *maturational*. The correlative logic of these maturational paradigms lies *on the wayside* of the Cause/Effect dichotomy. Whereas the "causalist" paradigm seeks to ascertain the identity of the cause and therefore clearly separate it from the effect, the correlative paradigm focuses on the interrelatedness and interdependence of cause and effect.

When the law of causality becomes substituted with the law of correlativity, the processual outcomes of strategic endeavors no longer represent desired or desirable goals, they become instead synonymous with "profit(s)", the canonical Early Chinese notion of *Li* (利).[88] This notion of *Li* (利) is critical to understand the maturational paradigm that underlies Classical Chinese strategical literature. The sinogram itself represents the idea of *reaping* insofar as it is an ideogrammic compound of the sinogram *he* (禾) which signifies "grain" and the sinogram *dao* (刀) which signifies "blade." This agricultural understanding of profit and efficacy as the reaping of matured grain embodies the Early Chinese civilization's strong grounding in an agricultural landscape. The agricultural grounding of Early Chinese civilization permeates the maturational understanding of strategic efficacy that it developed. In Early Chinese cosmological thinking, the careful detection of the *propensive conditions* favorable to a profitable process and the reaping of benefit(s) (利) are but a mere consequence of a greater process (always) already at play: the constant motions of the four seasons and the birth of all things. Instead of a teleological understanding of efficacy predicated upon projective modeling, the Early Chinese strategies of efficacy emphasize how to assess, detect, leverage, and inflect the *propensity at play* in any given situation so that it can yield the highest profit.

In the maturational paradigm, the strategist therefore does not have an aim in sight. He instead waits for the right moment to reap the profits of a situation already at play, just like a farmer collecting ripe fruits from his orchard, never too soon nor ever too late. The efficient general wins the battle before it is even engaged, attacking his enemies only when he knows that they are already defeated. His patient assessment and appraisal of the situation's potential allows him to reap maximal profits and suffer minimal losses from the battle or conflict. The great strategist "does not seek fame or praise," he is miles away from an inspirational and heroic leader.[89] Acting like an invisible shadow, he does not need to be courageous precisely because his strategy relies on the absence of risk-taking. The efficacy of the general in the maturational paradigm does not consist in his capacity to apply a predetermined plan of action. Instead, he leans into the *propensity* that is already at play in a conflictual situation. When the situation holds no potential, when engaging in conflict yields no profits, the strategist retreats; he waits for the factors and processes at play to generate more profitable situations further down the line. He is not a swaggering, braggadocious figure who relishes the dramatics of conflict: his presence remains nearly invisible, in the background.

Instead of opposing himself to the situation at hand, he works *in tandem* with it.

*

Early Chinese strategical treatises thus developed a general intelligibility of the seamless and effortless processes of war and combat: they deployed an intelligence of conflict hitherto *unthought* in the European context, where war and battle were associated with strife, effort, and difficulty.

It is worth pointing out (yet again) that our philosophical recourse to Early Chinese strategic literature is not driven by a desire to "compare and contrast" (Early) Chinese culture and the Western culture born out of Ancient Greece. What we find in the *Bin Fa* literature is an *unthought* approach to conflict which stresses not difficulty or adversity but instead ease and effortlessness. The recourse to Early Chinese strategic treatises helps us break the pre-conception associating the efficient with the difficult. Ancient China offers us instead an understanding of efficacy which emphasizes the *efficient unfolding* of the *sponte sua* processes at play in any given conflictual situation. In other words, the philosophical recourse to Early Chinese strategical treatises seeks to develop novel intercultural conceptual tools that can help us handle the strategic challenges and conflicts of the 21st century. As we shall see, these concepts can be used *across* eras and contexts, precisely because they are constructed to help us circulate *in between* cultures.

Setting up the field up for a strategic *encounter* where Ancient China and Ancient Greece can gaze into each other's *unthought* has the benefit of yielding high rewards for the one who is tempted neither by lazy cultural relativism nor by convenient, ethnocentric universalism. On the one hand, the intercultural perspective allows us to detach the efficient from the effective; it offers instead a processual concept of efficacy that differs from the action-oriented paradigm of effectiveness. On the other hand, the intercultural perspective highlights the importance of subjectivity in the action-oriented paradigm and the apparent lack thereof in the processual paradigm. Whereas the effective is (always) attributable to an observable action that can be ascribed to, if not a single cause, then at least a subject executing the action, the efficient has much more to do with the *maturation* of intertwining factors. In the paradigm of efficiency, it is difficult, if not impossible or irrelevant, to attribute an effect to a single actor or cause. The idea of an acting subject therefore does not emerge with ease in such a paradigm and in this regard, it is not so obvious that it is the strategist himself who reaps the profits of his strategy. It is precisely the strategist's *aimlessness* that makes him not an acting subject but rather an *agent of transformation*.

4/ *Wu wei* (無為), or the efficient Way(s) of the silent transformations.

If there is perhaps a single Early Chinese notion most associated with what sinology has constructed as "Daoism," it is assuredly *wu wei* (無為). *Wu wei* has most often been translated as "non-doing."[90] This habitual translation of *wu wei* as "non-doing" or inaction reflects the commonplace imaginary fetishization of an Oriental big Other: a conveniently detached mystical dreamer of "the Way" who serves as a foil for the industrious "doer" of the West, caught as he is in his worldly ways and affairs. Although the notion of *wu wei* is much more commonly associated with the techniques of the *Yang Sheng* paradigm discussed in the previous chapter, it is critical to emphasize the political context that this notion arose in.

a. Wu wei *as a political, as opposed to mystical, Way.*

No other formula sums up the logic of *wu wei* (無為) better than the one found in the 37th paragraph of the *Laozi*:

道 常 無 為 而 無 不 為

Dao chang wu wei er wu bu wei

> "The unchanging Way: to (always) do nothing but to (never)
> not let nothing be done."

This formula could be rendered with a deliberate, archaic inelegance as: "waying not (always) doing (some)thing and/yet not doing (no)thing." The key term in this formulation is the empty placeholder character *er* (而) commonly used in Classical Chinese to punctuate sentences and to endow them with a binary structure, its wide range of significations encompasses terms like: and/yet/or/also. While both translations, the archaic formulation and the succinct maxim, evoke a poetic approach to language that can be easily associated with the Western mystical tradition of "apophatism,"[91] they both seem far removed from the realm of governance and strategy that the *Laozi* was historically associated with in Early China.

The famous sentence of the *Laozi* indeed carries along with it a profound political significance that should not be lost on the contemporary reader. One can find a variation of this sentence in the Early Chinese text *Hanfeizi* associated with the autocratic "Legalist" tradition.[92] The "Legalist" tradition is perhaps most known for having supplied the philosophical and ideological apparatus of the Qin dynasty and of Early China's blood-thirsty First Emperor: Qin Shi Huangdi, the sovereign most famously associated with the buried terra-cotta army found in Xi'an in the 1970s.

The beginning of the 20th chapter of *Hanfeizi* is devoted to a commentary of the canonical characterization of *wu wei* found in the *Laozi*. These commentaries further discuss the relevance of *wu wei* within the context of the prince governing his Empire. In the *Hanfeizi*, *wu wei* thus becomes a vector of efficacy and governance, not only for the strategist but also for the Emperor himself.

In the political and strategic context, *wu wei* therefore becomes synonymous with a style of governance that leverages the situations, processes, and *transformations* or *hua* (化) that shape and affect a political terrain. The term *hua* deploys a vast array of semantic significations that allude to the transformation of water into ice, but also the transformation of life into death.[93] Comprehending the logic of

84

political transformations has everything to do with understanding the efficacy of *wu wei*. Only in light of a comprehension of *hua* can *wu wei* be understood as an efficient strategy of governance. It is easy to fantasize *wu wei* as a passive inactivity that resembles monastic renunciation and to thus mistake it for an ideal, and therefore inapplicable, model of governance founded upon a mystified and orientalist conception of "spirituality." The reference to *wu wei* in *Hanfeizi* shows us how the coherences found in Early Chinese thought deploy an uncannily efficient approach to governance that lies *on the wayside* of the Theory/Practice paradigm or of the Spiritual/Material divide.

Ancient China reflects back to Ancient Greece an understanding of "doing" that lies miles away from the heroics of action. There are no epics poems in Ancient China, nor is there a theatrical tradition of tragedy like in Ancient Greece: the taste for heroics, imitation (*mimesis*), and action that is so characteristic of these literary genres finds scarce equivalents in the Classical Chinese literature of the same era. In the political context, the processual understanding of (non)doing translates into a distrust of action for action's sake; it leads instead of the deployment of *wu wei* as an efficient and profitable strategy that yields the most effects with the least effort. *Wu wei* therefore has much more to do with efficacy and efficiency than with passivity or inaction, it involves tuning into the subtle transformations at play in a given situation so that they can be leveraged to yield maximal gain. *Wu wei* as it applies to the ruler involves the development of a vigilant gaze accompanied by an evenly suspended attention that can be attuned to the political terrain so as to best detect, assess, and leverage *potentialities.* These potentialities are not only the byproducts of transformation, at play in any given situation, they are also the *catalysts* that enable great political and strategic profit.

*

One can find in the *Mengzi* an agricultural tale that sums up the efficient (in)activity of *wu wei* and its capacity to generate profit.[94] In this anecdote, we see yet again how the Early Chinese developed an understanding of efficacy that is indissociable from the agricultural landscapes at the heart of their civilization. The tale tells us the story of an impatient farmer who wished to accelerate the growth of his crops: he became obsessed with the growth of the seedlings he had transplanted and would spend undue amount of time observing them. The more he gazed at the plants, the more impatient he grew. As his impatience grew, so did his desire to take action; he could not resist pulling the rice shoots up towards the sky to accelerate their growth. After a day spent frantically uprooting the rice shoots, the farmer returned to his home in a state of exhaustion. Confused by his unusual fatigue, his children asked him why he was so tired: they were mortified when they heard his answer. They rushed to the rice paddy to try and save the crop; but when they arrived, it was too late: the plants had already died and the crop was ruined by the impatient farmer's desire to act.

The farmer of the anecdote in the *Mengzi* sums up the inefficacy that results from the impatient desire to precipitate the natural processes of growth, transformation, and profit. Had the farmer followed the Way(s) of *wu wei*, he would have *nurtured and nourished* the *sponte sua* growth and transformation of the plants in a (non)effort to facilitate their effortless *maturation*. Master Meng even suggests that that the metaphor of the tutor meant to guide the growth of the plant is the most appropriate one when thinking of wu wei in the context of farming. The agricultural anecdote thus offers a wonderful example of *wu wei* as a path that is neither active nor inactive: there is perhaps no other activity than farming which better sums up the subtle blending of doing and non-doing that is required to reap what is sown. The farmer's task consists in favoring the maturation process of the seeds so as to collect the most bountiful harvest; there is indeed work to be done when it comes to weeding, nourishing the soil, and protecting the plants. Neither passive observation nor proactive intervention, the work of *wu wei* thus operates in an indirect and oblique manner, alongside the processes at play and not in reaction to them: it consists in doing the necessary minimum required to generate the maximum potential.

b. *Wu wei and the silent transformations: the example of Deng Xiaoping.*

The 17th century poet and scholar Wang Fuzhi used the following expression to characterize the historical motions of Chinese literature and History: "subterranean traveling(s) and silent transformation(s)," *qianyi mohua* (潜移默化).[95] The governing Way of *wu wei* has much to do with the Way of the silent transformations: it is a discrete path composed of barely perceptible movements. Nonetheless, its efficient motions leverage the transformations that are always already at play in historical and political situations.

If there is a contemporary figure who uncannily embodies the discrete yet transformational approach to governance and power so characteristic of Early Chinese political thought, it is assuredly Deng Xiaoping. Deng can indeed be thought of as a great "silent transform-er" who pulled China out of the ideological pitfalls of Maoism and into the global market economy, laying the foundation for the Chinese might of the 21st century. Although Deng Xiaoping did not explicitly refer himself to Wang Fuzhi's *chengyu* or to the idea of *wu wei*, call-ing him a "silent transformer" attuned to the efficacy of *wu wei* does not seem like a stretch: during his period of exile and disgrace during the Cultural Revolution, he cautiously *matured* his plan to *transform* China through gradual and almost imperceptible reform to make it the superpower that it is today.[96] Deng's ascent to power was neither a straight shot following a linear progression nor was it the product of a masterfully executed plan. Instead, it involved various key strategic phases of retreat, as well as an exceptional sensitivity to the shifting historical, political, and economic dynamics of 20th century China.

After Mao's death, Deng Xiaoping detected the *situation's po-tential* and leveraged it to quietly and efficiently rise to power. He did not need any of the bombast and bravado associated with heroic political action; his rise to power and the politics of transformation that he championed embodied an understanding of political efficacy that was neither purely idealistic and ideological, nor purely pragmat-ic and/or cynical. Deng's efficient approach to governance had much more to do with his keen sensitivity to transformation than with theo-retical projective modeling, be it ideological or economical. The People's Republic of China's curious blend of communist ideology and ultra-capitalist economic policies is a direct consequence of Deng's *transformational* policies.

5/ Governing without ideals or the limits of the politics of *Wu wei.*

a. Hanfeizi and the autocratic leanings of Wu wei.

It should be clear at this point that the efficacious Way of *wu wei* yields many profits for the one willing to follow it. Yet because the intercultural approach to philosophy is not comparative but rather reflexive, it is crucial to stress some of the key points that emerge after having measured the distance separating Early Chinese strategic and political literature from the philosophies of the *polis* developed in Ancient Greece. The logic of an intercultural philosophical strategy is to stress the resources belonging to each *language-thought*: one therefore shouldn't get the impression that the Ancient Chinese approach to strategizing the political is superior or inferior to the Ancient Greek strategies of modelization.

Early Chinese strategic and political treatises, despite their remarkable attention to subtle shifts and transformations, are indeed thoroughly lacking when it comes to developing an understanding of political freedom. It should not be lost upon us that the *Hanfeizi* and its inventive understanding of *wu wei* as an efficient strategy of governance served as the ideological bedrock of the ruthless Qin dynasty that emerged out of the lengthy Warring States period at the end of the third century BCE. The emperor Qin Shi Huangdi who founded this short-lived dynasty is not only famous for building the first stretches of the Great Wall and for the massive terra-cotta army defending his mausoleum, he was also well known for being ruthless and cruel with those who dared oppose him.[97]

*

The opening paragraph of the 5th chapter of the *Hanfeizi,* the

"Lord's Way" or *Zhu Dao* (主道), offers a striking description of the ways in which *wu wei* can be leveraged to instill an immense sense of fear in those who serve the Emperor.[98] By saying and doing nothing, the Emperor creates an open playing field for his servants: he allows their true intentions to mature and ultimately manifest themselves through their actions, without him having to ever intervene in the process. *Wu wei* therefore gives the Emperor an efficient way to ascertain the loyalty of his subjects and determine the right moment to eliminate those who oppose him. In this regard, the *Hanfeizi* lays the foundation for a proto-totalitarian regime wholly centered around the First Emperor's absolute power. Qin Shi Huangdi's approach to government was indeed characterized by its utter disregard for the sanctity of rituals and written culture: his book burnings and merciless executions of countless scholars and administrators set a troubling and traumatic precedent of ruthless tyranny.

The politics of efficacy outlined in the *Hanfeizi* and the brutality of the Qin Emperor thus demonstrate the limits of an approach to the political devoid of values and models: they show us the ugliness of a managerial approach to governance that dispenses itself of ideals and justifies violence in the name of order, efficacy and harmony. It is not a stretch to state that the politics of People's Republic of China in its worst moments, be it the Cultural Revolution or the ongoing ethnic cleansing in Xinjiang province and in Tibet, bear an uncanny resemblance with some of the governing principles outlined in the ancient Legalist texts that justified the ruthlessness of the First Emperor.[99]

b. The political power of the eidos and the construction of the common(s).

The ancient tales of the merciless Qin dynasty and the contemporary atrocities perpetrated by the People's Republic of China offer us valuable insight when it comes to the strength of the *eidos* understood as a political model form. In the same way that mathematical models offer us an ideal and modelized entry into the impossibility of the real, political models and ideals allow us to "get a grip" on the impossible and yet *necessary* reality of the political. The realness of the *eidos* lies not in its applicability but rather in its capacity to shape reality i.e. the world; much like the realness of mathematics shapes the reality of engineering, technology, and scientific innovation, the realness of ideals shapes the reality of political discourse and debate. Election programs are perfect examples of the political value of modelizations: by instilling debate in the public sphere, they forge the political and enable an effective construction of the *common* upon which democracy is founded. Much like Galilean science, democracy itself is unthinkable without an *eidos* or a modelized form, it is precisely the ideality of the democratic model which guarantees an *effective form* of "equality" for citizens of a democratic regime; without an ideal of equality, it is impossible to produce effective equality.

*

Modelization thus serves as the necessary foundation for debate and inquiry, be it scientific or political: its constructions acts like a regulatory horizon that directs action and fosters the construction of a *common*. The great general of the *Sunzi* treats his troops "like sheep," and handles them like non-humans as he lies and hides things from them.[100] He deploys a manipulative and authoritarian strategy of governance that leaves no room for deliberative processes, let alone democratic debate. The great democratic leader, on the other hand, offers his citizens an opportunity to act upon their subjective freedom and thus *contribute* to the political process of governance. The authoritarianism of Early Chinese strategic literature constitutes its most obscure and opaque point: it betrays an approach to governance where, from a Western liberal perspective, political subjects are rendered into mere objects destined to be efficiently manipulated. Any understanding of subjective individual freedom within the political context is squashed in these fascinating yet problematic texts.

Deliberation and debate are necessary to mobilize political subjects and transform them into free political agents: debating about projected ideals gives citizens a set of rallying points that empowers them and encourages them to *effectively* participate in the political process. Miles away from the authoritarian leanings of the processual understanding of strategy and governance developed in Early China, the democratic model forms of Ancient Greece thus offer us a precious conceptualization of the political *effectiveness* of deliberative processes founded upon ideality and modelization.

*

If we are to further examine the implications of this reflection on efficacy and effectiveness in politics and evaluate its significance for contemporary leadership, it becomes clear that the great leaders of the globalized world know how to simultaneously nurture maturational processes *and* offer projective models to rally their citizens. Because modelization constitutes the heart of democracy, it is critical for the democratic leader to embody and offer in some sense or another a *model* for the citizens he governs.

6/ Seizing opportunities vs launching transformation(s): strategy and the question of "Time."

As this chapter on strategy comes to a close, it should be stressed once more that highlighting the distance separating the Ancient Greek understanding of strategy from the Ancient Chinese one emphasizes a key moment inherent to *any* strategic process: the temporal moment of *decision*.

a. Aion, chronos, kairos *and* tuchè*: necessary philosophical models vs contingent political opportunities.*

The Ancient Greek conception of time is predicated upon a tripartite division which separates *aion*, eternal time, into two distinct parts: *chronos* and *kairos*. Whereas *chronos* represents the generic, calculable, and universal time of physics and science, *kairos* reflects the irreducible singularity of a given moment in time and of a given opportunity. *Chronos* belongs to the ideal, theoretical realm of the *eidos* and its model forms, while *kairos* can only be found in the elusive indeterminacy of contingent circumstances.

Although the 5th century BCE saw the emergence of the paradigm of the *eidos* with the advent of Plato's philosophy, it also represents a time where the efficacy of the theoretical "eidetic" models he developed was called into question by the rapidly evolving practical and "pragmatic" disciplines of rhetoric and medicine. The great Greek rhetorician Gorgias, who was also closely affiliated with the science of medicine through his brother, emphasized the primacy of the elusive opportunities of *kairos* over the truthfulness of theoretical and chrono-logical model forms.[101] In other words, doctors and rhetoricians in Ancient Greece didn't attribute much importance to the speculations of the Platonist philosophers, nor were they very interested in their theories about Truth, Beauty or Being. The Sophists and the Hippocratic doctors were men of action whose sole interest lay in the perfecting of their *technè,* their craft.

In a sense, Aristotle's departure from the literary stylings of Plato's dialogues and his subsequent elaboration of scientific logic represents an attempt to answer the (legitimate) concerns of rhetoricians and doctors. Aristotle's own singular style represents his attempt at producing a *technè* of modelization: a scientific *organon* or "instrument" designed to ground the contingent processes of knowledge in the necessary and repeatable structure of a model form of *logos* anchored in the measurable "time" (*chronos*) of "nature" (*phusis*). Aristotle's *Physics* even see him attempting to seize the "truth" (*aletheia*) of *kairos'* corollary: *tuchè,* most commonly translated as "chance."[102]

*

Yet Aristotle's attempt at producing a *technè* of logical modelization could not rid itself of the contingent constraints of *tuchè.* For the Greek philosopher, it was clear that the *indeterminacy* of chance constituted a significant obstacle for the construction of a systematized form of *logos* capable of producing efficient models of science and governance.[103] *Tuchè* contaminates *technè* for Aristotle because its singular contingency and its dependence on the time of *kairos* eludes the repeatable, predictable, and rational time of *anankè,* the necessary truth of science founded upon the divisible time of *chronos*.

b. "Sun-tah-zoo, the Chinese prince Machiavelli!" or Paulie Gualtieri and the Art of War.

Centuries later, the infamous Renaissance theorist of power Niccolò Macchiavelli turned Aristotle's cautious view of *tuchè* and *kairos* on their head when he developed an ethics of governance wholly founded upon their necessary elusiveness. In other words, Macchiavelli's political philosophy developed a genuine *technè,* not of modelization, but of *tuchè* and *kairos*, it incited rulers to become akin to gamblers in search of chance and opportunities.[104] The only truth that holds in the Machiavellian understanding of power is the truth of the roll of the dice, the irreducible veracity of chance and of the unpredictable potentialities it holds. Wielding power thus becomes like playing a game of cards where bluff, mind-games, and deception yield far greater profits than virtue, truthfulness, and integrity.

Popular TV shows like *Succession* convincingly portray the dramatics associated with the Machiavellian understanding of power: they portray a world ruled by *kairos'* "regime of opportunity," a world where the most efficient and profitable technique (always) consists in seizing *tuchè* or "chance" as it presents itself, regardless of human, let alone ecological consequences. Fictional characters like the patriarch Logan Roy, loosely based on Rupert Murdoch, illustrate a conception of strategy inspired by the Machiavellian sensitivity to *kairos* and *tuchè*, a grim worldview where personal interest remains, no matter the cost, the most decisive factor in any decision making. Are we then to believe another TV character, the comical and yet ruthless mobster Paulie Gualtieri of *The Sopranos*, who, after quoting the *Sunzi* (which he pronounces Sun Tah-zoo), proudly tells his fellow partners-in-crime that the Early Chinese strategist is like the "Chinese prince Machiavelli"?

At this point in our intercultural and philosophical itinerary, it should be clear to the reader that although Paulie's comparison might seem relevant upon a first glance, it does not do justice to Master Sun's text, precisely because the latter does not emphasize the primacy of personal, subjective interest in the way that Macchiavelli's Renaissance political philosophy treatise does. As we saw, the Early Chinese strategist is not a seizer of opportunities akin to a carnivore leaping on its prey. Instead, he ressembles the patient farmer attuned to the Way of *silent transformation*. Whereas *kairos* supposes a rupture in time, a disjunctive crossroads, the Way of the silent transformations supposes *continuity* and *regularity*. In the next chapter, we will further investigate the Western concept of "time" and examine how the distance separating it from the Early Chinese understanding of continuous processes and silent transformations can be leveraged to develop novel strategies for *living*.

CHAPTER IV

From "being here now" to living in/with the moment(s): wandering on the wayside of the philosophy of Time

1/ Semantic(s) of time(s): what does it mean when a language doesn't conjugate?

The question of Time continues to embody the obscure meanderings of philosophical inquiry to this day, almost as if asking questions like "what is time?" or "can we think without time?" had become comedy lines pulled out of an ironic YouTube philosophy clip. Why indeed ask oneself such questions, what relevance do they hold? Does the philosophical inquiry about time not simply lead to jargon-heavy, semantic dissections? After all, is the distinction we make between past, present, and future, here, then, and now not self-evident?

a. Physical time vs. lived time.

It is easy to leave the grand questions of Time unanswered, yet from a sinological and linguistic perspective there is one simple fact that cannot be ignored or unlearned: Classical Chinese does not conjugate and therefore does not differentiate between past, present, and future in the same way that inflected Indo-European languages do. Instead of designating verbal forms in a past, present, or future tense, Classical Chinese produces forms that can be likened to the infinitive form of the Indo-European languages, leaving it up to the reader to ascertain the "when" based upon context and not morphology. At a first glance, it might seem that such a linguistic consideration is just a matter of coincidental semantics and that the perception of time is in fact a universal *a priori* category of thought, to use a universalist, Kantian term.[105]

And yet, if we pay heed to the Classical Chinese verbalization of time without espousing the universalist lens of the Western philosophical tradition, we begin to detect the *unthought* intercultural *resources* of a *philosophy of living* that lies *in between* East and West, *on the wayside* of habitual patterns of thought.

*

Although we can easily admit that Western physics prove the material existence of time as the necessary condition of perception and observation, are we so certain that the measurable time of physics is the time that we *live* in? In other words, if physical time is real, what about the time we feel, our *own* time- the one we are given here on earth, the one whose expanse lies between life and death? What part of that subjective *feeling* of time is real? Without even traveling to Early China, it is clear that the question of Time remains elusive for us on a deeper, existential level. The elusiveness of Time has indeed made it a favored object of anguished philosophical inquiry in the Western tradition, precisely because its question addresses the existential angst best summarized by Virgil's melancholy adage- *tempus fugit,* time flies.[106]

Why do some moments seem to quickly pass us by while others seem to last forever? What does our own, immovable understanding of time have to do with the greater motions of creation, destruction, life and death? How is it possible to find permanence amidst the fleeting impermanence of our lives? Such is the grand mystery of time addressed by St. Augustine in the 11th book of the *Confessions* where he identifies that the root cause of our difficulties with time has everything to do with our way of *speaking* about it.[107] For Augustine, our confusion about time is rooted in our common usage of the the verb "to be" which divides time into what was, what is and what will be; past, present, and future. In other words, the problem of time therefore appears to be first and foremost a *semantic* one for Augustine, it is a marker of our embeddedness in the processes of language and its utterances.

The uttering processes of language being both meaningful and meaningless, it is no wonder that we become confused when we speak of the past and the future as if they existed separately from the present. The part of the past that remains in the present and the part of the future that the present holds both belong to the realm of "what is happening": they are in no way distinct from it. What has happened is therefore always what is *still happening,* while what will happen is always what *could* happen based on what we *say* is happening *now.* Yet the nature of the *now* is fleeting, it is an ephemeral point of passage. Thus, for Augustine there is nothing more real than a prayer, that moment in time where the intimate nature of a soul comes to embody the pure *presence* of uttered speech, wholly turned towards the infinity and eternity of God, beyond the rational dimensions of physical space and time carved out by the pagan philosophers. Augustine's faith in God requires an acceptance of the inherent mysteries of a fleeting physical time created by an eternal God. In a world where the Roman Empire was crumbling, the great Church Father invented a distinctly Latin and Christian conception of Time that would mark the centuries to come. With Augustine, Time ceased to be a god among others, it became the subjective, embodied, and, above all, *existential* manifestation of a single God whose *infinite* attributes bore no common measure with the polytheistic cosmologies of the Ancient Greeks (and Chinese).

b. Succession vs. alternation.

Even though the Ancient Greeks did not feel the gaping awe that Augustine felt when he confronted the question of Time, they nonetheless felt it to be a much more nebulous matter than the Ancient Chinese who, beginning with the *Yi Jing,* inscribed temporality within the continuous and endless alternation process that governs the shifts and transformations of the *Yin* and *Yang* polarities. As hinted at in the end of the previous chapter, the Ancient Greek understanding of time was predicated on a tripartite division separating eternal time, *aion,* into necessary time, *chronos,* and contingent time, *kairos.* The question and concept of time represented a pivotal point of inquiry for all the Greek philosophers, yet its significance varied greatly amongst them. The grand European philosophical divide separating materially oriented scientific thinkers focused on necessary and contingent time, from spiritually inclined metaphysicians turned towards eternal time began in Ancient Greece. Its influence is still felt today in contemporary debates about science and spirituality.

*

The conception of time that came to dominate Western physics is of course derived from Aristotle's understanding of nature, *phusis* in Greek, as a movement, *kinesis*, unfolding in time and space. In Aristotelian physics, time is a corollary to movement, a quantifiable property belonging to a body in motion. Time serves to delineate the beginning (*archè*) and end (*telos*) of a movement, yet it is not analogous to movement itself: it merely *represents* it. [108]

*

Unlike the Aristotelian representation of time as a finite movement ranging from point A to point B, the constant alternation of the *Yin* and the *Yang* polarities suggests the pre-eminence of continuous and uninterrupted *transformations* that govern the formless shifts of the Way or *Dao*, which knows neither beginning nor end. The Ancient Chinese understanding of *Yin* and *Yang* alternance fosters a qualitative and processual understanding of change that lies miles away from the quantitative conceptualization of time as the "measure of movement" pioneered by Aristotelian physics; that did not prevent it from *producing* an astounding body of technology and scientific invention that was arguably superior to Europe's until the Enlightenment.[109] The Ancient Greek and Ancient Chinese technologies born out of Aristotelian physics and *Yin Yang* cosmology thus evolved in parallel worlds, unbeknownst to each other: they offer, if not opposing, then assuredly *diverging*, perspectives of physical mobility, let alone metaphysical immobility.

98

c. Eternity vs. constancy.

As alluded to previously, speaking of metaphysics or the metaphysical in the Early Chinese context seems abusive given that there is no equivalent to those distinctly Greek terms in Classical Chinese. While it might be tempting to liken the limitlessness of the *Yin Yang* cosmology to the limitlessness of Greek *aion*, it is crucial to distinguish the eternity of becoming from the *constancy* of change.

Whereas Plato constructs the metaphysical, eternal Time of Becoming as a homogenous, divisible, and continuous succession that emanates from an immobile transcendent Being, the first aphorism of the Laozi stresses the paradoxical constancy of irregularity:

道可道，非常道.

dao ke dao, fei chang dao

"(a) way-able way, not (a) regular way"

This famously opaque sentence *negates* the very *possibility* of a single, permanent, immobile, "frequent," or "regular" (常) Way. By definition, the limitless plurality of Ways precludes the establishment of a single, "regular" Way. The image of the *Dao* found in the *Laozi* thus cannot be likened to a transcendent, metaphysical Being. In other words, the constancy of irregularity described in the first line of the *Laozi* bears little resemblance with the Platonic metaphysical eternity of becoming and contingency. The latter embodies a chaotic, immanent, and residual emanation of transcendent Being, whereas the irregular plurality of the "Way(s)"(道) of the *Laozi* manifests a paradoxical form of *constancy*: against all odds, it always remains *possible* (可) to travel alongside a "not common way (非常道)." The beginningless, endless, and, above all, *constant* advent of irregularity described in the *Laozi* thus lies miles away from any conception of Time as the byproduct of a transcendent act of Creation attributable to a supreme Being, be it the demiurge in Plato's *Timaeus* or Augustine's Christian God.

2/ A brief (pre)history of the "time" of the Greeks.

In an effort to better understand the opposition between the transcendence of eternity and the immanence of temporality emphasized by Greek philosophy and later Christian theology, we will conduct a brief genealogical investigation of the European philosophies of Time.

a. Time in Archaic Greece.

There is indeed a Greek understanding of time that predates the logical developments of Greek philosophy and the theological doctrines of Medieval scholasticism. Both of these thought-traditions contributed to the construction of a mythologized and personified conceptualization of Time found in ancestral cultural symbols, famous images like the Ancient Wheel of Fortune or the medieval Grim Reaper. Even in the Modern Era, the personification of time as a mythical figure persisted with the great romantic poet Baudelaire's cry: "*Le Temps mange la vie*" i.e. "Time eats life."[110] All three of these mythical and literary images emphasize the impermanence of worldly existence, the primacy of chance, and the inescapable eternity that marks the passage of life into death. As we probe the genealogical trajectories of this mythology of Time and examine its transformation into the universal philosophy of Time championed by scientific modernity, it becomes clear that the poetic weight of the archaic myths of Ancient Greece continued to influence the ulterior rational worldview of the philosophers, logicians, and scientists.

*

The foundational, allegorical myths of Ancient Greece as we find them in the cosmologies of Hesiod's *Theogony* or in the texts and rituals of the secretive Orphic traditions all point toward a homophonic confusion. What this means is that commentators of Late Antiquity were led to mistakenly identify Kronos, son of Gaïa and Ouranos

(Earth and Sky), the father of Zeus, with Chronos, the mythical god of Time, son of Gaïa and Hydros (Earth and Water). The term "time" itself is never used as the subject of a verb in all of Homer's works, it is only used in the dative form to indicate a delay, the same is true in all of Hesiod's works. It is only later in the 7th and 6th century BCE in the Pre-Classical period that the conceptualization and personification of Time begins to emerge alongside philosophical, political, and literary discourse.

Even though our knowledge of Pre-Classical Greece remains fragmentary due to the scarcity of original source materials, it seems clear enough that the great Ionian mathematician Thales is among the first to conceptualize and personify Time as a distinct entity, as an acting subject. Thales indeed states that "Time is the wisest because he uncovers (*anuriskei*) everything (*gar panta*)."[111] Time's capacity to uncover or reveal becomes an increasingly diffused idea in the Pre-Classical Era as evidenced by the statement of the great Athenian legislator Solon: "time shows truth." [112]

The concurrent personification and conceptualization of Time was also corroborated by the esoteric Orphic traditions that subsequently held a great influence on Greek tragedy in the Classical Era. Although our knowledge surrounding these esoteric traditions is imprecise and fragmentary, historical data seems to suggest that they emphasized a conception of Time that was at once divine and philosophical. Time was therefore both a divinity and a first principle (*archè*) in the Orphic traditions, this Orphic equation of time as being both the divine personification of the *theologoi* and the tangible representation of the *phusiologoi* is perhaps best captured by a little known and yet pivotal Pre-Socratic thinker: Pherecydes of Syros. In a sense, he was amongst the first to bridge the mythological worldview of Archaïc Greece with the philosophical worldview of Classical Greece. Pherecydes' works are only known to us through secondary sources yet the greats of Antiquity like Aristotle, Cicero, and Plutarch all had their word to say about him. He is perhaps most known for writing the first cosmogony in prose as opposed to verse and for offering the following hypothesis about the origin of the world: "Zeus and Chronos always were, along with Chtonia (the Earth)." (*Zas men kai Chronos èsan aei kai Kthoniè*).[113] Here again, the homophonic equivalence between Kronos, father of Zeus, and Chronos, "the Father of All" (*Chronos o panton Pater)* "[114] as the poet Pindar put it, reveals the Ancient Greek tension where a personified figure of Time stands at the intersection of mythological cosmogonies and philosophical conceptualizations.

b. Time in Classical Greece.

The literary and scientific developments of the Classical Era continued to further this equivalency between mythical time and philosophical time: the notion itself became increasingly equated with an immanent physical residue of an elusive yet necessary form of spiritual transcendence.

*

The figure that perhaps most assuredly marks the transition from a mythological personification of Time to a physical representation of time is the great "mobilist" Pre-Socratic thinker Heraclitus of Ephesus, most famously associated with the phrase "everything moves" (*Panta chorei*) and with the saying "you (can) never step in the same river twice."[115] The image of the river constitutes an allusive yet convincing means of conveying a consistent understanding of immanent temporality as the perpetual motion of physical things. Heraclitus' river crystalizes the idea of Time as a permanent marker of impermanence, the flowing passage of time governs the apparent eternal flux of the river; the empty figures of time are akin to a continuous, self-generating, and self-renewing substance that moves alongside a stream of physical forms and manifestations. Time thus becomes a corollary of life in the Classical Era, a silent and logical companion that lives alongside us, progressively dimming the brightness of the frightening mythological figure without ever fully effacing it.

*

The great playwrights of the Classical Era further this subdued yet tragic assessment of time as the silent companion that marks the inevitable passage of life into death. In Sophocles' *Oedipus at Colonus,* the destitute tragic hero says: "only the gods are free from old age and death; everything else is in the hands of Almighty Time (*pancrates chronos*)!"[116] In the tragic worldview, Time therefore becomes akin to an immanent residue of spiritual transcendence, an anonymous yet omnipotent divinity lying on the margins of the physical world. Although the "Almighty Time" of the tragic playwrights bears some resemblance with the mythologized figures of the archaic cosmogonies, it also demonstrates the influence of the more philosophical and abstract understandings of time as a necessary measure of motion first developed by the Pre-Socratic *phusiologoi* like Heraclitus and Thales, and later brought to its apex in the Classical Era by Aristotle.

*

In the 4th book of the *Physics,* Aristotle inscribes himself in the continuity of the Greek tradition that ascribes a residue of transcendence to the immanent unfolding of Time when he states that it "envelops" (*periechesthai*) all existing things.[117] Aristotle's philosophical conceptualization of Time therefore goes beyond physical time itself: Time acts like a greater category that envelops the *totality* of physical phenomena. Aristotle's understanding of time as the measure (*metron*) of movement (*kinesis*) marked a departure from the Pre-Socratic conception of Time as an elemental substance emanating from a physical principle like fire or water: it thus set a new benchmark for a more abstract and quantifiable understanding of Time as a *measurable corollary* of (meta)physical movement. Yet despite this significant departure from Pre-Socratic philosophy, Aristotle's conception of Time remains tributary to the cultural paradigms that it emerged in: it continues to associate Time with destruction and decay. This inscription of the Aristotelian understanding of Time within the cultural paradigms of Ancient Greece could not be clearer: the Greek philosopher himself states in the same passage that the common language is correct when it identifies Time as the cause of "ruin" (*phtoras*)!

Time therefore remains an aporetic category that is far less understandable than space in Aristotle's *Physics*: it remains a category of thought associated with a tragic and mythical rhetoric which predates the birth of philosophy. As we bring this brief history of Time in Ancient Greece to a close, it becomes clear that there is a continuous thread in the Western understanding of Time which runs all the way from Archaic Greece to 19th century Romanticism. From Hesiod to Baudelaire, Time's activity has constantly been likened to a divine reduction of the living into the dying, despite science's best attempts to construct Time as a quantifiable, abstract, and universal category. When turning our investigation towards Ancient China, it will be crucial to understand how the geo-historic distance separating the Chinese conception of seasonality from the mythical and philosophical representations of Time in Ancient Greece can help us develop a novel understanding of the temporal that lies *on the wayside* of the tragic *pathos* of the Western *tempus fugit* rhetoric.

3/ The legacy of early 20th century French sinology; or how did the Ancient Chinese (not) think about "time"?

The bold assertion that consists in stating that the Ancient Chinese civilization did not conceptualize an abstract understanding of "time" continues to raise sinological eyebrows. If the Ancient Chinese had no understanding of "time," then what led them to write down their history in canonical texts like Sima Qian's *Shiji* or the Ancient *Hanshu* or "Book of Documents"? Doesn't the *Shiji's* and the *Hanshu's* relating of synchronous and successive historical events reflect an understanding of simultaneity and chronology that presupposes a universal notion of Time? By espousing the legendary French sinologist's Marcel Granet's view that the Ancient Chinese did not conceive of an abstract category of "time," constructing instead a coherent and elaborate understanding of *eras* and *seasons*,[118] our investigation falls under the suspicion of sinologists like Wu Kuang Min who argue that the singularly "concrete" disposition of the Chinese people did not lead them to explicate their "implicit" understanding of the universal and necessary category of Time.[119]

a. On why intercultural philosophy cannot espouse a universalist or culturalist concept of "time."

A philosophical or sinological view which presupposes the universality of Time produces arguments that can be summed up as follows: Europeans produced an abstract, devitalized and yet *explicit* conception of Time while the Chinese produced a concrete, living, and yet *implicit* understanding of Time. Such lines of argumentation are misguided for two reasons:

1) They endorse the universalism of Western thought, specifically the Kantian paradigm and its phenomenological legacy positing the *a priori* universality of the subjective and psychological categories of Time and Space, all the while disregarding the singular history of these categories.

2) They essentialize Chinese culture and European culture, thereby constructing cultural stereotypes of the Chinese as being "concrete" while the heady Europeans meander in elusive abstraction.

The intercultural and philosophical investigation surrounding the notion of "time" seeks to avoid both of these pitfalls: on the one hand, we've been careful to showcase the singular history of Time in Western thought in an effort to demonstrate the situated and *constructed* nature of the universalist paradigm that posits the existence of Time and Space as universal categories of thought; on the other hand, we seek to avoid at all costs any form of Orientalism that fantasizes Ancient China, let alone the Chinese people, as some exotic Other.

*

As stated in previous chapters, an intercultural strategy for philosophy consists in deploying and promoting the *unthought resources* that lie *in between* the Ancient Greek and the Ancient Chinese worlds. The ethical commitment to interculturality precludes us from endorsing both facile universalism and lazy relativism. We can therefore neither admit the position that Time is universal, nor can we affirm that the apparent lack of an abstract formulation of "time" in Ancient Chinese culture reflects an "implicit" ethnic and cultural characteristic of the Chinese people. The intercultural approach to philosophy seeks not to stress the "difference" separating Ancient China from Ancient Greece but rather to emphasize the linguistic, geographic, and historic *distance* that separates them. Positing difference as a first principle (*archè*) amounts to re-espousing the categorical worldview that the Moderns inherited from the Greeks, whereas underscoring distance simply consists in pointing out factual evidence. Emphasizing distance as opposed to difference allows us to avoid both the pitfalls of universalism and cultural relativism: it signals the *possibility* of the constructible, promotable, and shareable *common(s)* of intelligence that lies *in between* cultures and the distances that separate them. The construction of this intercultural common(s) requires a patient and constant form of philosophical, pedagogical, and political *translation* that lies *on the wayside* of the hyper-specialized academicism that has become all too dominant in the globalized and digitized Humanities.

b. Marcel Granet's genius or the socio-anthropological approach to sinology.

By following Marcel Granet's footsteps, intercultural philosophy deliberately inscribes itself not in a specialized but rather in a *generalist* approach to sinology heavily influenced by the proto-structuralist, sociological, and anthropological theses of Emile Durkheim and Marcel Mauss.[120] Despite their brilliance, Granet's works now bear little influence on contemporary sinological scholarship. Few of them have been translated into English and they have fallen into relative obscurity as there is little secondary literature devoted to this giant of 20th century intellectual history who nonetheless bore a decisive influence on Claude Levi-Strauss' paradigm-shifting structural anthropology.[121] Although Granet's theses on Ancient China are of course historically dated, his eloquent formulations display his vast erudition as well as his remarkable sensitivity to the singular *coherence* that tied together literary and scientific modes of reasoning in Classical Chinese *language-thought*.

The erudite French sinologist born in 1884 lived a short yet eventful life. He witnessed not only the end of over three millennia of Chinese imperial power with the fall of the Qing Dynasty in 1912, but also the first World War in which he served; the legend has it that he died in a fit of rage when he heard the Nazis marching into Paris in 1940. Granet's key thesis concerning Ancient China and "time" consists in the following assertion/observation found in the first chapter of the second tome of his *magnum opus* entitled *La Pensée Chinoise*. In this work that has yet to be translated in English, Granet writes: "no one in Ancient China thought to conceive of Time as a monotonous duration constituted by the succession of qualitatively similar moments attributable to a uniform movement."[122] Rather than conceptualizing temporality in the universal, Aristotelian terms that make Time the measure of a movement unfolding in Space, Granet suggests that the Ancient Chinese thought the *temporal* on the basis of an ensemble of *eras*, seasons, and epochs; Space in turn was thought on the basis of *fields*, climates, and cardinal directions. In accordance with Granet's intuition, we will advance in this reflection by examining how the Early Chinese thought of "time" and "space" not "in and of themselves," but rather in terms of *occurrences* and *sites*.

4/ Season(s) and duration(s): cursory overview of a structural paradigm.

When taking a closer look at the terms used by the Ancient Chinese to designate temporal phenomena, we find two correlated, paradigm-defining notions: *shi* (時), which can be translated as season, moment or occurrence, and *jiu* (久), which refers to duration. On an etymological level, the latter term points towards the image of a man crossing a distance while the graphemes of the former term *shi* (時) connote both the sun and vegetation.

a. Seasons and rites.

It should not surprise us that in the predominantly agricultural Early Chinese civilization one of the key usages of *shi* (時) refers to the alternation of the four seasons, the *si shi* (四時). The occurrence of the four seasons and the individual moments that each one represents played a foundational and structural role in Early Chinese civilization, influencing not only agricultural but also political life. The passage of one season into another served as the formal basis for the codification of the rites and rituals expressed by the sinogram *li* (禮). These rites and rituals acted as a structural matrix for Ancient Chinese society, their careful observance governed the daily living of both the illiterate farming classes and the literate ruling classes, all the way up to the Emperor himself. The notion of *li* bears a far greater cultural significance than the notion of rite or ritual in the Ancient Greek world. The claim that the Ancient Chinese forbode abstraction thinking in favor of concreteness of daily life does not hold up when we examine the elaborate thinking used by the Confucian Xunzi to formalize the notion of *li* and transform it into an abstract notion that pertains not just to quotidian living, but also to political governance.[123] The logical and epistemological developments of the Later Mohists whose style of argumentation most resembles the style of the Ancient Greek philosophers also testifies that the Ancient Chinese were not foreign to abstract thinking.[124]

*

One could even argue that the *inkling* of an abstract understanding of "time" can be found in the 17th chapter of the *Zhuangzi*, yet the philosophical text's elaboration on the notion of *shi* (時) does not fully separate "time" as a formal category that exists on a distinct plane of its own. In this chapter of the *Zhuangzi*, the term *shi* refers to duration and thus remains correlated to existing "things," *wu* (物).[125] *Shi* is therefore never fully dissociated from the processes of existence, nor is it abstracted into an independent term that exists outside of these processes. Although the *Zhuangzi* develops an abstract understanding of *shi* as duration, thereby demonstrating a capacity to conceptualize the temporal in abstract terms, the conceptualization of *shi* found in the text always refers to the duration *of something*. In other words, it seems as though, even in its most abstract and conceptual developments, Early Chinese thought did not require the development of

108

"time" as a distinct entity that exists on an independent level.

b. Yuzhou 宇宙 *or the world as it is extending, the world as it is lasting.*

If we are to better understand how the Ancient Chinese reflected upon the correlation that binds seasons and moments, *shi* (時), to duration, *jiu* (久), then it is critical to probe Ancient Chinese texts for clues that can help us decipher their profound relationship to the temporal, which flourished *on the wayside* of the tragic European rhetoric of Time. Investigating the usage of the Early Chinese compound form *yuzhou* (宇宙), which has been commonly used to translate an abstract understanding of "space-time," can provide us with preliminary perspectives. Yet as the sinologist A.C. Graham astutely notes, these terms were never conceived as abstract dimensions of Space and Time, detached from the physical world: both terms, which originally designate parts of a roof, remain undetached from their supportive and constitutive processual rooting. The significance of these terms more closely resembles the following conceptions: "the world as it is extending" and the "world as it is lasting."[126] In other words, they reflect a *processual* as opposed to *disjunctive* understanding of the spatial and the temporal.

*

If we turn to an important formulation found in the 18th paragraph of the 11th chapter of the *Huainanzi*, an eclectic text of the 1st century BCE which blends together various strains of Early Chinese thought into a composite ensemble, we find a striking example that helps us better understand the processual relationship to the spatial and temporal that the *yuzhou* (宇宙) compound designates:

往 古 來 今 謂 之 宙, 四 方　 上　 下 謂 之 宇, 道
在 其 間, 而 莫 知 其 所

> *wang gu lai jin wei zhi zhou, si fang shang xia wei zhi yu, dao zai*
> *qi jian, er mo zhi qi suo*

"Going towards old and coming towards current is what we call *zhou*
(宙), the four directions and above/below is what we call *yu*
(宇), the *dao* lies in that between, and/yet no one knows that place."[127]

This essential formula in our investigation requires careful translation and is subject to varying interpretations; hence why we thought it so important to highlight the text character by character so that the reader can appreciate for himself the subtle correspondences and parallelisms that play such a crucial role in Early Chinese philosophical writing. As per our usual habit, we prefer to offer a literal and inelegant translation to stay closer to the archaic rhythmicity of the formulation. Respected translators like Christoph Harbsmeier fall prey to the habitual European understanding of time as a tripartite structure divided into past/present/future when they translate the first part of the sentence in the following manner: "the past, the present, and the future are called *zhou*."[128] Such a translation not only departs significantly from the Early Chinese syntax and its structural correspondences, it also neglects the bipolar, as opposed to tripartite, division of the temporal found in this passage. There are indeed only two terms associated with the temporal in this sentence, *gu* (古) which refers to the "old" or "what is going," and *jin* (今), which refers to the "now" or "what is coming." The relationship that binds these two terms together has much more to do with the *opposing and yet complementary* relationship that binds the *yin* to the *yang* than with the nominal relationship that makes past, present, and future subdivisions of the general category of "time." The sentence characterizes the temporal relationship that *zhou* (宙) designates as a *constant transition*.

The formulation that ends the sentence is critical because it designates the spatial and the temporal as manifestations of the all-encompassing processes of the *Dao* (道). The temporal and spatial manifestations of the *Dao* (道) lie *in between* (間) sites and occurrences; in a place that can be trodden and named, but not known. Thus, neither temporal duration nor spatial extension are thought of as being distinct from the greater processes that compose the fabric of the real:

the proceedings that fabricate the real therefore inhabit the processes of duration and extension, without occupying a specific moment or place. This passage of the *Huainanzi* highlights the constant folding and unfolding of the Way and of its continuous processes: the characterization of *yuzhou* (宇宙) found in this text thus appears to confirm our view that the abstract concept of "time" did not emerge, as such, in Early China, as if the Early Chinese had not felt the need to establish a clear distinction separating the temporal from the *processual*.

*

It indeed appears as though the Ancient Chinese never produced an abstract understanding of "time" because they did not seek to extract the temporal from what they conceived to be the constant course of renewal pervading the world: the *Dao* (道) or the Way(s). Even Early China's experts of abstraction, the Mohists, never detached the temporal and the spatial from the processual. In the 40th and 41tst paragraph of their *Canon,* they offer a lapidary, abstract and, above all, *processual* characterization of duration, *jiu* (久), and extension, *yu* (宇): "Lasting (久) (corresponds to): filling (彌) differing (異) moments (時). Extending (宇) (corresponds to): filling differing places (所)."[129] The eloquent simplicity of these formulations matches their efficient capacity to capture two parallel yet correlated processes; both assertions underscore the activities of filling, *mi* (彌), and differing, *yi* (異), as being the common denominators that bind together temporal and spatial processes in an opposing and/yet complementary tandem, in a ceaseless and/yet constant relationship that knows neither beginning nor end.

c. 時間 *as "time": a 19ᵗʰ century invention.*

The capacity that the Ancient Chinese possessed to approach the world through the lens of abstraction therefore makes the absence of a formalized and abstracted understanding of "time" even more surprising considering that they were known to use water clocks beginning in the second millennium BCE and incense clocks beginning in the 6th century CE![130] The elaborate calendars and historiographies of Early China also seem to contradict our assertions regarding their relationship, or lack thereof, to abstract "time." Yet these apparent contradictions obfuscate a simple historical fact: the words used to translate the European notion of "time" into East Asian languages, *shijian* in Chinese or *jikan* in Japanese (時間) is itself largely a 19th century creation. The attentive reader might be able at this point in our investigation to identify the two sinograms in this compound and translate it in the following manner "moment(s) in between." The Meiji-Era Japanese translation of European "time" into *jikan* is first attested in 1872 according to dictionaries and was popularized by cultural figures like the novelist Natsume Sôseki, while the first attested presence of *shijian* in China dates back to 1908.

In other words, the very fact that it was deemed necessary to compound two notions found in sinographic writing to encapsulate the single, European concept of "time" demonstrates not only the apparent lack of such a concept in East Asian cultures, but more importantly the geo-historic singularity of the European understanding of "time" as the measure of differing intervals. Whereas European thought attached a particular importance to the measurability of temporal intervals, positing that the determination of a beginning and an end marks in and of itself the movement from a point A to a point B, Early Chinese thought emphasized continuous, processual *transitions*. The 19th century invention *jikan/shijian* therefore seized a spatialized dimension of the temporal understood as a *distending*, measurable interval that had remained unthought in East Asian culture, much like the processual, continuous, and *transitional* understanding of duration and seasonality expressed by *shi* (時) had remained largely unthought in Europe up until the works of Marcel Granet.

5/ Distending vs. transitioning: from being present to living alongside change(s).

Having now emphasized the distance separating the Ancient

Greek understanding of Time from the Ancient Chinese understanding of duration and seasonality, we are led back to the initial protagonist of our investigation: St. Augustine.

a. Time as "distending" or the origins of the "be here now" mantra.

Augustine was one of the few great thinkers of Antiquity who did not know Ancient Greek, which makes the understanding of Time he developed all the more interesting to us. Whereas the Greek philosophers thought of Time as a divisible (*meristos*) substance, a corollary of movement, Augustine was among the first to establish that an indivisible and individuated soul lies at the heart of the subjective perception of Time. For Augustine, the soul's subjective *experience* of Time differs from the divisible, regular, and objective "time" of physical science. In the 26th chapter of the XIth book of the *Confessions*, Augustine emits the hypothesis that when we measure Time as we speak, saying things like "that was a long time ago," or "this event is right around the corner," we measure nothing more and nothing less than the *distension* of our very souls. He then goes on to argue in the following two chapters that memory (or remembrance) consists in distending our present soul towards the past whereas thinking about the future (or expectance) consists in distending our present soul towards the future. Augustine's reflection on Time ends on a meditative yet exhortative note that suggests that our confusion surrounding Time, which is largely attributable to our embeddedness in the processes of language, can be remedied through the cultivation of an attitude that embodies *presence*. In an allusion to *Phillipians* 3:12-14, the early Church Father admonishes the faithful to be forgetful about things past and to be unconcerned about the transience of what lies ahead, professing instead the virtues of a life wholly turned towards the "extending and not distending" (*extentus sed non distentus*) presence of an eternal and infinite God that transcends the determinations of material existence. [131]

*

Although Augustine remains fully engrossed in the tragic *tempus fugit* rhetoric, his original assessment of Time as the *distending of the soul* lays the ground for a subjective and phenomenological appreciation of spiritual presence that continues to bear a strong influence, not only on philosophical discourse, but also on contemporary psychotherapeutic discourse as it relates to the medical practice of "mindfulness meditation." It isn't too far off to say that the psychedelic guru Richard Alpert aka Ram Dass' influential book *Be Here Now,* which greatly contributed to the popularization of meditation techniques in America, can be read as a riff on the Augustinian understanding of the experience of presence as an embodiment of the distending of the soul. In other words, the exhortation to "be present" or to "be mindful" advocated by a certain vein of spirituality heavily inspired by the Orientalist leanings of the American intelligentsia of the 1960s and 1970s remains a centuries old riff inscribed in a metaphysical, if not mystical, European Christian tradition that preaches the virtues of "presence." Thus, even when great minds like Ram Dass endorse the philosophical mantle of non-European wisdom traditions, they remain tied to the very European metaphysical presuppositions that the verb "being" has been carrying along since the Ancient Greeks!

b. Transitioning and transforming or the operations of change: bian tong. 變通 vs bian hua 變化.

On the wayside of the preaching, if not downright preachy, rhetoric of distending time, being and presence, Early China developed a subtle understanding of the continuous, *transitioning* and *transforming* processes that structure the *operations of change*.

*

The daunting wealth of vocabulary used to distinguish the diverse processes of change in Classical Chinese befuddles even well-trodden sinologists. In the context of this summative book, it is only possible to offer a cursory overview of the rich semantic resources offered by Classical Chinese: we will therefore only signal the existence of the binome *bianhua* (變化) while mostly focusing on the binome *biantong* (變通) as it is deployed in the *Great commentary* of the *Yi Jing* (易經) or "Book of Changes." Both binomes agglomerate two synonyms signifying "change," *bian* (變) being the constant denominator. On an etymological level, the character *Bian* (變) connotes threading, silk, gestures, and speech: it denotes a process of exchange and *modification*. *Hua* (化), a term we've encountered in previous chapters, most commonly rendered as "transformation," evokes the passage of *yin* into *yang*, of liquid into solid, of dying into living. In the context of the translation we offer here of the *Great Commentary*, we suggest understanding *hua* (化) as a *governing transformation*. The association *bianhua* (變化) has received a significant amount of sinological attention insofar as it appears in a great variety of Classical Chinese texts and traditions which range from the literary and philosophical, like the *Zhuangzi*, to the scientific and medical, like the *Huang Di Nei Jing Su Wen* or "Yellow Emperor's Cannon"[132]

*

Rather than delving into the wealth of existing commentaries that examine the relationship tying together *bian* (變) and *hua* (化) into the compound form *bianhua* (變化), we will concentrate on the lesser commented relationship that links *bian* (變) to *tong* (通), which refers to the notions of passing through and *continuation*, particularly as we find it in the first part of the *Great Commentary* of the *Yi Jing*.[133] In the 6th paragraph it is said that "modifications continuing make up the four seasons, (變通配四時),"[134] thus suggesting that the transition from one season into another is made up of *continuous* processes of modification. Further in the text, the 11th paragraph offers the following statement to allude to distinction between modifying, *bian* (變), and continuing, *tong* (通): "one closing/one opening, that is called modifying; going/coming without depleting, that is called continuing (一闔一闢謂之變；往來不窮謂之通).[135]

Whereas *bian* (變) refers to a revolving and alternating binary process, *tong* (通), refers to a continuous process made up of three terms. If we return to the comment of the 6th paragraph, it therefore becomes clearer how the 4 seasons, *si shi* (四時), are made up of a conjunction of modification and continuation. Indeed, spring "continues" in summer with the progressive increase of *yang* heat, the advent of autumn then "modifies" the *yang*-dominant governing transformation, *hua* (化), by inverting its pattern; in the same fashion, autumn "continues" in winter with the increase of *yin* coolness, while spring then "modifies" the *yin*-dominant governing transformation of "cooling" with the *yang*-dominant governing pattern of "warming." The *Great Commentary* indicially points toward an understanding of temporal transition as a simultaneous process of *modification-continuation* that shapes and regulates the governing transformations, *hua* (化), that characterize the 4 seasonal phases and moments, *si shi* (四時).

*

The formulations of the *Great Commentary* thus give us the *inkling* of *living change(s)* that lies *on the wayside* of the European rhetoric of distension and extension. If the Augustinian understanding of time as distension brought us closer to an understanding of what it means to *be present*, the *Great Commentary* of the *Yi Jing* appears to have given us a stronger grasp of what it means to *live alongside change(s)*: the meeting of these two paradigms seems to draw into focus the emergence of a hitherto *unthought* approach to *living* that lies *in between* customary ways of thinking, be they Chinese or European- the thought of *living in/with the moment(s)*.

6/ Living in the present vs. living in/with the moment(s).

Our intercultural and philosophical investigation of the question of "time" has led us to now focus our attention on the emergence of two critical terms: *presence* and *living*. At this point in our reflection, it seems appropriate to probe the meaning of presence and to examine to which extent fostering a capacity to live in the present correlates to the *experience* of presence itself. In other words, does the concept of presence itself simply refer to the *possibility* of being present or does its signification encompass a more experiential and existential dimension of living? Can presence even be conceptualized if the present is but a mere point of passage? What consistency does the present hold if its existence is only revealed by its passing? If the present cannot extend and if the sensation of presence is but a pure subjective distension, then can presence as such truly *exist*?

a. Presence vs. the present: Aristotle, the Stoics, and the problem of what it means to "be present."

The paradoxical relationship that binds the subjective experience of presence to the objective understanding of the present as a formal, mathematical point in "time" can be traced back to Aristotle. There indeed appears to be a discrepancy between his definition of the present as an inconsistent present instant (*to nun*), and his assertion that the instant of pleasure represents the experience of an indivisible totality (*holon ti*) that lies outside of Time. [136]

For Aristotle, the experience of pleasure points towards a totality that is neither *eidos* nor *telos*, rather it equates temporal instants with each other and in a sense abolishes Time itself. And yet, when pleasure ceases, we return to the inconsistency of the passing present instant. The Aristotelian conception of pleasure as an experience of totality that abolishes Time and yet remains subjected to the ephemerality of the temporal points toward a tension that dissociates the scientific present instant of physics from the existential and ethical instance of pleasure. The question of what it means to be present, of what it means to experience presence as pleasure thus becomes equated with the possibility of *extending* the present. If we can only live in the present, then is it possible to extend it?

*

The Stoics offer in this regard an alternative to the dissociative ontological assessment of Time offered by Aristotle. Instead of offering a metaphysical philosophy of time that incorporated the mythical representations of Time as a transcendent Being, they sought to cultivate a pure philosophy of immanence based on a paradoxical logic devoid of any reference to transcendence. The Stoics developed an original understanding of opportunity with the notion of *eukairia,* which refers to the idea of an opportune point or moment.[137] For the Stoics, the possibility of extending the present is tied to the paradoxical possibility of a free act that *seizes* the right opportunity at the right time. It is the Stoic practitioner's capacity to *conform* his actions with the necessary order of the physical world that guarantees the rightness of his conduct. He can only live in the present because he knows that the past and future do not exist as such: for him, they are mere *distensions* of the present instant and are therefore subjected to illusive and elusive emotions. The emotions associated with the past and the future get in the way of taking the right decisions in the *now,* the only place in time we *know* to be real.

The Stoics viewed living in the present as a fundamental example of how seizing opportunity can be understood as a capacity to *act.* If I am thinking of going for a walk, my present situation is not walking; I am simply thinking of walking. Walking only becomes present and real when I *decide* to effectively walk. The capacity to live in the present for the Stoics is thus directly tied to a capacity to take deliberate, ethical actions and decisions: to live in the present from the Stoic perspective means to *choose* to do so. The highly injunctive approach to the ethics of presence that the Stoics developed is tied to maxims that order the practitioner to follow the codes of right conduct: "cease to fear, cease to regret, resist the pull(s) of trouble and worry, do not think about the past or the future, the present is all that there is, be here now, etc…" The stoic injunctions and imperatives offer an alternative and in a sense a solution to the dissociative ontological assessment of the physical present and the ethical present offered by Aristotle. Nonetheless, they lack the intimate, phenomenological subtlety of Augustine's later ontological assessment of Time and presence as the existential markers of a subjective experience of the distention of a mortal, finite body containing an immaterial soul turned towards the eternity and infinity of God.

By suggesting that extending the present can be achieved through deliberate actions and a proactive lifestyle, the Stoics offered an ethical answer to the question of living in the present that did not encumber itself with the mythological and theological legacy of the philosophical problems of Time. And yet, they failed to account for the irreducible *singularity* that characterizes an individual's relationship to presence, thus bringing to light once more the *tension* that burdens the European understanding of living in the present.

b. 20th century philosophies of Time or living as a trajectory.

While the tense and injunctive maxims of the Stoics progressively became more and more associated with literary discourse, as opposed to scientific inquiry, the tension of the subjective and distended paradigm of Time pioneered by Augustine continued to bear a significant influence on European philosophy well into the 20th century. Its assessment of the present as an inconsistent, distending, halo-like surface, simultaneously retracting towards the past and protracting towards the future, bore a significant influence on Edmund Husserl's phenomenology.[138] Husserl's phenomenological analyses of Time remain critical reference points across the social and natural sciences to this day: his key concept of intentionality plays a critical role in Philippe Descola's universal anthropology[139] and the emerging field of "care studies" has long nourished a dialog with the existential philosophy of Husserl's most (in)famous student, Martin Heidegger.[140]

Without entering into the details of Husserl or Heidegger's philosophies of Time, we will limit our observation to the following remark: both emphasize an understanding of living as a *trajectory*. Both Husserls' understanding of intentionality and Heidegger's assertion that existence represents a "being-towards-death" stress a *directionality* that reflects the *distensive* understanding of the present that underlies them; as if living could only be understood as a trajectory beginning at a point A and moving *towards* a point B. Thus, even important philosophers of the early 20th century frame the existential question of living in terms of provenance and destination, as if the questions "where did I come from and where am I going?" remained the pivotal point of any philosophical reflection on living.

The understanding of what it means to live in the present that Husserlian intentionality and Heideggerian existential phenomenology offer appears to be yet another iteration of the grand European philosophical gesture that lauds the contemplative mysteries of the "journey of life." Does the universalizing semantic elaboration of these seminal European philosophies of Time not occult the *qualitative* and sensitive, if not sensual, features that *govern the transition* from one moment in "time" to another? Is there not a philosophical and intercultural conceptualization of *living in/with the moment(s)* that lies *on the wayside* of the familiar tropes of philosophy that liken living to journeying?

7/ Wandering on the wayside of the injunction to "be here now," living in/with the moment(s): welcoming occurrence(s), nurturing availability, and connecting with breath(ing).

How does *living in/with the moment(s)* allow us to *wander on the wayside* of the dramatics of the journey of life and of the stoic injunction to "be here now"? Can a *philosophy of living* devoid of references to "being" truly take shape and shake up the assumptions, not only of facile ethnocentrist universalism, but also of lazy cultural relativism? Is it really sufficient or honest to state that the Early Chinese conceptions of duration, seasonality, transition, modification and continuation offer us a way out of the limits of European thought? Providing concrete examples and references remains the only way to answer such important questions.

a. Montaigne and the forebodings of the philosophy of living: cultivating availability.

When we talk about a good moment, we are not talking about it in quantitative terms but rather in qualitative ones. While the European philosophical notion of Time distends our understanding of reality, stretching our perception across the two opposing poles of past and future, thus leaving us at the confusing and empty crossroads of the present, the realness of the qualitative *experience* of the moment is at once firm and unassuming. Even without wandering as far as Early China we can already find a superb expression of what it means to *live in/with the moment(s)* in Michel de Montaigne's unclassifiable and forever delectable *Essays*. At the end of this massive work, in the 13th chapter of the third book entitled *On experience*, the French Renaissance writer offers the following assessment of the immediate experience of the moment as it relates to living and Time:

> "When I dance, I dance: when I sleep, I sleep. As I wander off alone in a beautiful orchard, my thoughts can, from time to time, become entertained with foreign occurrences; other times, I bring them back to the wandering, to the orchard, to the sweetness of this solitude, and to myself [...] The glorious masterpiece of man, to live in congruence (vivre à propos)"[141]

Although Montaigne's nearly tautological reasoning can appear to be nothing more than a well formulated, and yet ultimately daft and trite blend of the Epicurean and Stoic wisdom traditions, there is a subtle sharpness in his thinking that places him miles away from the two millennia of philosophical reflection on Time that precede him! In this passage, Montaigne displays an understanding of living as a *welcoming of occurrences*. Unbothered by the occurrence of distraction, he emphasizes the inherent fullness of the *lived moment*. Whether a moment is spent in the deepest rest or deepest activity, dancing or sleeping, welcoming the singular occurrence that it offers guarantees a sense of fluid and carefree appeasement for the one who can to *live in and with the moment(s)*.

Time ceases to be a point of preoccupation and care, it is no longer spent but rather *lived*, pleasantness and unpleasantness alternate like sunshine and rain. By wandering *on the wayside* of the logical dissections of the philosophy of Time and by embracing instead a literary and yet philosophical approach to writing, Montaigne pioneered a carefree philosophy of living that refused to be preoccupied with the passage of Time. Instead, he offered instead a novel understanding of how simple activities like dancing, sleeping, and wandering constitute opportune moments to nurture *availability*, moments that can help us develop a capacity to remain *open* to the randomness of occurrence.

b. Zhuangzi's availability: breathing "by way of the heels" or the seeds of carefree living.

It would be uncouth to end this lengthy chapter that began with a sinological remark without circling back to Early China. After all, had Montaigne said everything that needed to be said about Time and nurturing availability, we would not have embarked on such a daunting investigation! Our translation of Montaigne's *"vivre à propos"* as "to live in congruence" suggested that it is not so much the exertion of a Stoic capacity to conform with the moment that facilitates carefree living, but rather the cultivation of a capacity to remain open to the *occurrence of the moment-* what we call *availability*. Given the paradigmatic significance accorded to notion of "moment(s)" *shi* (時) in Classical Chinese literature, it comes as no surprise that we might find in its texts a more substantial grasp of availability understood as a capacity to remain *open* to the occurrence of the moment.

*

One can indeed find a strong understanding of what it means to foster availability and to welcome the moment in the 6th chapter of the *Zhuangzi* where it is said the masters of yore were: " readily coming and/yet readily leaving" (翛然而往, 翛然而來).[142] The highly idiomatic nature of this sentence makes it difficult to offer a literal translation due to the important number of "empty" placeholder characters. The adverbial form *xiaoran* (翛然) which we translate with the adverb "readily" evokes the image of the fluttering wings of a bird, available for takeoff, flying and landing; it is at once the most critical and the most opaque term of the sentence. Our translation here aims to emphasize the Sage's capacity to remain *available* to the coming and going of the moment: in the same way that the bird's wings are available for taking off, flying and landing. While it is the birds' wings that make him readily available and open to the occurrences moment, the Sage's cultivation of availability remains intrinsically tied to his *breath(ing)*: " The Sage breathes deeply deeply, authentic men breathe by way of the heels, common men breathe by way of the throat (其息深深, 真人之息以踵, 眾人之息以喉)."[143] The striking image of "breathing by way of the heels" poetically evokes how the simple, automatic, and unconscious activity of breathing deploys an attunable and modulable field of *aperture*. Opening and closing, inhaling and exhaling, contracting and expanding, coming and going, such are the activities of the Sage who nurtures his availability and therefore his capacity to attune himself to the occurrence of the moment(s).

*

The understanding of availability found in the in the *Zhuang-zi* thus outlines a strong *philosophy of breath(ing)* that *nurtures and nourishes* a capacity for carefree living that lies *on the wayside* of dogmatic injunctions and dramatic preoccupations. The continuous and constant renewal of breath plugs itself into the *actuality* of each moment: breath belongs to the moment, it does not precede or succeed it, it does not hold onto a precedence, nor does it anticipate a succession. The regulating alternation of breath matches the *phasing* and *variation* of the moment: both of its core movements, inhalation and exhalation, necessarily call upon one another. *Breath(ing)* as such represents the vital expression of the rhythmic *coming and going* that structures the processes of living. *Breath(ing)* establishes the most primary form of communication between "outside" and "inside," it represents an initial and fundamental point of *opening*; "breathing by way of the heels" therefore signifies that nothing interior remains closed off to constant renewal that comes from the exterior. The radical opening of the breath is inscribed in physicality yet it does not limit itself to the physical: the term "radical" needs to be understood here in its literal acceptance as a signifier that refers to the notion of a "root."

Nurturing availability by way of the breath needs to be understood in terms of a capacity to let oneself be traversed and irrigated by the very source of living: *breath(ing)* as such, *Qi* (氣). Traversed and irrigated by his *breath(ing)*, attuned to the flowing of *Qi* (氣) as they unfold both in and with the moment, the available human dissolves contraction and (dis)tension, finding instead relaxation and ease. Wandering *on the wayside* of injunctions and orders, the humans that *live in/with the moments* connect with the constancy of *breath(ing)*. Remaining carefree and available, indifferent to fleeting dramatics of presence, being, becoming, and Time, they tap into the infinite *resource(s) of breath(ing)*; learning how to breathe "by way of the heels" as the Zhuangzi suggests can indeed help us wander through life with efficiency and ease, alongside the silent transformations that pave the Way(s) of living.

8/ Global and continuous, or the silent transformations: an intercultural concept fit for 21st century living?

As we bring this chapter to a close, it becomes clearer that it is indeed possible to envision a *philosophy of living* that does not encumber itself with the vicissitudes and mysteries of the philosophy of Time. Born out of a strategic operation that stressed the distance separating the Ancient Greek understanding of Time from the Ancient Chinese conception of the moment, the emerging philosophical concept of the *silent transformations* offers us a tool that assists us in better understanding the processes at play in our world. It allows us to practice living *in between* cultures, an essential skill that should be, if not required, then assuredly cultivated if we wish to navigate the inherent complexities of 21st century living with the efficiency and ease of the Sage!

*

A silent transformation moves along without making a sound, remaining unheard, undiscussed and unnoticed: it does not draw attention to itself, but its operation is always visible, yet only after the fact. When the results of a silent transformation are felt as a sonorous event, the more the proceedings of the transformation are discrete and unnoticeable, the more the clamor of the event becomes palpable. Global and continuous, the silent transformations envelop the maturational and evolutive processes of living, ranging all the way from the individual process of aging to the global process of climate change. Far from the dramatic rhetoric of epiphanies and revelations, the discrete and efficient logic of the silent transformations is always at work in the processes that fabricate the world. More than ever, the interconnectedness of our globalized world leads us to think of change and transformation, not from the perspective of dramatic events, but in terms of continuous transitions that encompass a wide range of intertwining and correlated factors: AI, social media, climate change…

If anything, the concept of silent transformations, crafted out of necessity to translate the subtle logic of Classical Chinese into European languages, offers us a strong tool to approach the critical historical, political, economic, and ethical junctures of the 21st century. Lying *on the wayside* of boisterous Events and Revolutions, silent transformations bring into a focus an *unheard* dimension of *living*: whereas the Event and the Revolution are often associated with brazen esthetics that proclaim the urgency of a changing *now* (the art of the 20th century), the *barely perceptible* sensory operations of the silent transformations reveal an effective and actual *passing* that the Ancient Chinese would not have been afraid to describe as being both *bland* and *without flavor*.

CHAPTER V

The bland, the nude and the beautiful: intercultural perspectives in esthetics.

1/ The moral resource(s) of blandness or the psychological virtue(s) of flavorless character(s).

The notion of blandness bears a mostly negative connotation in our day and age; it evokes indistinction and boredom. The fact that Ancient China developed a positive understanding of blandness as a structuring esthetic and moral value might seem surprising for the contemporary reader.

a. The centrality of blandness: neither Confucian nor Daoist.

Once again, the *geo-historic distance* that separates the contemporary reader from Early China offers a singular point of entry into an *unheard* thought of blandness capable of destabilizing the thrill-seeking thinking of the 21st century. Blandness, *dan* (淡), is indeed praised early on in Ancient China as many of the classic texts found across the schools of thought can attest. In the 33rd paragraph of the *Zhongyong*, a treatise "on the usage of the middle" (中庸) and one of the four canonical "Confucian" texts that served as the basis for the mandarinal examinations, blandness is assimilated to one of the key moral attributes of the Sage following the *Dao* (道).[144]

Traditional sinology has often opposed the "Confucians" and the "Daoists," emphasizing their divergent usage of the term *Dao* itself. And yet there is remarkable convergence of the two "schools" when it comes to their appraisal of the bland texturing that seems to characterize and underlie the processual fabric of reality. In the 35th paragraph of the *Laozi,* it is said that the *Dao* passing by way of the mouth is at once bland, *dan* (淡), without flavor, *wei* (味), and yet inexhaustible in its usages.[145] Both the straightforward assertions of the "Confucians" and the sybilline statements of the "Daoists" allude to a neutral, indeterminate, and superior *openness* of blandness that eludes the confines and determinations of identifiable flavors and characters, however strong they may be. Blandness and its indeterminacy thus embody the openness of the Sage's disposition across Early Chinese schools of thought; "neither approaching nor leaving," *buji buli,* as a later Chan Buddhist formulation elegantly states it, the Sage remains entirely *available* to the moment and to those around him.[146]

*

The Sage's bland and available disposition assures his constancy and reliability; not gravitating towards extremes, he welcomes all his fellow humans as they present themselves to him. Blandness in Early China wasn't just a moral virtue, it was also understood to be a psychological phenomenon, an identifiable and desirable trait of character. A little known yet perspicacious psychologist of Ancient China, the 3rd century CE government official Liu Shiao,[147] offers the following assessment of the Sage's character in his only written work, a dense treatise entitled *Ren Wu Zhi* (人物志), which was translated into English as the *Study of human ability*:

> *Generally speaking, when it comes to human character, it is balance (understood as the capacity to remain "at center,"* 中 *zhong) and harmony that are most prized. Yet a centered and harmonious character needs to be flattened, bland, and flavorless: such a character can combine the five capacities and adapt with ease when necessary. This is why when one observes a man and judges his character, one must evaluate his ability to be flat and bland before going on to inquire about*

his intelligence.[148]

In the conflictual era of the Three Kingdoms, blandness was therefore seen as a key harmonizing psychological attribute that endowed the Sage with a capacity to diffuse tension and aggression. Much like the bland flavor is the only flavor that leaves enough space for all 5 flavors to coexist -bitter, sweet, acid, spicy and salty- the bland character is the only one that allows for the peaceful coexistence of emotions. The bland neutrality of the Sage's personality prevents him from fixating himself on a particular disposition of character or emotion, it allows him to maintain a state of perpetual availability, giving him the capacity to harmonize the fluctuating push and pull of opposing forces.

As Buddhism and its metaphysical understanding of "nothingness" began to penetrate and permeate the philosophical and esthetic elaborations of the Ancient Chinese literate classes over the course of the rule of the later Han dynasty, its psychological characterization of emptiness and flavorlessness had no difficulty folding itself into the pre-existing texts and traditions that were then beginning to be classified as "Confucian" and "Daoist." [149] The archetypal image of the available, reliable, and yet bland Sage, whose very facial features embody the serene, soft and self-effacing disposition seen in Buddhist statuary, bore a strong influence on the thinkers and artists of the literate classes who were seeking to find a renewed sense of inspiration in the Chinese classical texts, some of which were nearly a thousand years old at the time of the fall of the Han dynasty.

*

During the turbulent Three Kingdoms era that succeeded the fall of the Han dynasty, the great commentators of the *Xuanxue* (玄學) or "profound learning" tradition were influenced by Buddhist philosophy's conceptual leanings and offered a syncretic re-reading of the classic Chinese texts. These erudite scholars and men of government stressed not the opposition of "Confucianism" and "Daoism" but rather their interrelatedness. Wang Bi, the most brilliant commentator of the *Laozi* and *Yijing* who died at the early age of 23 and Guo Xiang, the man responsible for the canonical edition of the *Zhuangzi,* were arguably the two most important commentators of the Three Kingdoms era. Both offered a philosophical appreciation of emptiness and blandness that would anchor the morals and esthetics of East Asian cultures for centuries to come. Combining the traditional image of "the flavorless food and the muted music" found in the Ancient rituals described in the *Liji* or "Book of Rites"[150] with a philosophical assessment of the interrelating properties of sound and silence derived from close readings of the *Laozi* and the *Zhuangzi*, the *Xuanxue* commentators outlined how emptiness, flavorlessness and silence could constitute an indeterminate and limitless *resource* for morality and esthetics.

The limitless esthetic savoring of the bland and the empty became a core value integral to the *Yang Sheng* practices that flourished in the Three Kingdoms Era. In a troubled time where the world order was shifting, the literate classes could fold back into the empty and/ yet nurturing-nourishing practices of *Yang Sheng* that encompassed not only breathing and postural exercices, but also poetry, painting, music, and calligraphy. Blandness thus became a lifestyle practice endowed with its own iconography and soundtrack, its esthetic appreciation came to embody the ambivalent relationship to the political that haunted great figures of the *Xuanxue* tradition like the poet, musician and scholar Xi Kang mentioned in the second chapter.[151] Even though there were political and esthetic currents that rejected the bland neutrality valued by the erudite commentators of the *Xuanxue* tradition, their moral, political, and esthetic preference for emptiness and blandness continued to bear a decisive influence on music, painting and poetry centuries after their passing.

2/ Bland sounds and bland images: reverberation(s) and negative space(s).

That the ruling classes should possess the privilege and/or the leisure time necessary to codify and regulate the practice of the arts seems to be a common social phenomenon found across pre-modern cultures; in this regard, the culture of Ancient China seems no different from the culture of Ancient Greece. The regulation of music, the transmission of its correct phrasing from master to disciple, and the significance of its role in the grooming process of the young members of the ruling classes is a literary and philosophical trope shared by both geo-historic worlds. The third book of Plato's *Republic* famously seeks to regulate the different modes of music associated with various geographic locations of Ancient Greece, suggesting that some modes and rhythms might be more appropriate than others when considering the education of the city's ruling class.[152] Music played a crucial role in Greek tragedy and in the political life that revolved around the theater, its significance was not lost upon the likes of Aristotle who theorized the "purgative" virtue of music with the concept of *katharsis,* a term which would later be recouped by Freud to develop the "cathartic" method of the "talking-cure" in psychoanalysis.[153]

a. The sound of the Guqin: 大音希聲 or "great sound, rare tone".

Thousands of miles away from the philosophers of Ancient Greece, the scholars of Ancient China were known to play a 5 (and later 7) string zither still played today, the *Guqin* (古琴).[154] *Guqin* technic was codified early on in the Ancient Chinese texts since it played a critical role in the execution of rituals; its practice was not just a privileged avenue of relaxation for the governing elites: zither music literally *set the tone* of government rule. The playing of zither and the savoring of its sound fading into silence provided a welcome distraction for the administrators of the Empire, it also offered the *sound-image* of a form of *constancy* whose aim was to reflect the celestial order ruling the world, especially in times of turmoil.

What did the bland and flavorless zither music of the scholars described in the *Book of Rites* sound like? By turning to the 41st paragraph of the *Laozi* we might find an indication if we take the time to decipher the evocation of a "great sound" with a "rare tone":

大音希聲

dai yin, xi sheng

"Great sound, rare tone"

We find in this formulation a typical rhetorical process of Classical Chinese where two synonymic characters are juxtaposed in a compact formula: *yi* (音) and *sheng* (聲) are indeed both synonyms of sound, tone, music, and noise. In appearance, the sequence of words is nearly nonsensical; yet if we play close attention to both these sinograms and their qualifiers, *dai* which means "great," "big," and "ample" (大), and *xi* which means "rare," "precious," and "reduced" (希), it becomes possible to uncover a remarkably subtle philosophical appreciation of sound and music. Whereas *yi* (音) refers etymologically to *emission* of sound as it exits the mouth, the character *sheng* (聲) refers etymologically to the *reception* of sound as it reaches the ear; the term *xi* (希) used here as an adjective suggests the idea of a precious craft as it is composed of the sinograms *jīn* (巾), which refers to a silk garment, and *yao* (爻), which denotes the idea of threading. What constitutes the greatness or amplitude of an emitted sound therefore is its capacity to transform itself into a *rarified* received sound. This means that the great sound bears no excess, it is engaged in a process of *rarefaction* wherein the duration and subtlety of its *fading* constitutes the marker of its strength. In other words, the rare tone which evokes greatness and immensity lies *on the edge* of sound; it reveals its might as it becomes *nearly imperceptible*, fading into the limitless and indeterminate *ground(s) of silence*.

This brief yet dazzling passage of the *Laozi* gives us a strong sense of the esthetic constructs that underscore traditional *Guqin* playing to this day: it demonstrates the central role played by silences and reverberations when it comes to the execution and appreciation of the subtle, understated, and/yet powerful tones that reverberate from the instrument as its sounds fade into silence. The bland music described in the *Book of Rites* should therefore not be understood as a trite, formulaic, or insipid rendition of ritual tunes. Instead, it corresponds to the *silent music* that deploys itself *in between* notes.

b. The blandness of landscape(s).

The esthetic appreciation of blandness as a marker of a philosophical and artistic sensibility focused on emptiness, phasing, and *liminality* thus bore a strong influence, not only on the music but also on the prose writing, poetry, and painting of the literate classes of Ancient China. The patient practice of calligraphy and the compact, allusive, and evasive formulations of many styles of East Asian poetry both carry the mark of the esthetics of understated majesty alluded to in the 41st paragraph of the *Laozi*.

Centuries after the Three Kingdoms period, the stylistic traits associated with the esthetics of blandness and silent music carried on in the Chinese tradition of "mountain(s)-water(s)" landscape painting known as *Shan Shui* (山水).[155] The 14th century painter Ni Zan's (Fig. 1) paintings perhaps best capture how bland and empty landscapes convey a unique sense of openness and availability. Ni Zan's paintings rarely portray human beings. Full of void spaces, there is nothing in particular in them that pulls the eye; and yet, they seem to diffuse an expansive sense of emptiness and harmony. The bland landscapes of Ni Zan's paintings aren't landscapes devoid of feelings and resonances; on the contrary, the negative space within them deploys subtle yet strong feelings of contemplation and belonging. Ni Zan's esthetics represent first and foremost his singular understanding of painting, yet they effortlessly *inscribe* themselves in well-trodden literary and philosophical tropes that stress the moral and esthetic virtues of blandness.

Nonetheless, one should be wary of hasty generalizations as there were obviously artists who explored divergent esthetic paths. The painter Wang Meng (Fig. 2), a friend and contemporary of Ni Zan, known for his dense and almost oppressive paintings, is a perfect example of an esthetics of fullness that contrasts with the emptiness of the esthetics of blandness. The point of this brief overview of the role of blandness in Classical Chinese esthetics was not to stress a specifically Chinese nor East Asian "cultural trait." Instead, our aim was to offer a thought-provoking perspective on the untapped and unheard *resources* of a characterization of blandness that lies *in between* the negative preconceptions of one culture and the positive valuations of another one.

*

Fig. 1 Ni Zan, 14th century CE, *Six Gentlemen*, Shanghai Museum, China

Fig. 2 Wang Meng, 14t$^\text{h}$ century CE, *The Simple Retreat*, Metropolitan Museum of Art, NYC

3/ Impossible nudes or when the model forms of metaphysics don't exist.

As we continue to probe the esthetic categories that define geo-historic areas and eras across the globe to challenge received ways of thinking, both culturalist and universalist, we are led to a striking observation: "the nude" does not exist in the art of Ancient China.[156] While there are of course representations of nude bodies in Chinese art, as evidenced by the erotic art of the Ming dynasty (Fig.3), the *ideal representation* of the nude human body as a simultaneously scientific and artistic model of anatomical perfection did not exist, as such, in the sculptural and pictorial traditions that emanated from Ancient China journeyed across East Asia.

Fig. 3. Ming Dynasty erotic print.

On the one hand, the nude body was the object of life-like representations very early on in Ancient Greek art (Fig.4); it became a staple of European sculpture and painting. On the other hand, the artists of Early China, and later East Asia, devoted far greater attention to life-like representations of animals, landscapes, and textures, while exhibiting little interest for figurative representations of the nude human body (Fig.5). As we stretch the geo-historic distances separating

136

the European world from the East Asian world to signal the absence of "the nude" in Ancient China and East Asian art more broadly, it becomes clearer how the cultural pathways taken by these worlds diverge at a critical point of juncture: the understanding of the human "body" itself.

That the nude body would not emerge in Ancient China as a category of scientific and artistic inquiry should not surprise us: we have seen that the term "body" itself, derived from the Ancient Greek *soma*, is a far less univocal notion in Classical Chinese.[157] The models of anatomy bore little influence on Early Chinese scientific, medical, and esthetic thinking: the idea of the body as a single, divisible "substance" finds no exact equivalents in Classical Chinese medical and scientific texts where a plethora of terms come into play to describe the corporeal. If we look at the visual representations of bodies in Classical Chinese medical treatises, we see that the anatomical or "organic" components of the body are barely depicted, they are left at the stage of outlines, while the points of the *mai* (脈) "channels" or "meridians" are named and charted with minute detail (Fig.6).

What Classical Chinese medical texts and images tell us is that "the nude" as an esthetic and scientific category worthy of inquiry did not emerge as such, *precisely* because the scholars and artists of Ancient China were focused on *interrelatedness* and *not* separateness. In other words, the emergence of "the nude" as a foundational esthetic and scientific principle, or *archè,* of the Western world appears to be entirely correlated to the history of Being and to the construction of "Man" as a constitutive category of thought. The question that therefore emerges from the basic and factual observation that "the nude" does not exist, as such, in Ancient China is the following one: what were the *conditions of possibility* of the nude in Ancient Greece and the conditions of its *impossibility* in Ancient China?

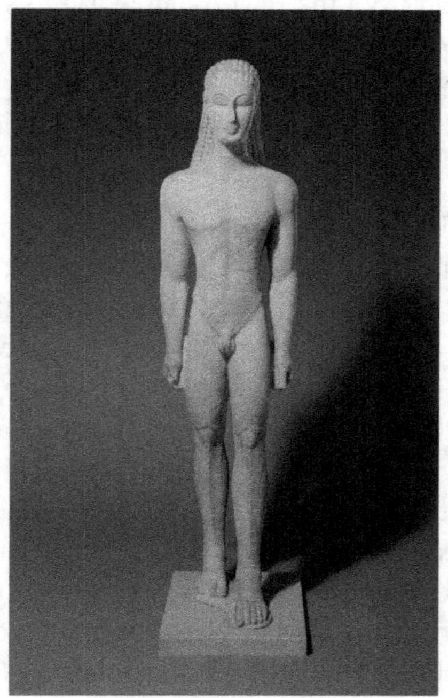

Fig.4. Greek nude *kouros* statue, 5th century BCE.

Fig. 5. Edo Period (17th century CE) Japanese painting of a tiger.

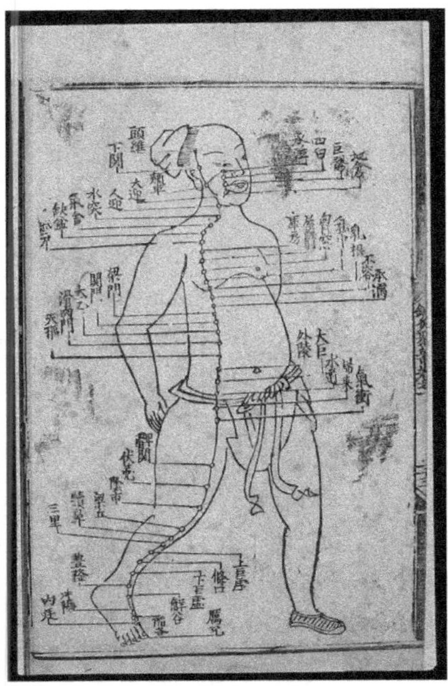

Fig.6. Ming Dynasty (16th century CE) Chinese acupuncture chart.

a. "the nude" as an ontological representation of morphè and eidos.

The three distinctly Greek terms and notions that seem to permeate and underpin the artistic and scientific understanding of "the nude," are, without a doubt, the "model form," or *eidos,* "essence," *ousia,* and the notion of Being itself, *to on.*

In a modelized nude form, the human being is idealized and abstracted from temporal and societal determinations. The representation of the nude body represents, not a social or historic function (i.e a portrait of a ruler, of a saint or of a layman at a given moment in time) but rather the idealized *essence* of a generic and universal human being. The notion of a modelized ideal or *eidos* that embodies a permanent essence of the human being conditions the scientific and artistic representations of the human body in the West from Plato onwards. The image of the nude mirrors the representation of a paradigmatic anatomical body abstracted from determinations: it *projects* an essentialized and idealized understanding of the human being. In Plato's philosophy, the existence of the intelligible model form, the pure *eidos*, is thought to precede the existence of the sensible form: the ideal and intelligible model forms of Beauty and Love literally pre-figure the forms of love and beauty experienced in the sensible realm.[158]

Even though Plato's student Aristotle is known for his far more materialistic and empirical outlook, he also attributes great importance to the notion of model form when he states that the circular shape of the kidneys illustrates "matter's desire for form (*kinei hos eromenon*)."[159] In other words, the imperfectly circular shape of the kidney represents for Aristotle the *aspirational motion* of matter as it aims to reach the *perfect ideality* of a circular and self-identical model-form. In Aristotle's teleological worldview, the materiality of figure (*morphè*) aspires to the intelligibility of form (*eidos*). The aspirational pull of *morphè's* transformation into *eidos* represents the primal genesis of an initial impulse-movement (*kinesis*) that orients immanent becoming towards the transcendence of Being. The pursuit of model-forms through art and craft (*technè*) thus becomes a mediating ground between the sensible and the intelligible: the artist depicting the nude becomes a craftsman whose direct action consists in carving out an intelligible form, an identifiable and life-like representation made of inert sensible matter (pigment, stone, or metal). The nude literally embodies the ambivalence of form and its precarious journey from the sensible to the intelligible, from figure to form: it is a *hypostatic* and nearly incarnate representation of Being itself.

b. The indeterminacy of xing *(形) or the wayside of anatomic morphology.*

Miles away from the hypostatized understanding of the nude as a paradigmatic ideal form that represents an abstract(ed) understanding of the human being, the civilization of Ancient China developed the notion of *xing* (形). Xing can be translated as "actualized form"; as we've seen, it can also be translated as "body," "bodily form" or "situation." The distance that separates *xing* from *eidos* is great insofar as *xing* never represents a hypostatized essence: it only reflects a process of *actualization.*

The notion of *xing* (形) thus challenges the morpho-logic understanding of the body that conditioned the scientific and artistic paradigms of Ancient Greece. Morphology indeed refers to "the logic of figure" and it is not hard to understand how its corollary, anatomy, can be thought as a decomposition of figures into forms. Leonardo Da Vinci's anatomical drawings are perfect examples of the decisive influence that the morphologic paradigm inherited from Ancient Greece bore on the construction of artistic and scientific modernity. Leonardo's keen interest in mechanics and optics illustrates how the understanding of a modelized, idealized, and divisible ideal form shaped, not only the artistic representations of Early Modernity, but also its technological developments. The Renaissance's revalorization of the culture of Ancient Greece resulted in a scientific and esthetic paradigm where artists were encouraged to become geometrists in the name of life-like representation, thus furthering the idealization of the nude human body as a hypostatized essence turned towards immobile and transcendent Being. If we think of the suffering that nude models endured throughout the history of Western art, having to remain immobile for prolonged periods time, supported and chained by elaborate systems of ropings and pulleys, we begin to measure how the abstract idea of an immobile model form had very *real* implications for the human beings who literally put their living bodies at the service of art and science!

In an esthetic paradigm where a hypostatized model form of the nude body represents the ideal image of the human being, the physical living body can only be apprehended as a means destined to an end. In other words, the nude as a physical embodiment of transcendent Beauty itself reflects an aspirational motion that pulls immanent matter towards pure spiritual form through a web of causal principles and relationships. Here again, the nude and the essence of Beauty that it carries along with it seem to embody the paradigmatic categories of Western thought on both a literal and metaphorical level.

4/ Representing the Beauty of form(s) vs depicting vapor(s)-breath(s) and mountain(s)-water(s).

Instead of anatomical models of the body derived from the naturalist philosophies of Ancient Greece, the civilization of Ancient China developed a schematized and schematizable understanding of the circulation of *Qi* (氣).[160] On the one hand, the nomenclature of anatomical models aims to designate identifiable components whose sum literally forms the physical essence of the human body. On the other hand, the schematic drawings found in acupuncture treatises offer a series of cartographic outlines that map the passage of *Qi* through the *mai* channels. Acupuncture charts detail precise points endowed with evocative names like "gateway of life" or *ming men* (命門); the usage of these points and charts in the Chinese medical tradition dates back to the Han dynasty era.[161] It could be tempting for the modern reader to dismiss acupuncture and Chinese medicine as a pre-scientific approaches to the human body, yet doing so would betray a lazy universalist perspective: such a perspective fails to account for the singular *cartographies* of *Qi* found in Ancient Chinese medical texts. It glosses over a complex and precise approach to the processes of *circulation* and *exchange* that connect the internal to the external, the empty to the full, the visible to the invisible, the formed to the formless.

*

Ancient Chinese views on the circulation of *Qi* as a process of simultaneous forming and deforming find their esthetic apex in the landscape painting tradition of *Shan Shui*. In *Shan shui* painting, rocks cease to become inert and lifeless being, they are traversed and inhabited by the formless *Qi* of the wind and the water that shapes them into distinct, actualized forms (形). Misty hazes and floating clouds circulate across the visual field, as if these paintings offered us a point of viewing in which a mere image could be infused with the *pulsating breath(ing)* of *Qi*. The diffuse lines that compose the paintings depict a process of transformation wherein one form transitions into another, they are unconcerned with depicting the defined contours and forms of an identifiable, hypostatized, and self-identical "model form" or "entity."

The transitioning and circulatory processes of transformation featured in *Shan shui* paintings recall the 15th paragraph of the *Laozi* where the *Dao* is said to be "vacant like a valley and muddled like mud."[162] *Shan Shui* paintings portray both dense, compact, and nearly muddled images within and alongside vast expanses of pristine negative space; they effortlessly capture the flowing motions of a cloud, the flutter of a whisker, or the folds of a piece of silk. The (de)pictorial process of the painter in this esthetic paradigm is an art of both obfuscation and clarification: painting becomes a simultaneous exploration of form and formlessness, it mirrors the uncreated and endless *(de)formation(s)* of the "great formless image(s)" so poetically evoked in the 41th paragraph of the *Laozi*.[163]

*

Whereas the Classical Chinese notion of *xing* (形) emphasizes the primal *indeterminacy* of *forms*, as well as their capacity to transform and transition into one another, the esthetic tradition of "the nude" emphasizes the distinction of *a* form extracting itself from matter. A strong relationship binds *morphè*, the shaping form or "figure," to *eidos*, the model or "ideal" form. These two complementary terms detail the way in which Ancient Greek thought viewed material form as a circumspection that outlines intelligible form: the sculptural productions of the artists of Ancient Greece embody the tension of a paradigm where a work of art should *represent* both material and intelligible perfection. "The nude" thus acts as a *representative vehicle* that brings forth the ideal form of the Beautiful into the world via the artistic shaping of forms: the tangible form or figure of the sculpture, its *morphè*, therefore outlines its intelligible form or *representation*, the *eidos* of Beauty.

The representative and morphologic paradigms of Ancient Greek art set the stage for what will become a centuries long pursuit of Western art: representing and outlining Beauty through the representation of beautiful forms or figures. What begins to emerge from this staged encounter, where the Ancient Chinese paradigms of *transformation* meet the Ancient Greek theories and practices of *representation*, is a keener appreciation of the singularity of a constitutive and central category of Western thought- the Beautiful. At this point in our inquiry, the Western attention to the nude body and the lack of nudes in East Asian arts should compel us to ask ourselves the following question: was thinking the Beautiful even *necessary*?

5/ The strange idea of the Beautiful: Being (the) Beautiful vs. transmitting spirit(s).

Interrogating the Beautiful might seem to be a fruitless endeavor: on the one hand, it seems as though modern art has relinquished the Beautiful as a meaningful category; on the other hand, there appears to be a universal understanding of the Beautiful that transcends cultures, eras, and subjective judgements. The critical theorist Theodor W. Adorno best summed up the problem of the Beautiful when he stated that the Beautiful constitutes a necessary and universal category of thought that protects us from cultural relativism and from an uninteresting universalist ideology devoid of identifiable content. Adorno eloquently sums up the conundrum of the Beautiful in his *Aesthetic Theory* with the following sentence: "We cannot define the Beautiful yet we cannot let go of the concept of the Beautiful; it is the perfect example of an antinomy."[164] Adorno's position has become in a sense so obvious in our globalized world that it now makes sense to question it using the intercultural approach to esthetics developed throughout this chapter.

a. Defining the Beautiful: the story of a well-trodden philosophical concept.

The first point of reflection that needs to be interrogated is *how* the adjective "beautiful" becomes substantiated into "the Beautiful." When the adjective "beautiful" becomes "the Beautiful," there is an implicit passage from a descriptive usage of the term to a conceptual one. Unsurprisingly, the Ancient Greeks were the first to leverage the conceptual resources of the Beautiful. In Plato's *Hippias Major*, the philosopher attempts to distinguish what is beautiful from *the* Beautiful, as such. The questions tackled in Plato's dialogue outline the steps of an *onto-logical* mode of reasoning which seeks to understand how one moves from a concrete and material *sensible comprehension* of beautiful things to abstract and ideal *logical intellection* of the Beautiful itself. For the idealist philosopher, the discovery of a pure *idea* or model-form (*eidos*) is intrinsically tied to the logical apprehension of the idea of the Beautiful. The notion of an indissoluble bond tying the Ideal to the Beautiful has haunted and confounded Western thought since then; nearly 2000 years after Plato, the French Enlightenment thinker Denis Diderot continued to remain perplex when faced with the impossible task of defining the Beautiful: "how is it that almost all men agree to say that the beautiful exists, how is it that so many of them feel as if they truly know where it lies and yet that so few of them know what it truly is?" [165]

*

Classical Chinese offers us an alternate point of entry into this seemingly insoluble question as it does not establish a morphological distinction between the adjective "beautiful" and the substantiated noun "the Beautiful." The character *mei* (美)[166] can indeed refer to both the adjectival and the nominal form. Because of this linguistic indetermination, the hegemonic conceptualization of "the Beautiful" that dominates Western thought did not unfold as such in Early China where a great variety of semantic options were used to designate phenomena that are lumped in the West under a single, subsuming conceptual category. Following its habitual custom, Classical Chinese favored the usage of correlative and bipolar *binomes* rooted in the *yin/yang* opposition rather than in a single, definitive category: "flourishing/delightful," "smooth/pretty," "secret/elegant..." such were the binomial formulations used to describe what the West designated under the single term of the Beautiful. Other expressions like "superior," "alive," "excellent," "well-executed," "inextinguishable," "penetrating the spiritual," were held on equal footing so that *mei* (美) never assumed the dominating role held by the Beautiful in the West.

From Plato onwards, the West detached the intelligible truth of Being from the sensible realm of experience: the idea of the Beautiful thus emerged as a paradigmatic category of Western thought because it was the only idea that could lead to an *a-rising* of the intelligible within the sensible. The Beautiful is said to be *ekphanestaton,* its a-rising represents a detachment and projection out of the sensible into the intelligible.[167]

The Beautiful operates as a fundamental building block of metaphysics: shining like a well-worn patina, it attempts to tie back together the disjointed and cleaved planes of sensibility and intelligibility, transcendent Being and immanent beings, spiritual forms and material figures. Plotinus pursued the Platonist hypostasis of the Beautiful when he characterized the work of the artist as a process wherein the luminous and ideal form of the Beautiful is *impressed* upon obscure and resistant matter. The 3rd century CE philosopher even asks: "where would the Beautiful be if it was deprived of Being? Where would Being be if it was deprived of the Beautiful?"[168] In the Neo-Platonist worldview, "Being" is nothing more than "being beautiful" and conversely "being beautiful" is simply "Being."

b. Resonance and the transmission of spirit(s).

Classical Chinese did not produce such a dualist and spiritualist philosophy of mutually exclusive, hierarchical opposites; rather, the notion of the invisible-immortal spirit, *shen* (神), is thought to be a refined and subtle form -quintessence- of the seminal-mortal spirit, *jing* (精).[169] In texts like the *Zhuangzi,* the spiritual reflects an *internal* process contained within material processes, it is in no way the marker of an *external* source of spiritual transcendence. The "spiritual" dimension of *Shan shui* paintings therefore does not consist in their ability to depict an otherworldly transcendence via a projected and

146

projective symbolization process. Instead, it resides in their *capacity* to *transmit* the subtle internal *shen* spirits that emanate and emerge *from within* a depicted image. *Shan shui* paintings do not seek to represent the Beautiful or to modelize beautiful things; rather, their social and esthetic function is to *transmit spirit(s)*, chuan *shen* (傳神).[170]

In lieu of a hypostatized, metaphysical, and conceptualized understanding of the Beautiful as the *archè* of art, we find in the many Classical Chinese treatises discussing the art of painting a two-character expression that could be literally translated as "spiritual color(ing)," *shen cai* (神彩).[171] *Shen cai* does not hold the hegemonic power that the Beautiful holds over Western esthetics, it is not a concept as such but rather a structural feature of an artistic process. *Shen cai* instead depicts the ways in which a sensible experience of esthetic appreciation can subtly *diffuse* a distinctly *spiritual* fragrance; the expression conjures *a web of spirit(s)* that the senses simultaneously *receive and deploy.*

The Classical Chinese art of *transmitting spirit through coloration* thus isn't an art of *resemblance* or *mimesis* but rather an art of *resonance* or *yun* (韻). The fifth and sixth century CE artist and literati Xie Hie summed up the art of painting in the following formulation that has since then been copiously commented upon:

氣 韻 生 動

qi yun sheng dong

"Breathing resonance and generating movement."[172]

In a literal translation this formulation could be rendered as "breathing resonating birthing moving." This emblematic formulation showcases the ways in which pictorial production in Pre-Modern China bore little concern for "the representation of the Beautiful." Because Chinese painting techniques evolved *on the wayside* of the hypostatized essences of Western metaphysics, painters and critics were not preoccupied with the Greek question *of mimesis*. Instead, their attention was wholly turned towards the *transmission* of a diffuse yet pregnant, varying yet constant, ceaseless flux of *breath(ing)-spirit(s)*.

6/ Exiting the hegemony of the Beautiful in an effort to restore its strangeness.

Exiting the hegemonic influence of the concept of the Beautiful requires a thorough critique of the three pillars of classical Reason upon which it stands: *representation, judgment,* and *satisfaction.* Hegel was among the early detractors of the first pillar when he criticized representation's failure to account for its infinite determination. In other terms, the necessarily contingent aspects of the represented object cannot, as such, embody the transcendence of the *eidos.*

a. Depicting vs representing, savoring vs judging.

Our exploration of Classical Chinese esthetical traditions and of their indifference to the   conceptual problems of representation and *mimesis* forged in Ancient Greece also offers a point of entry into the critique of representation. Representation thus isn't only suspect because its abstracted, isolated, and substantive features *mask* the contingent determinations that produced them in the first place; it also betrays a securitarian distance and mastery aimed towards its object. In other words, the emergence of the represented object and the overflowing that results from this emergence cannot be neatly subsumed by the mastery of a representing subject. A function of the (de)pictorial activity that cannot be reduced to the grasping motion of *mimesis* indeed lies *beneath* the subject/object distinction. The rupture of representation also induces the rupture of *judgment* insofar as the latter presupposes the idea of a sovereign entity that is immediately and entirely present to itself, the Cartesian subject encapsulated by and within the *cogito.* Does the appreciating and *savoring -wei* (味) in Chinese- of artistic productions not entail a lengthier and largely unconscious process of *infusion* that necessarily eludes the cognizing activity of a rational, conscious, and judging subject?

When the figure of the subject ceases to dominate the practice of esthetic appreciation, the individual satisfaction or pleasure of the viewer or listener becomes secondary to the experimental and experiential processes that orient esthetic activity itself, be they creative or appreciative. Modern Art has indeed questioned the relevance of subjective pleasure in the creation and reception of artworks and has instead emphasized the processual underpinnings of the creative and critical process. Yet one can legitimately question Modern Art's near utter refusal of satisfaction: how viable is it to promote such a radical recusal of form and such a blatant endorsement of process? Does an appreciation of the material and processual *labor* of the artist truly represent an alternative to the metaphysical pursuit of an intelligible form of the Beautiful carved out of beautiful figures? In its constructed effort to slay the Beautiful and in its quest to replace it with the notions of the sublime, the formless, the ugly, and ultimately with the concept of Art itself, Modern Art has both achieved its goal and drawn itself into a corner. In a sense the metaphysical pursuit of the Beautiful and the mythological representation of the artist as a devoted craftsman extracting intelligible Beauty from formless matter has been replaced by another mythology: the one of the heroic laborer-artist engaged in alternative processes of creation meant to represent a radical critique of culture itself. Despite its audacious brilliance, a deconstructive and critical work of Modern Art like Duchamp's urinal furthers the image of the artist as a radical, stubborn, and paradoxical proponent of an alienated and inaccessible form of Anti-Culture.

b. On the wayside of the "natural" and the "artistic."

Classical Chinese esthetics offer a welcome counterpoint to Western art's tired philosophical debates insofar as they produced an understanding of process that is neither critical nor deconstructive. As we saw, the Western ideal of the Beautiful and its subsequent deconstruction in the Modern Era has much to do with an equally Western concept: "nature." Whereas Western art sought to extract the distinctly human essence of the Beautiful from the indistinct beauty of the natural world, Classical Chinese esthetics never drew such a stark distinction between a human understanding of the Beautiful and the beauty of nature itself. Because the concept of "nature" as such did not exist as such in Classical Chinese, a plurality of semantic options was (once again) used to describe what was lumped under a single term in the West. The notion of tian (天), commonly translated as "Heaven," its coupling within the bipolar binome *tian di* (天地), "heaven-earth," the notion of spontaneous advent, *ziran* (自然), and even the notion of *Dao* itself evoke the processual underpinnings of "nature." And yet, none of these terms are quite equatable with the massive univocity that this paradigmatic concept of Western thought carries along with it.[173]

The concept of "art" itself was never fully developed in Classical Chinese where the notion of *yi* (藝), which refers to craft, did not hold the same prominence in intellectual debate as it did in the West. It was only in the 19th century that *yi* was rendered an equivalent of the Western concept of art. The artists of the sinosphere did not view themselves as "creators" caught in a metaphysical search for Beauty: if we pay heed to the language they used, we read that they engaged in a process of "fabrication-transformation," *zhaohua* (造化), the one that underlies the "spontaneous advent," *ziran* (自然), of all things.[174] The notion of the image thus becomes identical with the notion of the phenomenal, both are expressed by the term *xiang* (象). There is no need to develop a separate plane of representation, be it transcendent or transcendental, a plane where the *noumena,* the "things as such" are distinguished from the *phenomena,* the "things as they appear. Here again, the 41st paragraph of the *Laozi* perfectly sums it up: "the great image has no form, *da xiang wu xing* (大象無形)."

In summary, the *internal interplay* of polarities within images and phenomena (appearing/disappearing, soft/hard, bright/dark etc.) *transmits their spirit(s)* and *enlivens* them without the need to designate an external, symbolic, and transcendent point of reference like the Beautiful.

c. Neither universal nor cultural, or the de-centering Adorno's antinomy of the Beautiful.

The decentering of the Western fixation on the Beautiful *via* Classical Chinese esthetics is salutary not because it offers a "solution" to all the negative attributes we want to pin on Western civilization. Rather, it offers us a philosophical passageway that allows us to dissolve Adorno's remarks on the seemingly insoluble conundrum of the Beautiful which is both crudely and yet accurately summed up by the popular American expression: "ya can't live with it, and ya can't live without it."

While Adorno seems to remain bogged in the aporetic stance that ends the *Hippias Major* regarding the impossible definition of the Beautiful,[175] he also posits that the Beautiful acts as a necessary scientific hypothesis when thinking about the positive valuations granted to artifacts throughout history and across the world. For Adorno, without the hypothesis of the Beautiful the esthetic interest in historical artifacts would be "senseless and blind." And yet, within the confines of his scientific perspective and paradigm, the discipline of esthetics becomes nothing more than "a formless, historical, and relativistic description of what was considered beautiful here and there in a diverse range of societies and across a diverse range of styles." Adorno sees an "antinomy'- and thus a logical problem- within the conundrum of the Beautiful because he still holds it to be, if not in essence, then in right, a universal category found across cultures; he still believes, as he puts it himself, in the "fatal universality of the concept of the Beautiful."[176]

*

If we were to remain betrodden to the limitless universality of the Beautiful as Adorno outlines it, then the weight of such a responsibility would surely be "fatal" and crush us. Yet if we turn our attention to the cultural inventiveness, resourcefulness, and *strangeness* encapsulated within the concept of the Beautiful, it becomes possible for us to reflect on the conditions of possibility that fostered its emergence. We can then gain a newfound appreciation of the hitherto *unheard possibilities* that it holds. Without veering into ideological universalism and/or lazy cultural relativism, the singularity of the idea of the Beautiful can be appreciated for all its limitations *and* qualities. If we skirt around the Beautiful's falsely evident universality, we can then preserve its uncanny *operativity*.

The fallacious self-evidence of the Beautiful indeed continues to permeate contemporary debates, not only in the social sciences and humanities, but also in the field of "neuro-esthetics" where devoted scientists program a battery of sophisticated neurophysiological tests that seek to find empirical foundations that could confirm that the Beautiful can indeed be perceived, and thus exist, as such. The baseline assumptions of the crudest forms of Platonism are not far away and, despite the incredible advances in technology we've experienced over the past millennia, it seems as though Modern Science truly cannot rid itself of its Greek heritage… Even more preoccupying than the rehashing of Platonist metaphysics in the field of neurobiological research is perhaps the staggering diffusion of the Beautiful as a uniformizing common measure of human experience.

*

Paradoxically, as the West began to lose interest in the Beautiful as a relevant category of esthetic and artistic inquiry, the concept itself spread its wings across the world, uniformizing diverse ways of thinking along the way and imposing the fallacious self-evidence of its universality. It is now commonplace in China or Japan to translate "esthetics" as *bigaku* in Japanese or *meixue* in Chinese (美學), literally "beauty-study," when, as we saw, the notion of 美 did not hold a central place in the esthetic and artistic tradition of these cultures until very recently! The subsumption of these rich esthetic traditions under the uniformized umbrella of the globalized concept of the Beautiful translated as 美 leads in turn to a culturalist stance where certain commentators like the Japanese philosopher Kuki Shuzo go on to argue that *only* the members of a given culture can appreciate the singular understanding of the Beautiful developed within that culture. Kuki argued that a true understanding of the Beautiful articulated within the Japanese esthetic tradition of *iki* would be, in effect, impossible for a non-Japanese person.[177]

Such a culturalist understanding of esthetics betrays two tendencies: on the one hand, it showcases an uncritical and uncriticized usage of the universalizing concept of the Beautiful that negates and obfuscates, its singular history; on the other hand, it highlights an isolationist ideological stance that refuses to engage in cultural dialogue.

152

Rather than servicing the exchange between cultures, the culturalist stance that posits that each culture possesses its own singular, culturally determined, and ultimately ineffable conception of the Beautiful shrouds the artistic traditions of all cultures in a veil of metaphysical mystery all-to-betrodden to the imperialist tropes of Western thought; it functions like a barrier that prevents meaningful and important intercultural dialogue. Now that the demise of the hegemony of the Beautiful has been fully carried out in the Western world, now that we realize that the heroic overthrowing of the Beautiful does not constitute a recusal of its conceptual premises and foundations, now that we see that the very project to deconstruct the Beautiful from within leads to an unspoken acceptance of its fallacious and seemingly self-evident neutrality, it is possible to uncover and highlight the *implicit* evidences that the idea of the Beautiful carries along with it. Doing so will allow us to both measure the fecundities of the Beautiful and what it leaves *unthought*, it will give us the means to distinguish which avenues of thought it opened and which pathways of thinking it closed. In short, it will allow us to reflect on the strange and adventurous pathways espoused by the idea of the Beautiful across its history, and renew our understanding of the possibilities it holds for the 21st century without adhering to the ideologies of facile universalism and lazy relativism.

*

The following chapter will continue to question the fundamental categories of Western thought as so to develop an intercultural concept of the *intimate* that lies on the *wayside* of the overplayed dramatics of "Love." Instead of falling into the tired universalist trope that emphasizes the "One Love" that pervades the world, we will explore how European authors like Augustine and Rousseau developed an *existential* understanding of the intimate that is best appreciated when we stand *in between* cultures. As we shall see, Classical Chinese literary culture also touched upon the existential *resources* of the intimate; and yet, it did not explicitly thematize them in the way(s) that thinkers like Augustine and Rousseau did.

CHAPTER VI
Resource(s) of the intimate.

1/ Charting the intimate: an intercultural perspective.

a. Historicizing European categories of thought, on the way-side of the grand myth of "Love."

As we saw in the previous chapter, an intercultural approach to philosophy can find many strong groundings in Classical Chinese esthetic culture, particularly because the latter challenges the hegemonic supremacy of the universalist Western concept of the Beautiful. If we are to continue our exploration of the *wayside* that lies *in between* cultures, then it makes sense at this point in our inquiry to turn our attention towards an all-too-neglected category of Western i.e., European culture- the *intimate*. In an era where European-born categories of thought standardize and uniformize the world, it is more important than ever to historicize them. Our exploration of the intimate as a concept will serve precisely this purpose: we must indeed save the world from boring and uniform thought which mistakes itself as being universal. To do so, we must find a point of entry into our *unthought*. In other words, it is imperative to return to those obvious elements of our thinking which we take for granted and that we no longer even think to question.

*

"Love," that grand mythical category of European thought, remains to this day one of these major unthought building blocks of our thinking that is ripe for this kind of in-depth (re)questioning. Yet how can we *step outside* its mythical vicissitudes? How can we cease to be *bogged down* in the tired rhetoric of this foundational category of our thought? Once again, we will need to follow neglected threads of thinking and turn our attention towards lesser explored categories and concepts: the intimate will offer us a privileged avenue to *wander on the wayside* of the syrupy noisiness of Love.

b. The paradox of the intimate: sharing what is "most interior" with what is "most exterior."

The meaning of the intimate is paradoxical and twofold. On the one hand, it refers to the most interior dimension of subjective experience (the "intimate conviction" that one can have about something or someone). On the other hand, it refers to a *sharing* (as in "we are intimate *together*"). The intimate indeed refers to a superlative interior: the Latin word *intimus* is itself the superlative of the term *intus* or "inside," it denotes that which is "most within" (the comparative form of *intus* is *interior,* which means "more within'). And yet, paradoxically, this "most within" the Self leads us straight back to an Other; as if the profundity of the inner was directly correlated with the expansiveness of the outer. The definitive formulation of the intimate as it relates to the porous boundaries separating Self from Other can without a doubt be found in St. Augustine's *Confessions*: "*tu autem eras interior intimo meo et superior summo meo,*"[178] which can be translated as "[God], you were more inside me than the most inside of me, and more superior to me than the most superior to me." What is interesting in this crucial sentence is that the superlative nature of the intimate here has nothing to do with the concept of "Love." Instead, the intimate signals a profound experience wherein the bottomless depth of the inside becomes tied to the limitless height of the outside. By compounding the superlative (*intimo*) with the comparative (*interior*), Augustine sets the stage for a groundbreaking and inventive conception of the intimate that departs from the Greek language of Being. The intimate experience of God that he outlines is not caught in a dialectic prison of being vs. non-being, existence vs. non-existence: it is instead a *lived* experience wherein the boundaries separating the Self from the Other are dissolved.

156

2/ Floating living, or when the intimate does not take hold.

At this point in our enquiry, it might be worthwhile to examine whether this radical experience of the intimate might have emerged in other cultures. As per our usual habit, we will turn our attention towards Classical Chinese literature to explore this intercultural line of philosophical questioning. If there is one Classical Chinese text which neighbors the European conception of the intimate, without ever fully touching upon the boundlessness that it supposes, it is assuredly Shen Fu's (沈復) *Six Tales of the Floating Life* (浮生六記 or *Fu Sheng Liu Ji*).[179] As we shall see, this text's superb poetic evocation of intimacy in married life does not quite capture the *infinity* of the intimate *realized* by Augustine, and later Rousseau, in their respective *Confessions*.

a. The intimate complicity of shared living.

Written at the end of the 18th century under the rule of the Manchu Qing dynasty by a scholar-esthete who pursued a mediocre career in administration, *Six Tales of the Floating Life* is an immensely touching and poetic work of literature that highlights a stylized form of Classical Chinese that has yet to be influenced by the esthetic and philosophical conceptions Western culture. The tales themselves are not so much linear narratives as they are *fragmentary inscriptions* gleaned on a quotidian, day-to-day basis. This text, written in the first-person and in the form of "notes," marks a departure from the heavily normed, ritualized, and codified relationships that are habitually associated with male-female interactions in Classical Chinese literature. The author of the text inscribes himself in a moment where the grand normative features of Chinese civilization were becoming more contested and where the literate classes were seeking to distance themselves from the authoritarian rule of government in an effort to assert their individuality. In Shen Fu's time, there was a strong stylistic and esthetic emphasis put on the notion of *pu* (樸),[180] which suggests a kind, sincere, simple, and unfiltered *emotionality*. The simple *pu* emotionality (樸) of Shen Fu's esthetics evokes a kind of "lonely outpouring of natural brightness" (獨抒性靈),[181] it holds a genuine literary *force of resistance*. However fortuitous, tenuous, and marginal this force may have been, it nonetheless challenged the sclerotized stylings of official literature embodied by the dissertation exercise required for the mandarinal examinations, a gruesome formality that had become even more rigid and ossified during the ultimate Manchu Qing rule of China.

Shen Fu himself was a man of letters but he did not pursue a glorious career; he lived modestly and avoided lavishness. His attention was therefore entirely turned towards what can be retained from the particularity of life. In his writings, life is fragile and it never ceases to dissipate itself: it is a "fugitive" form of life that is uncovered once one has pierced through the illusions of the order imposed by the government. "Floating living" (浮生) or *fu sheng* possesses no constancy nor consistency, it holds no great goal that one can devote oneself to, no reputable or noble cause that is worthy of attachment, it is unstable and evanescent; in such a life everything passes on by, nothing remains. Amidst such impermanence, wouldn't the intimate be that modest and minimal anchor that can preserve a sense of constancy and permanence?

The first chapter of Shen Fu's work offers a significant appraisal of the importance of *shared living* in the context of a couple. The title of this chapter brings us close to the intimate: "Notes on the Joy of the Small Bedded Chamber" or "*Gui Feng Ji Le*" (閨房記樂), which in this context needs to be understood as an allusive reference to "married life." Against the impermanent backdrop of a "floating life" limited to the private sphere, devoid of illustrious deeds, and where nothing memorable, historical, or important can leave a mark, the only thing that matters is the small story, the one that is shared by the two individuals in a couple. The story of the couple is written *on the wayside* of the lives of others, it is detached from the vast familial networks of traditional Chinese culture and dissociated from the noise of the events and great tremblings of the world- Shen Fu never mentions family nor worldly affairs in his text. He focuses instead on those fugitive emotions which can only arise when there is a strong ground of mutual understanding. It is when the spouses find vacant spaces that allow them to step outside the floating nature of the world that they can find the complicity of the kind of *shared living* which finds its nourishment in retreat, tacit union, and a shared sense of understanding. These moment-emotions can only be perceived by two people at once, they are the result of the complicity that forms the *in between* which "holds" a couple together, all the while maintaining the individuality of each person. It is that feeling of *sharing together* which makes these moment-emotions salient, even though they are in appearance insignificant.

Shen Fu's text avoids a linear, narrative form precisely because its concern is not "telling a story;" it instead develops a literary style which gleans the exceptional within the anecdotal. As it follows the flowings and markings of "brush-ink" or *bi mo* (筆墨), the text highlights the *singular value* of unassuming and accidental moments in the shared life of a couple. It is the discretion of these moments which makes them the most unique markers of the singularity of the couple: they carry within them a form of unfiltered, unprocessed, and fortuitous emotion that resists the imposed perspective of society which constructs -and thus rigidifies- the couple's relationship in the form of an identifiable "entity" or status. Shen Fu advises us to keep only what appears most inessential within the "floating life": life can only be retained within these alveolar moments of nothingness which mark the evanescent and yet constant formation of the quotidian, it can only be held within the creases of the smallest and most insignificant of deeds. However fugitive and furtive this kind of floating emotionality may be, its "natural brightness" (性靈) or "unfiltered authenticity" (樸) distinguishes itself from the semblance and facticity of the forceful societal conventions imposed by Imperial Rule.

b. Floating vs existing.

Yet why does it seem like this text somehow falls short of the kind of radical and existential subjective experience of *standing out* captured in Augustine's conception of the intimate? It holds so many ingredients of a consciousness of the intimate and yet the intimacy of the "floating living" or *fu sheng* (浮生) it depicts opens up nothing-onto nothing- and thus does not appear to *take hold*. The conditions and manifestations of the intimate are indeed found in Shen Fu's text, often in very typified terms, but these figures of the intimate remain dispersed throughout the pages and ultimately, they do not point to-wards a possible *outlet*:

自此耳鬢 相　磨，親同　形. 影，愛戀. 之情. 有.
不可以 言. 語. 形. 容 者

*Zi ci er bin xiang mo, qin tong xing ying, ai lian zhi qing you
bu ke yi yan yu xing rong zhe*

"And so now, hearing the hair of our temples mutually pressing upon each other like mill stones, intimate shared living ties us together like the shadow is bound to the bodily form; the affection and yearning that we feel we possess bears no possibility or consequentiality in terms of words, languages, situations, or even appearances."[182]

A remarkable and deeply moving ephemeral tenderness *bonds* the spouses together: the Chinese text delicately tells us that "intimate shared living" (親)[183] ties them together like "shadow(s)" (影) to "bodily form(s)" (形). As they "hear" (耳), the "hairs of their temples" (鬢) pressing upon each other in a "mutual way" (相) just like "mill stones" (磨), they are nonetheless confronted with the ephemerality of the "fondness," "love," or "affection" (愛)[184] and "yearning" (戀) that characterizes the "feeling" (情) they "possess" (有) when they are together ; this floating emotion represents neither a "possibility" (可) nor a "means" (以) that can be assimilated to "speech" (言), "language" (語), "bodily forms" (形) or even "appearances" (容). Thus, the "intimate shared living" (親) so poetically evoked in Shen Fu's writing remains a quotidian experience of *subjection* to ephemerality and impermanence. It opens up no possibilities, it does not *deploy living*.

We are told that the spouses married young following the mutual agreement of their families: their relationship at times feels inexorably tied to the imposed bonds of kinship (Shen Fu writes that his wife is too attached to rituals and codified gender roles), it does not seem to stem from an individual, subjective experience of *freedom* like the one Augustine described in his existential approach to the intimate. There is indeed no event that surges and changes everything in these notes, no instance of a brutal shift where the indifferent outside becomes the bottomless inside of the intimate. There is no moment of decision- no adventure nor risk- that signals a *conversion to the intimate* where the latter is detached into a singular, *unheard* form of *(non)experiencing* which "exists" or *stands outside* the constitutive framework of "experience" (Time and Space, Subject and Object, Self and Other). We find no uncanny instance of a *tipping point* where two individual subjects begin to "exist" or *stand outside* the imposed order of the world as they cross the limit where the most inner part of themselves becomes subsumed within the most outer or "Other" part of themselves, thus uncovering a hitherto *unheard possibility* of *sharing-living* that bears no common measure with the "intimate shared living" of domestic partnership.

Although the complicity of gestures that forms the fabric of "intimate shared living" is beautifully captured in the text -the hand caught under the table, the tacit harmony of the wedding ceremony, the careful asides in the corridor to avoid the intrusion of others- these instances and gestures remain akin to markers of inclination and affection: they do not coagulate into the *existential option* of the intimate. In other words, the tender exchange of kind gestures and thoughtful moments amidst the washing away of impermanence cannot constitute itself into a *dissident possibility* which challenges the established order of the world and of the choices/non-choices of others. It is this "possibility" of the intimate which forms the *existential mooring* upon which *unheard living* can *take hold* and thus revolutionize our lives; such a possibility cannot be found amidst the ceaseless impermanence of "floating living," *fu sheng.*

*

The universal impermanence that is so poetically captured by Shen Fu's evocation of "floating living" of course belongs to a religious and historic context that bears no common measure with the Early Christian context where the intimate emerged as a foundational subjective experience. The text's characterization of "floating living" finds its stylings in a syncretic moment of the Classical Chinese literary tradition that arguably represents its final stage of development before the collapse of Imperial Rule nearly one hundred years later. Allusively blending Buddhist conceptions of "impermanence"[185] with more "Daoist" literary leanings that evoke the style of the *Zhuangzi*,[186] the "notes on floating living" foster a seemingly infinite *savoring* of the ceaseless *emotionality* that can be uncovered in the mundaneness of quotidian intimacy. And yet, they do not open onto the possibility of a new paradigm for experience nor culture in the same way that the irruption of the Augustinian, Christian intimate in Late Antiquity does.

The striking purity and coherence of Shen Fu's text threads a clear link with a two-thousand-year-old writing tradition and arguably brings it to its, if not poetic, then assuredly stylistic apex. Nonetheless, it does not suggest how hitherto *unheard* styles of writing could be uncovered or invented. The allusive and evasive formulations of Shen Fu's writing cannot evoke the radical experience of "existing" or *standing out(side)* that the intimate supposes, precisely because the text's modes of operation and signification lie *on the wayside* of onto-logical reasoning: the diffuse, evasive, and un-seizable nature of impermanence cannot be subjectively grasped in the same way that the intimate experience of "being" can.

Whereas the Augustinian advent of the intimate signals the transformation of Classical Greek ontology into a new mode of reasoning -Latin theology-, thus forecasting the emergences of the new Empires of the Middle Ages -Byzantium and the Roman papacy-, Shen Fu's poetic appraisal of impermanence seemingly foreshadows the crumbling decay of a millenary mode of governance -the imperial rule of the "Mandate of Heaven"[187]- and of a centuries-old bureaucratic apparatus of scholar-administrators and ritual executors -the "mandarinate." Written at the dawn of the final Qing dynasty's rule, the *Notes on Floating Living* seem to reverberate a profound sense of nostalgia, as if they evoked and signaled the end of an era that could not possibly renew itself into a "new" one that would be any less impermanent and meaningless than the one preceding it. Augustine's *Confessions* on the other hand triumphantly declare the advent of the

"Good News" of an *intimate* Faith capable of transforming the world and humanity, they are a marker of new beginning in the literary and intellectual history of the West.

3/ Augustine and the anchoring of the intimate.

If we return to Augustine, we can see that his characterization of the intimate offers a violent rupture with the delicate "intimate shared living" depicted in Shen Fu's text: to remove his existence from the quivering state in which it vacillated for years on end, the Church Father chose to definitively tie it down. Augustine attaches his existence to a form of eternity that is personal, he integrated his life in the course of a greater History yet he remained committed to a form of individual Salvation which could serve as the sheath and as the receptacle for his drifting sense of interiority. His life ceased to be tenuous and instead became resolved. The Church Father's *Confessions* mark a point of articulation which signals the entry into a truly European form of culture: written after nearly two centuries of Early Christian patristic tradition, they lie *in between* ontology and eschatology, between Being and the End, between the foundation of Being (which comes from the Greeks) and the affirmation of Meaning (the Judeo-Christian heritage). Augustine's story can be entirely held in the abrupt decision, which is as total as it is arbitrary, to *put an end* to the "rolling and tumbling" of life- to *anchor* life. It is the meeting of these two traditions (Greek and Judeo-Christian) which gives him the intellectual, moral, and existential *resources* necessary to cement the radicality of his newfound orientation. The Church Father's choice (Faith in the Christian God) is clearcut, he does not cease to repeat and justify his gesture: it is this motion of anchoring which establishes the "truth" he holds within him. In a sense, Augustine is doing nothing more than showing us the port where one can dock, put down an anchor and exit the "floating" of life.

*

All positive predicates are pulled out of ephemerality and ambiguousness, they are absolutized because they are the only ones that truly "are": Being, the Eternal, and the absolutely Good. Yet, thanks to Christianity, the ideality of theses notions that were dear to the Greeks inscribes itself in an Alliance where each individual life can find its meaning. This meaning is found by talking to a Person that anyone can address. The Person of God isn't a theoretical principle but an incarnate Subject, the one from which all subjectivity proceeds. Instead, Being has become the "Other," the "Other" has become the "You" or "Thou" of prayer. The absolute is no longer reached by means of theorization and abstraction, as it was in the Greek context, but by confiding in "Him," the God of "life." Once the resolution to choose God has been taken, all life -especially one's own- lets itself be carried away by this adhesion.

When Augustine turns "God" into the place of all beginnings and endings, his resolution is equatable with a conversion. His reasoning can be summarized in the following manner:

> I need to anchor my life and put an end to its "floating" transience so that I can remove it from insignificant flux; positing the absoluteness of God allows me to do so. "God," as Other and as Exterior, is/names the bedrock of my life: I am no longer living a life that "goes" but a referred life, one that is inexorably drawn to what fixates it; it is this indexation that I call "faith." I do not ask myself whether I "believe" in God, this question can only appear in an aftermath, in a retrospective discourse of justification. Since I have decided to make "God" my partner in life and my sole point of reference, I am no longer caught in "floating" ephemerality.

Augustine never departs from this arbitrariness which founds his decision to choose God. The *Confessions* are, in a sense, just a commentary which justifies *a posteriori* the existential turning point that led him to espouse the Christian faith. He is unbothered by the question: "does God exist" and by its converse: "what if God doesn't exist?" More exactly, this question does not intersect with his need to pour the innermost part of himself-the intimate- into God's absolute

Exteriority.

4/ Resources of Christianity, without resorting to Faith.

It is Augustine's singular and revolutionary experience of "God" which opened- and uncovered- the possibility of the intimate in the West. The time has come where we no longer have to approach Christianity from the perspective of dogma and faith (to "believe" in it or not); which isn't to say that we should understand it only in relationship to the history of religions and societies (as a form of monotheism or as it relates to the development of the political in Europe, for example). Finally, we can also cease to consider Christianity from the perspective of intellectual history which stresses its influence on the development of secular philosophy in Europe (we know for example that Descartes's *cogito* finds its roots in Augustine).[188]

a. Towards a philosophy of Christianity.

It is useful to distinguish traditional Christian philosophy from a *philosophy of Christianity*. Doing so allows us to consider Christianity from a point of view that is neither purely internal (dogmatic) nor purely external (socio-cultural). Instead, it could provide us with interesting avenues to ask ourselves what resources and possibilities Christianity promoted within the human: the ways in which it "formed us," as Nietzsche used to say, independently from any kind of explicit belief, in other words the ways in which it transformed and *mutated* human experience itself.

*

It appears as though Christianity promoted the intimate in a threefold manner. Firstly, it carried along the idea that there is an *event* of the intimate which changes everything and which holds the power to tip over existence. Secondly, it established this event of the *encounter* with the intimate as a moment where the barrier separating the Self from the Other is lifted. Thirdly, it produced a specific *place* where the intimate can take hold and deploy a form of infinite subjectivity (prayer). The inventiveness of these conditions of possibility of the intimate needs to be fully appreciated, regardless of one's personal beliefs or relationship to the Christian faith.

*

Christianity indeed gave us the consciousness (confidence) that a moment of decision *can* irrupt into our lives: it suggested that the *eventfulness* of this moment holds the power to carry everything away with it (The legendary image of St Paul on the road to Damascus, *Acts 9:3–9*). But what does this "everything" mean? It signifies that an *eventful tipping*- or even capsizing- can operate within a relationship to the "Other." This instance of tipping represents a conscious choice, a moment of deliberate risk-taking: one lets the "everything else" invade oneself, it thus ceases to be the "everything else," to the point where one becomes dispossessed from a sense of "self" altogether, all the while gaining greater access to a Divine Self which communes in God. Following the event, everything depends on the tipping instance, nothing is separated from it. What I could not imagine- nor even dream of- effectively realizes itself when the event of the intimate tips my existence over and plunges it into the Other, into "You." A hitherto *unheard possibility* suddenly opens itself up before me.

What Christianity teaches us is that life-changing events can only result from the intervention of an Other. And yet, after these events, nothing seems to have changed in the eyes of others. The more things seem to follow their ordinary course, the less need there is to broadcast the magnitude of the intimate tipping event; the greatest of internal upheavals becomes barely perceptible from an external perspective. The Christian invention of the intimate operates on the level where that which is "most inside" the self- that deep sense of "I"- is turned inside/out as it *encounters* God, the ultimate Other or paramount "You." After the *intimate event* of my *encounter* with "You," nothing will ever be the same, even though others might not see it that way.

*

The Christian Faith invented this "moronic," and yet self-aware, dimension of the intimate event when it conceded the "foolishness" of the Calvary of the Cross (Corinthians 1:18), *môria* in Greek, all the while still proclaiming the Salvation announced by the Event of the Resurrection. The only thing needed to gain access to God's Grace was the *intimate* and apparently "insane" *conviction* that the faithful profess to this day every Easter: "He is not here, for He has risen [from the dead]" (Mathew 28:6). Christianity implanted the possibility of a miracle that comes from the Other, that is to say the possibility of an *intimate event* -the irruption of an Other "more inside than the most inside" *into* me, an experience which can thereafter only be apprehended from a *subjective place* of decision/acceptance. The intimate event as Christianity envisions it shows that the *unheard-* or even the unbelievable- *can* indeed happen: it shows that the effraction-mediation of the Other into me can *alter* the course of my life and usher in a different kind of "existence." This "existence" which suddenly *stands outside* the life I previously lived is not shaped by my individual volition. Instead, it is the product of the contingent *encounters* that paved the path of my life and that led me to God, to the Other, to "You."

Augustine's *Confessions* thus can only begin with the following words: "You are great, Lord." One cannot speak *of* God (he immediately retracts into the ineffable if one does) but one can, on the other hand, never cease to speak *to* God. God is not described but rather *addressed*: he *is* the *Other* to whom I am speaking. He is therefore the person before which I uncover myself: it is by addressing "you" that I find myself within "me." Because a "you" (God) is erected (felt) as the initial point of my existence (which means that I am "created), I can thus effectively exist, and my sense of I ("myself) can install itself. God, "seeing" every part of me ("you who counts all the hairs on the head" Luke 12:7), is conversely the same genitor who makes possible the advent of an effective subject. God ("You") is what allows me to see my truth, he is the one that guarantees that "I" can hold the possibility of truth: "Who else could show me the truth if not the One who illuminates my heart and dispels its darkness?" (Corinthians 2 4:6). What God knows of "me" offers the anchoring ground where *I* can find consistency: this depth of me that He opens within "myself" has become the most solid point that *I* can speak of and can now be erected into a "temple" where *I* praise Him when *I* address him as "You."

b. The Christian invention of the Self and the Subject or the advent of the human intimate.

In his notes on the "floating life," Shen Fu pays no heed to his sense of "self," even though he is writing an autobiographical text. The Buddhist context in which he is writing of course bears a strong influence on this absence of "self" in the text: one of the key doctrines of Buddhism is indeed "no self." From a Buddhist perspective, the sense of "self" is understood to be an illusion generated by the veils of deceit- it reflects the illusory nature of desire.[189]

In contrast, if we look at Christianity and strip it of what it dissimulates when approached, we can begin to find new resources to approach the question of "self" and subjectivity. The "truth" of Christianity is indeed this *possibility* that it opens: an "I" or a "Self" can "exist" or *stand outside* the "floating" and quivering of living, thanks to a "You" or an "Other." It is because this You ("God") has constituted itself with "me" that a subjectivity of the Self can be deployed, thus overflowing the contingent "me" or "self" made incarnate by the subject of enunciation ("I"). In other words, it is by way of the intimacy of God as he lives within me, which corresponds to a "more inside me than the most inside of me," that "I" can access Being. The intimate experience of God first described by Augustine establishes a crucial precedent in the history of humanity: an individual speaking subject or a "self" (an "I") can know "himself" as he accesses "his" subjective truth when addressing a "You" or an "Other." The knowledge that is gained from the access to the intimate is at once infinite (it never ceases to become and expand) and singular (it is tied to a unique individual experience of the world).

Once this source of the intimate appeared in History, the only thing left to do, if we dare say, was to cease to refer it to the Divine and to exploit it on a properly *human* plane. The extraction of the intimate from its theological (and thus dogmatic) origins took many centuries in Europe. In a sense, so much of the intellectual labor of the European tradition can be tied back to this process wherein the universalizing features of *intimate living* untie and extract themselves from the overplayed "foolishness" and drama of the Christian faith and *un-cover* in that process *existential resources* available for *all* humans, not just Christians. So much of the intellectual labor - perhaps all of it? - of Europe can be brought back to this core philosophical problem: detaching the truth of the Christian intimate from the contingent arbitrariness of dogma.

Such is the thread that leads us from Augustine's Confessions to Rousseau's Confessions. Whereas Shen Fu's art consists in gleaning personal impressions amidst the impermanent flux of the quotidian, Rousseau's art does not just consist in trying to "know himself" as a long European tradition which leads back to Montaigne would have it: it also promotes an enlightened and universalizing *human intimate* detached from the velleities and dogmas of the Christian faith. Rousseau maintains Augustine's apparatus of the intimate: an "I" who stands in front of "God," in front of "You." But with Rousseau this "you" progressively detaches itself from the God that first promoted it. This detachment from the divine is the story of our modernity as it begins with Rousseau.

5/ Rousseau, or the advent of the Modern intimate.

a. Rousseau and the unheard of intimate.

Even though they obviously inscribe themselves in the continuity of the tradition set forth by Augustine's *Confessions*, Rousseau's *Confessions* represent a turning point in European literary and intellectual history. Rousseau's work maintains the Augustinian textual and enunciative apparatus wherein an "I" addresses and invokes a "You" identified as an "eternal Being." And yet, it changes the stakes: instead of referring himself solely to the divine figure of God, the confessional apparatus that Rousseau's writing deploys addresses itself directly to his *fellow humans*:

> I am forming an enterprise which is without example and whose executions will know no imitators. I want to show my fellow-men a man in all the truth of nature: this man shall be I.
>
> I alone. I feel my heart, and I know men; I am not made like any of the ones I have seen; I dare to believe that I am not made like any of the other ones that exist. If I am not worth more than any of them, then at least I am other (*je suis autre*). Whether nature did good or bad in breaking the mold in which she threw me, one can only judge of that after having read me.
>
> Let the trumpets of the final judgment sound when they shall and I will come, with this book in hand, to present myself before the sovereign judge. I will loudly say: here is what I have done, what I have thought, and who I was. I have said good and evil with the same earnestness. I have not silenced the bad, nor have I added goodness [...]. I have shown myself as I was: despicable and vile sometimes; good, generous, and sublime at other times: I have unveiled my interior as you have seen it yourself, eternal Being. Gather round me the innumerable crowd of my fellow-men; let them hear my confessions, let them gasp at my indignities, let them blush at my miseries. Let each one of them find their turn in discovering his sincere heart at the foot of your throne, and let one of them, if he ever dares, tell you: *I was better than that man.*[190]

Even though Rousseau sticks to some of the tropes of his predecessor Augustine, he is keenly aware that the text he is writing bears no common measure with the text of the Church Father as evidenced by the very first sentence of the book. Commentators and critics are quick to dismiss these famous opening paragraphs of Rousseau's *Confessions* as a supposed illustration of his megalomaniacal and pedantic character: these hasty moral judgements diminish in no way the true and singular *invention* that lies at the heart of the Enlightenment philosopher's thought, particularly when it comes to the way in which he revolutionizes the approach to the intimate.

Augustine's intimate address to God allows him to transcend the transience of the world and to find peace in the eternity of Being.

In this regard, Rousseau is no different since he also addresses an "eternal Being" as a "you" to tell him that he has "unveiled" his "interior." And yet, the aim of this address is not to escape the transient vicissitudes of the world of men. Instead, Rousseau wishes to "gather round" him the worldly mass of humanity's "innumerable crowd." Rousseau's experience of the intimate thus isn't a vehicle that is meant to transport him into a sublimated relationship with a Divine Being. Rather, it is what allows him to *freely confide* in his fellow-humans without any filter or aim. In other words, Rousseau establishes the intimate as a place that can be *shared*; not only with God but also, and more decisively, with all our fellow-humans, regardless of their condition or origin.

Truth be told, Rousseau *needs* to write in this apparently mad and arguably pedantic style to get his point across. One has to understand why he, throughout the entirety of the *Confessions*, evolves logically from one literary register to another: why he needs the theatricality, the cover of drama, the invocatory exclamations, or the tearful grandiloquence. The reason why he requires such bombast is at once simple and *unheard*: the booming excess is needed to protect its opposite, the *hushedness* of the intimate. One is necessary to cover and brood the other. One is the screen under which the other can hide. The overblown makes room for the discrete. One has to tap into the most declamatory part of oneself to offer -undercover- the most intimate part of oneself. All this theatricality needs to be spent so that, on its *wayside*, or in its *in between*, in tension with it, sheltered by its overbearingness, its contrary can also follow its own singular path. Because it is that path, the discrete one hidden by bombast, which is *the* path that the effraction of the intimate reveals. It is in this regard that Rousseau opens the pathway for romanticism and modernity: one needs the declamatory and the exclamatory -even Baudelaire doesn't shy away from them- to bring about their opposite- the hushed infinity of the intimate.

b. The intimate and the human.

What exactly is this intimate which at a first glance seems so insignificant and so fugitive? Why do we barely ever notice it? Why do we almost never bother to pay heed to the subtle shadings of its *humanity*? How can we pull it out of this disinterest, out of its unexpected emergence? How can we envision grasping it, or better yet collecting it? How can we say it, or better yet *whisper* it? How can we let it arise and probe within it a truth that annuls the need for explanation, not by rendering it false, but by making it useless?

Rousseau gives us a clue to approach these questions at the beginning of the *Confessions* when he evokes the forgotten memories of the nursery rhymes that his aunt Suson used to sing to him. He bluntly recognizes that he is infinitely touched by the emergence of these memories and yet he does not explain *why*, he needs no reason nor justification:

> [...] I was always with my aunt; I would watch her embroider and would hear her sing as I sat next to her or stood beside her; and thus, I was content. Her playfulness, her softness, her agreeable figure left such strong impressions within me; I can still see her face, her look, her attitude: I remember her caressing small talk [...]

> [...] She knew a prodigious amount of tunes and songs that she sung with her very soft and silken voice. [...] Her singing was so attractive to me; a few of her songs have never left my memory. To this day, some of them come back to me even though they had been lost and completely forgotten since my childhood; as I grow older, these songs retrace themselves within me with a charm that I cannot express. Will they say that I, an old dotard, gnawed with worries and sorrow, sometimes surprises himself crying like a child, muttering these little tunes with a voice that is already broken and trembling? I can remember the entire tune of one of these songs and yet, despite all my efforts, I cannot recollect the second half of the lyrics, even though I can confusedly recall the rhymes. [...] I am searching for the endearing charm that my heart finds in this song: it is a folly that I do not comprehend in any way; and yet, it is impossible for me to sing this song without crying.[191]

This moving passage of the *Confessions* perfectly captures the *risk* of the intimate. Rousseau indeed takes the risk of ridiculing himself ("I, an old dotard, gnawed with worries and sorrows") in front of all of his fellow-men when he exposes this intimate experience and yet he takes that risk to *share* the profundity of this experience with us. It is clear when he evokes the child-like "muttering" of the nursery rhymes that he is not trying to convince or explain anything to us ("It is a folly that I do not comprehend in any way"). Instead, he *shares* the teary tenderness of the moment and lets us hear "a more within than the most inside." The intimate tenderness that Rousseau shares with us finds its roots beneath a defined sense of "self": it detaches the "I" from the crampedness of a "me" or a "myself." Even though Rousseau's "tears" might be melodramatic or rhetorical, they highlight a crucial "endearing charm" of the intimate that was never mentioned by Augustine. This "endearing" dimension and resource of the "most interior" that Rousseau unveils before us does not lead to a retractive shutting off. Rather, it offers the anchor for an *expansive opening* that cannot be codified, explained, or dogmatized; it is so discrete that it cannot be reduced to a usage or to a finality. Christian thinkers like Augustine could not let this "endearingness" of the intimate arise: since they could not retain or grasp it, they let it slip away into oblivion until the advent of modernity.

Recalling a tune that an aunt sang in our childhood, feeling its throbbing melody penetrates our memory as we approach old age, not being able to remember all the lyrics… Like so many things in life, this feeling and this memory begins to take the form of a discontinuous, dotted line: Rousseau allows us to recognize this tenuous trait, this discrete emotion, without insisting upon it. He does not impose it (with explanations) and is fine with just putting it out there: available for each and every one of us. It is clear that, despite its tenuousness, this anecdotal story allows us to see- enables the arisal of- a common *ground of humanity* that exceeds the confines of introspection. However singular it may be, the anecdote is immediately shareable ; or rather, it is its "endearing" and trivial nature which opens us up to the *possibility of sharing*. The story effaces the borders of the self-interest and of the "for oneself" that govern self-centered living, its trivial nature both touches us and disarms us as it takes us beneath the separation which demarcates an "I" and makes it distinct from a "You." The in appearance trite story of the childhood songs sets the *tone* of the intimate: it pushes the reader out of his "outsidedness" and plunges him into a shared sense of "insidedness," thus creating a form of human "concord" that requires no explanation. This endearing and trivial trait of the intimate does not instruct us, its purpose is not to convince us. Instead, it creates- from the get-go- the *conditions of intimacy*.

*

c. Neither love nor friendship.

In Rousseau's *Confessions* the intimate is both nameless and fixated by a proper noun that serves as its eponym and consecrates it: Madame de Warens. In the third book of the *Confessions*, the utmost originality and the non-demarcated dimension of the intimate surface, both of which hinder its recognition as a proper philosophical concept. Rousseau can only envision the intimate by way of the negative: he can only identify it by stating what it is not, thus undoing the old opposition of love and friendship as he puts the two terms back-to-back:

> And so I was finally established with her [Mme de Warens.] This establishment was nonetheless not the one that I look upon as the happy days of my life, but it served to prepare them. Even though this sensibility of the heart, which truly makes us more than enjoy ourselves, may just be the work of nature, perhaps a mere product of organization, it needs [concrete] situations to develop itself. Without these occasional occurrences, a man born with great sensibility might never feel a thing, and could die without ever having known his [intimate] being. I had been much like that up until then, and I might have always been that way, had I never known Mme de Warens, and if, even having known her, I had not lived long enough beside her to contract the sweet habit of the affectionate feelings that she inspired within me. I will dare to say it: the one who only feels love does not feel what is softest in life. I know of another feeling, less impetuous perhaps, but a thousand times more delicious; sometimes it is tied to love but, more often than not, it is separated from it. This feeling is not friendship alone, it is more voluptuous, more tender [...] None of this is very clear,

but it will become so later; feelings are only described well by their effects.

Rousseau does not conceptualize the "affectionate feelings" that this paragraph gravitates around but we can do it for him; let us name these "feelings"- the *intimate*. Rousseau grants the intimate all his attention, he puts it at the forefront of this description, and yet he cannot name it. He has not yet found it as a *concept* and is thus obligated to tackle it via the *in betweenness* that lies *on the wayside* of the habitual oppositions that this feeling eludes (love vs. friendship, male vs. female, sensual vs. intellectual). The *in between* that the intimate introduces into his life is not a form of equilibrium nor is it some kind of reasonable middle path or halfway point. And yet, it also presents itself as less than one and more than the other: less "impetuous" than love, but more "voluptuous" than friendship. The intimate is not a mellowed-out or resorbed form of love that has become less intense, it also holds a form of preeminence: it is "a thousand times more delicious" than love. The experience of the intimate is not a form of sublimated spiritual bypassing: its "voluptuous" nature maintains it in the order of the sensual and the pleasurable. Rousseau tells us that none of this is "very clear." Let us then try to clarify it for him.

If we follow Rousseau's intuition, the intimate belongs to neither love nor friendship. In the Classical European tradition, a tripartite division separated *philia* (friendship or "brotherly love") from *eros* (lust or "sexual love") and *agapè* (charitable or "divine love").[192] *Philia* involves a fortuitous encounter with a *peer* (someone who is similar to me), *eros* an encounter with (sexual) *desire* (someone that I lust for), and *agape* an encounter with a divine big Love (God's Love). Much like Love in all its forms, the intimate involves an encounter with an Outside: it involves opening up to this exteriority or "outsidedness" that the encounter with another, if not an Other, brings forth into our lives. And yet, instead of wanting to absorb the exteriority of the encounter into oneself and thus possess it for oneself (the "I want to make you mine" of erotic love), instead of maintaining an agreeable distance with the encountered other (the "you do your thing, I'll do my own, and we can both respect that" of brotherly love), and instead of letting this exteriority of an encounter with a big Other completely strip us of any sense of individuality (the "You are

I, I am You, and We are One" of charitable or compassionate love), the intimate makes us tip over *together* into a *shared inside*. This inside is no longer given to us as in friendship- the "we met each other and just happened to share the same interests," example: Mick Jagger and Keith Richards, old grade school pals, fortuitously meeting each other at the train station with the same treasured blues records under their arms. Nor does the inside of the intimate become the object of an erotic quest hell-bent upon making the Outside the Inside, an elusive attempt to possess the Other's inside(s) - "I want to be inside you or I want you inside me." Instead, the *inside* of the intimate is a byproduct of *sharing*. This common inside of the intimate is not conquered via a form of seduction that pits "me" against "you" (the classical libertine trope of eroticism as military conquest), nor does it involve a hierarchical relationship where Your (God's) supremacy and pre-eminence supersedes my own (the religious conception of Obedience). It involves instead a willingness to *share together* a common *within us* that belongs to neither of us. The common that the intimate builds is both a product of an arbitrary contingency (the randomness of two separate individuals encountering each other), and of a necessary, *shared initiative*: the common *decision* that leads *us* to build upon this intimate, *together*- not for, but *with* each other.

6/ On why the intimate isn't bound to Love's lustful desire.

a. Living beside you vs. desiring you.

Analyzing the intimate is a delicate affair because it compels us to untie the connection which binds pleasure to desire and which subordinates the former to the latter. What singularizes the intimate is that it is no longer tied to the *lack* which structures desire. The intimate therefore isn't concerned with the quest and bondage of the infinite cycle of satisfaction-disappointment that conditions the search for Love. The lack that lies at the heart of the quest for the beloved object of desire is perhaps most succinctly captured by the title and lyrics of the rocking but otherwise horrifically sexist punk-metal tune

"The Chase is Better than the Catch," a B-side off of Mötörhead's legendary 1980 album *Ace of Spades*:

Silver-tongued devil, demon lech

I know just what I'm doing

I like a little innocent bitch

You know I ain't just screwing, I ain't

I love you baby, love you too much

I like it fine, I feel your touch

But your appearance don't hold no class

You know the chase is better than the catch, you know

The garish sexism of the lyrics offers a blunt take on the limits of the view that would want us to bind Love to lust and desire. The very fact that lyrics like "I like a little innocent bitch" can be combined with "I love you baby, I love you too much" highlights how the search for Love inevitably leads to a form of projection and objectification where the other is transformed into a mere *object*. What is even more problematic is that this transformation of the other into an object of desire can only result in disappointment and thus lead the desiring subject down a Sisyphean path where he will be led to yet another object of desire that will inevitably disappoint him. In other words, the intertwinement of Love and desire produces a dynamic of entrapment where one is doomed to project one's own inadequacies onto another and thus turn them into an object of desire/disappointment. Even the seemingly innocent declarative sentence: "I love you" holds within it this kind of dramatizing dynamic where the "you" is performatively rendered into an object upon which a subject - the "I"- *projects* his desire. Lacan's clever take on Love offers a remarkably synthetic overview of the ineptitude of the tired image of lustful desire that form the problematic lyrical material of Mötörhead's pulsating yet lurid song: "Love is giving something you don't have to someone that doesn't want it."[193] The intimate on the other hand is precisely not an act of giving but instead an act of *sharing*: what is shared in the intimate isn't an object which takes the form of desire, lust or love, it is the simple act of *living beside* the Other.

If we turn our attention back to Rousseau's relationship with Mme de Warens, it is clear that Rousseau is unconcerned with "possessing" her: unlike Lemmy Kilmister from Mötörhead, Rousseau does not transform Mme de Warens into the mere object of a lustful chase, nor would he ever think to qualify her as a "little innocent bitch." What matters for Rousseau isn't the kind of desire and possession that characterizes Love (nor is it the crassness of unfiltered eroticism). Instead the *sharing* that can be discovered "beside" Mme de Warens. It is this "beside her" or "beside you" of sharing that Rousseau first experienced with his aunt Suzon and that he renews during his time with Mme de Warens which constitutes the inexhaustible fund of the intimate. When I am living *beside you* and thus constructing a form of *shared presence* with you, I am no longer trying to "make you mine;" nor am I in a position where I might no longer want you because I could harbor desire for someone else. Living beside you amounts to sharing my life with you in a way that does not require that I view you as an extension of myself or as an object that I seek to possess. Beside each other, *we* can share an intimate space that belongs to neither of us and that remains nonetheless a space that can only be produced when we are *together*. Even though this shared space of the intimate cannot be entirely shielded from the "floating impermanence" of the world that Shen Fu so poetically captured, it nonetheless opens *both of us* to an *infinite* that lies wholly *within* this life- the one that lies *between* You and I, the one that we can keep on *sharing,* even after one of us departs from this world.

b. intimate vs. "extimate," or relating to the big Other.

As we bring this chapter to a close, it should be clear that the intimate represents a strikingly *unthought* theme in philosophy even though it appears to yield significant existential resources which lie *on the wayside* of the rhetoric of Love. While the existential resources of the intimate are undoubtedly intercultural, our inquiry showed that its fecund subjective experience was thematized more explicitly in the European confessional tradition that finds its roots in Augustine and in Rousseau's writings than in the literati Classical Chinese lite-

178

rary tradition that Shen Fu belonged to. That being said, it would be dishonest to suggest that the confessional intimate invented by Augustine and brought to its apex by Rousseau holds no limitations. In doing so, we would deny the ways in which its limitless "inside-ness" itself reflects the universalist ethnocentrism of a European tradition that has been all too content to analyze the world solely through its own categories for nearly two millennia. Much like remaining exclusively within the confines of one cultural tradition suffocates intellectual *initiative*, remaining within the existential confines of the intimate can all also lead to a form of emotional breathlessness.

*

Whereas the great drama of Love plays itself out in the alternation of passion and disinterest, one could say that the story of the intimate and of its limitless Inside can quickly come to an end if it does not maintain itself in a relationship with an Outside that we shall call, following Lacan's suite, the "extimate." Lacan coined the ingenious concept of the "extimacy" but, as is often the case with him, he remained allusive when sketching out his ideas and did not offer many concrete examples, thus providing us with a welcome opportunity to do so in his place.[194]

In the context of the couple, the intimate refers to that *shared inside* which "exists" or "stands outside" the exteriority and ephemerality of the world and thus allows us to *inhabit together* a space which is "more inside than the most inside" of either of us. The shared Inside of the intimate is what anchors the couple. And yet in order to remain afloat and alive, the couple needs to periodically *venture together* out into the *unheard possibilities* of the "extimate" Outside: a docked or anchored ship will inevitably decay if it is not regularly taken out at sea. The exteriority of the extimate prevents the interiority of the intimate from collapsing onto itself: sharing things or people *outside* of "us" or of "our relationship" (movies, books, music, experiences, friends, families, children, pets etc.) allows us- "you" and "I"- to renew the seemingly infinite possibilities held *within* the limitless *inside* which first emerged when we *encountered* each other.

The confrontation of "our" inside with the "extimacy" of an ever-impermanent outside world is what allows *us* to *share living*, it is both what nourishes "our" capacity to share and what prevents "us" from devolving into a fixed, and thus morbid, "relational" status. In other words, the extimate helps maintain the Other within the intimate and prevents the latter from veering into the claustrophobic dynamics of assimilation: when there's only an inside shared by the two of us and when there is no confrontation with an outside that we could potentially share together, it's easy to fall back into the lackluster dynamics of desire ; I begin to assimilate your inside to mine and thus become estranged from its inherent otherness, which then leads me to defensively shut myself off from that big Other that *our encounter* first brought forth into *our* worlds.

*

It's not surprising that the existential theme of the Other and the intellectual figures most associated with it (Sartre, Levinas, Derrida, Lacan, Fanon, to name but a few...) emerged in a philosophical moment that bore the traumatic marks of its geo-historic context: the European Post-War. The atrocities of the Second World War carved a solid dent into the metaphysical worldviews and concepts that had anchored Europe's often delirious self-confidence: the notion of a universal God in particular was questioned with a newfound strength in a time where "His" much touted Goodness and Magnanimity had lost an already well-worn luster of preeminence and prestige. And yet, despite all of their respective and indisputable brilliance, none of these inventive thinkers who conceptualized the Other at great lengths took the time to confront themselves to a thought tradition that lies wholly *outside* the intimate confines of their own focus, the great Greek question of Being. Apart from Lacan, none of these thinkers went as far as to expose themselves to the outsidedness of the Classical Chinese tradition to introduce an "extimate" element within the intimate European confines of the "onto-theological" tradition that they all sought to overcome. Although the relevance of Lacan's sinological adventures remains a matter of scholarly debate, there is no doubt that in invoking "China" and more importantly Chinese writing as an important, if not essential feature of what he then dubbed the "lacanian" discourse on the Other, he inscribed himself in the continuity of previous European intellectuals like Montaigne, Pascal and Montesquieu who were unafraid to consider with lucidity the way in which East Asian civilization represented an "alternative" to the European model of civilization.[195]

In the following chapter, we will explore how canonical Classical Chinese texts - the *Classic of Poems* and the *Yi Jing* among others- can offer us valuable insights on the deployment, or lack thereof, of the *idea of God* in the European and Western contexts and in the Chinese and East Asian contexts. Doing so will give us newfound means to approach the existential question of the Other or of "Otherness," a hotly debated topic in contemporary academic and lay discussions regarding issues of gender, sexuality, race, power, and politics.

CHAPTER VII
When the idea of God does not unfold

1/ When the idea of God does not unfold: intercultural reflection and the metaphysical minimal.

If there is a historical fact that remains indubitable, it is the genuine surprise of the Jesuit missionaries who arrived at the Ming court in the 16th century. While the ruling classes of China seemed to bear a genuine interest in Western science and particularly in geometry, they remained largely *indifferent* to the religious discourse of the Catholic priests and to their *intimate* faith in an eternal and transcendent God. The dizzying perplexity and shock felt by the Jesuit scholars betrayed the emergence of a fundamental question that Western civilization had left largely *unthought* up until that point: instead of obsessing over God's (non)existence, could it be possible to think of a world where humans do not even *need* God?

a. Montaigne and Pascal: differing (French) perspectives on a Godless world.

The notion of the divine, *theos* in Greek, acted as a structural backbone of Western thought from Plato onwards. Alongside *logos* and *eidos,* it represents one of the fundamental building blocks used to construct thought in the Western world. That a millennial and technologically advanced civilization like China could develop for centuries without fostering an anguished and obsessive philosophical concern over the alleged (non)existence of the divine startled the Western intellectuals of the late Renaissance and early Modern era. Thinkers like the forever astute Michel de Montaigne were quick to notice that the Chinese world represented a viable alternative to the civilizational models hitherto developed by the West. In the final chapter of the *Essays* "On experience" previously discussed in the 4th chapter, Montaigne offers the following consideration regarding the civilizational significance of the Chinese world:

> "In the kingdom of China, the governing policies and the arts, having neither knowledge or commerce with ours, surpass our examples in diverse fields of excellency, its [China's] history teaches me how much more ample and diverse the world is than either we or the ancients [the Greeks and the Romans] could ever fathom."[196]

Montaigne was amongst the first to measure the vast *distance* separating the Chinese understanding of civilization from the Western one: far from adopting a supremacist stance, he recognized the exceptional *viability* of China's approach to governance, esthetics, and craft. The Renaissance thinker sensed that the Chinese world had not needed the "examples" of the West to achieve the degree of "excellency" that he so admired: Montaigne understood that it was indeed possible for a supremely civilized and ordered world to develop *on the wayside* of the theoretical and practical models so diligently forged for centuries by the Western philosophical and theological traditions.

*

A generation after Montaigne, another great French mind of the Early Modern era, the genius physicist turned mystical theologian Blaise Pascal, confronted himself with the puzzling indifference of the Chinese elites to the question of God. In Pascal's posthumous magnum opus *Pensées* ("Thoughts"), we find an anguished yet perspicuous author who laid out in dramatic, oppositional terms the genuine alternative that the Chinese civilizational model seemed to represent for the Western intellectuals who had been raised to *believe* in the transcendence of God: "Which of the two is more believable, Moses or China?"[197]

Pascal's radical either/or formulation encapsulates the dizzying effect that the discovery of the mere existence of the Chinese civilization could have had on any learned Christian person in an era where faith in God was deemed a necessary prerequisite for human existence itself. The 17th century Jesuit scholars that Pascal read to learn about China – folks like the brazen father Martino Martini who had translated the Chinese imperial chronologies and been captured by pirates for two years on his journey East- were at times led to believe that the antiquity of the Chinese civilization predated even ancient and immemorial biblical events like the dispersion of languages at Babel and the Great Flood. They were also keen to assume that the Chinese had also worshiped a single God in the past but that they had, over the course of their history, become "atheists."[198]

Suddenly, at the other end of the known world, the faithful discovered a global and continuous understanding of History that ran parallel to theirs and that could not be neatly integrated into it. Religious scholars and scientists like Pascal discovered a History in which their historical gods and their transcendent God, born in the Fertile Crescent and in Ancient Egypt, diffused through the waterways of the Mediterranean and roadways of the Roman Empire, were both absent and ignored. How could Western thought, imbued with its own belief in the professed universality of its univocal and unequivocal Truth, not be shaken up and *rattled* by this fateful *encounter* with a world that remained indifferent to the Supreme Being, God himself?

*

The exteriority of Chinese civilization's History acted like a wave of seismic shocks for Christian intellectuals like Pascal. The structural categories of "universal truth" upon which the edifice of their knowledge had been founded suddenly *crackled*: devout and learned Christians were forced to fathom the existence of a world that in no way required, let alone espoused, their faith in a universal God. Pascal's dramatic opposition remains asymmetrical because it puts on equal footing a mythical and symbolic figure like Moses, whose singular story embodies the fabled adventure of God's "true believers," and an entire civilization reduced to a single, nebulous name- "China." Pascal's dramatic question was left open and never answered. The scholarly editor of the *Pensées,* Leon Brunschwicg, did not think too much of Pascal's interest in China and viewed it primarily as an idiosyncratic example of the French thinker's insatiable curiosity. Yet it is precisely the fragmentary dimension of Pascal's thoughts on China, their unfinished aspect, which opens up a door for an intercultural reflection capable of highlighting the fertile *unthought* that lies *in between* the world(s) of the faithful and the world(s) of the faithless.

b. Encountering the Other: an intercultural perspective.

Pascal himself was weary of hasty generalizations: he was conscious that his forever forlorn enquiry on Chinese civilization could only be achieved through patient and minute work. In his preliminary exploratory notes, he writes that any approach to the question of God in China can only be a "detailed one, requiring us to put our papers on the table." The illustrative materiality carried along by the formulation "to put our papers on the table" suggests the careful nature of a workflow embedded in the idiosyncratic subtleties of human languages and, above all, in the creative/destructive process of *translation*. It suggests a technical line of labor defined by concurrent processes of research, analysis, and problematization. The work of intercultural reflection thus cannot be dissociated from a historiographic, philological, and philosophical process wherein the baseline assumptions that govern cultural patterns and frameworks are both reflected upon and questioned. If we are to take seriously Pascal's recommendations and pursue an intercultural line of inquiry that investigates the vast *distance* which separates Moses' world from the world of the mythical Yellow Emperor, then it is critical to painstakingly detect the at times infinitesimal points of tension that separate cultures from one another. Only then can we begin to delineate the ever-fluctuating boundaries of a *common* meeting ground, a *constructed* site of *encounters* that lies *in between* them.

The intercultural, as opposed to comparatist, approach to the question of God outlined in this chapter does not seek to construct differentiated, static representations of Chinese and/or Western "cultures," let alone "religions": our point is not to argue that there are essential features attributable to the distinct entities of "Chinese religion" and "Western religion"(culturalist position), nor do we affirm the existence of a universal substrate of subjective human experience rooted in the psychological phenomenon of Faith or "belief" (universalist position). Instead, the evaluation of the semantic and geo-historic distance separating Pascal and his contemporaries the *Ru* (儒)[199] scholars of the Ming court offers a strategic point of entry into a philosophical concept that continues to bear a decisive and dominant influence in academia and in media culture: the "Other."

As we patiently and carefully measure the distance that separates Pascal's world from the world of the *Ru* scholar-administrators, as we begin to turn our ears towards the *unheard aftershocks* of their *encounter*, a previously *unthought possibility* for thinking arises: an intercultural concept of the "Other" that is neither psychological nor sociological, but rather, in the most minimal meaning possible, *metaphysical*.

*

Examining the status held by the idea of God in Chinese civilization and Western civilization constitutes a privileged point of entry into a conceptualization of the Other that anchors the *philosophy of living* in an intercultural and existential *metaphysical minimal*. As we shall see, the "metaphysical minimalism" of the philosophy of living lies wholly *on the wayside* of (Indo-European) metaphysical traditions and of their most hegemonic concepts, Being and God.

2/ (non) existence vs. (non) unfolding.

When we begin to approach the question of God within the context of Indo-European languages, we are inexorably drawn to the question of existence and Being; it is indeed impossible to avoid the "to be or not to be" logic that underlies the structural features of this linguistic family.

a. Protagoras' conundrum.

From Ancient India to Ancient Greece, the question of existence envelops the question of the Divine. In the Sanskrit-speaking world, divinity becomes tied to the notion of existence early on: two adages of Vedanta philosophy, *"tat tvam asi"* or "thou art that,"[200] and *"Ayam Atma Brahma"* or "This Self is the Supreme Being,"[201] famously associate the notions of existence and Being with the concept of the Divine.

In Ancient Greece, it is the Sophist Protagoras who best summed up the insoluble conundrum of the (non)existence of the gods that has haunted Western thinking for centuries. In the following sentence attributed to him by the historian and "doxographer" Diogenes Laertius, Protagoras lays out the fundamental terms of the ceaseless debates that animated Western ontology and theology well into the era of the Enlightenment:

> "Regarding the gods, I am unable to know whether they exist (*eisin*) or do not exist (*ouk eisin*), nor what they are like in form (*idean*); for the things preventing knowledge are many: the obscurity of the question and the brevity of human life."[202]

Although Protagoras' status as a sophist led to the minoring of his philosophical influence, the concomitant radicality and simplicity of his assertion perfectly illustrates the fundamental ambivalence that underscores any inquiry that seeks to prove the (non)existence of God.

*

Over twenty centuries after Protagoras, Kant finally settled the score once and for all when he concluded that it was impossible, if not futile, to attempt to prove the existence of God. For Kant, "existence is not a predicate"[203]: philosophical arguments that aim to prove the (non)existence of God are null and void because existence is observed and not logically deduced. Kant's critique of metaphysics and theology effectively ended Western thought's attempt at reconciling

188

ontology, the philosophy of Being inherited from the Greeks, with the Judeo-Christian mytho-theology of the Bible. After Nietzsche's famous insistence on the "Death of God,"[204] the attention that the idea of God received was mostly critical: as the 20th century marched on, the idea of God was progressively reduced to a purely sociological -Durkheim in the *Elementary Forms of Religious Life*- or psychological -Freud in *The Future of an Illusion*- "data point," a name like any other, a sign devoid of any intrinsic *meaning*.

The story of the idea of God follows the dramatic and predictable "rise and fall" narrative arc that seems to characterize the Western tradition. As the scientific and the technological revolutions of the Modern Era carried on their unstoppable march, the cultural significance of the great question of God's (non)existence that had animated Western thought for centuries was never fully resolved. Rather, it simply *dissolved*.

b. The land of "master-emblems".

Miles away from the tragic narrative of the "rise and fall" of the idea of God in the West, Classical Chinese civilization offers us a point of entry into the question of God that allows us to elude the dramatics associated with the impossible proof of his (non)existence.

When Western scholars first sought to find equivalents to the notion of God in the Classical Chinese canon, they were confronted with a plurality of "master-emblems" as the great Marcel Granet so elegantly puts it.[205] At the time of the Ming Dynasty, the literature of the *Ru* scholars of the court available to the Jesuit priests made little reference to a single entity that could easily be assimilated to an identifiable Divine, let alone human, Being. Instead of an all-seeing and all-powerful figure of God easily assimilated to a single name, the Jesuits found in the Classical Chinese texts a set of closely interrelated terms: *Dao* (道) or the Way(s), *tian* (天) or Heaven(s), and, of course, the famous and ubiquitous *Yin* (陰) and *Yang* (陽).

As the Jesuits learned to read Classical Chinese texts, they also came across the expression *Shangdi* (上帝), or "Lord Above," predominantly found in the earliest Chinese Classics like the *Shijing* (

詩經*) or* "Classic of Poems*"* and the *Shujing* (書經) or "Classic of Documents." These ancient sources are among the few that explicitly refer to the archaic oracular and sacrificial practices of the mythical Xia and the historical Shang Dynasties dating back to the the 3rd and 2nd millennium BCE. While the Jesuits were quick to notice the existence of this *Shangdi* figure in these texts, they were also confronted with its relative insignificance within the dominant strains of thought found at the court of the Emperor. The "master-emblems" *Dao, Tian* and *Yin-Yang* held far greater currency than the notion of *Shangdi* in the *Ru* tradition that infused the intellectual life of the scholar-administrators servicing the Ming Emperor. For these learned government officials, the question of whether the (non)existence of *Dao, Tian* or *Yin-Yang* needs to be proven or not was neither here nor there. What need is there to prove that the sky above our heads exists when we feel the rain falling on our heads as it drips from above? What need is there to prove that the way or *Dao* we walk on exists, given that we are already walking on it? What need is there to prove that the sky or *Tian* above our heads exists when we feel rain falling on our heads as it drips on from above? What need is there to prove that *Yang* light and *Yin* darkness envelop our waking and sleeping lives?

3/ Fixation vs resorption.

a. When the figure of "Heaven" supplants the "Lord Above".

The figure of the *Shangdi* lies *on the wayside* of the familiar images associated with the divine in the West: revelation, mythology, and creation. In other words, the *Shangdi* does not have an origin story: it is not revealed to a group of faithful followers, nor is it thought to be the principle at the origin of the world. The worship of *Shangdi* is mentioned in a cursory fashion in the early Classics and, as time goes on, it is referenced less and less. With the fall of the Shang dynasty and the advent of the Zhou dynasty (between 1025 and 1050 BC) the figure of *Shangdi* is supplanted by another figure that the Jesuits associated with their Christian understanding of "Supreme Divinity": *tian* (天).

There is good reason to speculate that the Shang dynasty also worshiped 天 in their rituals. The Chinese historiographical traditions insist on the continuity from one dynasty to another, and it is obvious that the image of "Heaven" enters into a form of competition with the "Lord Above" early on in the Zhou era. Indeed, the "Lord Above" is progressively equivocated with Heaven and it becomes increasingly marginalized as the centuries pass on without ever being the object of explicit criticism or denunciation. There are no traces of theological debates asserting the pre-eminence of "Heaven" over the "Lord Above." And yet the latter becomes absorbed and then deactivated by the former as the Zhou dynasty cements its decisive influence.

b. The "Mandate of Heaven" and the moralization of conduct.

The promotion of "Heaven" and the deactivation of the "Lord Above" during the advent of the Zhou dynasty coincides with the first moralization of History found in Chinese literature. This moralization of history can in large part be attributed to the Duke of Zhou who played an essential role in the governmental transition that led to the end of a dynasty and to the foundation of a new one. The Duke of Zhou's father, the King of Wen, defeated the Shang rulers and instatuted a new dynasty using the following justification: the Shang were defeated because their corruption progressively led them to lose the "Mandate of Heaven" or *tianming* (天命).[206] The Zhou justified their accession to the throne by claiming that they were the rightful heirs of the "Mandate of Heaven" due to their moral virtue, thus establishing the idea that the course of History itself was regulated by the natural motions of Heaven. In other words, the turnover from one dynasty to another was justified as an essentially natural phenomenon that reflected the *coherence, li* (理), of Heaven's inherent, self-regulating order.[207]

The advent of the notion of *tianming* with the Zhou dynasty signals the birth of an ethical and political ideology founded upon the tutelary figure of *tian* that will last well until the 19th century CE.[208] While the "Mandate of Heaven" firmly associates the moral with the political, it does not leave space for a purely theological approach to the divine because the figure of *tian* itself corroborates the idea that morality is *correlated* to the coherence of a spontaneous, "natural" world order. The moral "Mandate of Heaven" of the sovereigns of Ancient China therefore bears little resemblance with a theocratic absolute monarchy, precisely because their power was aligned with a "natural" as opposed to "supra-natural" force: their right to rule was not derived from a transcendent entity like the "Lord Above" but was instead attributed to the immanent *processes* that characterize the fluctuating motions of (the) Heaven(s).

The resorption of the figure of the *Shangdi* into the figure of *tian* thus marked the advent of a political regime where questions of transcendence and *meaning* dissolved under the influence of a worldview founded upon the *coherence* of notions that articulate an *internal* order of constant renewal. While the West constructed a vision of the political predicated upon an *external* source of transcendence (Truth, God, Justice), the sovereigns of Ancient China forged a managerial approach to governance rooted in a top-down moralization of conduct that extended from the ruling classes down to the laboring classes. The understanding of moralized conduct and of governance developed by the ruling classes was derived from an intricate appreciation of the *correlative webs* that constitute phenomenal processes: there was no distinction made between human law and divine law since all law was thought to be derived from the constancy of a continuous set of interweaving processes. The ruling classes of Ancient China did not need to appeal to a single, external symbolic point of reference to justify their exercise of power. Instead, they developed a complex and totalizing web of emblems and symbols that both *mirrored* and *performed* their processual understanding of the world.

Ruling in Early China was not a dramatic or heroic affair subjected to human whims, it was not a theatrical scene thought to represent the alleged propensity of men to aspire to goodness or to fall prey to Evil: it was instead a discrete occupation that required vigilance, modesty, and above all a profound sense of *responsibility*. The scholarly governing classes of Ancient China thus displayed an internalized sense of morality. This sense of duty was founded upon their coherent understanding of the world which stressed the *internal order* of cosmological processes. The scholar-administrators codified and performed their internalized sense of morality through the performance of *Li* (禮) or "rites": a vast ensemble of codified customs, gestures, and ceremonies which deployed a set of *behavioral norms* that effectively shielded the ruling classes from the "fear and trembling" that led so many rulers and thinkers of the West to invoke the Divine as their supreme point of reference and ultimate source of authority.

4/ Rites, emblems, and behavioral norms vs. prayers, narratives, and utterances.

One of the first Westerners to astutely notice the capital importance of rites in Chinese society and government was the Enlightenment-era political theorist Montesquieu:

> "The legislators of China did just that: they confused religion, law, morality, customs and manners; all of these were equated with morality, all of these were equated with virtue. The precepts that concerned these four points were called "rites." It was through the exact observation of these rites that the Chinese government triumphed. One would spend all of one's youth learning them and all of one's life practicing them. The scholars taught them and the magistrates preached them. And, since they enveloped all the minute aspects of life, when it was possible to have them correctly observed, China was well governed."[209]

Although Montesquieu understood the foundational role of performative practices in Chinese government and society, his analysis remained entrenched in Western categories and he did not accurately measure the abstraction that the Chinese notion of *Li* (禮), commonly translated as "rites," carries along with it. When Montesquieu states that the Chinese "confused religion, law, morality, customs and manners," he betrays above all his own confusion and his incapacity to neatly translate the Chinese notion of *li* with the Western term of "rites"! The notion of *li* has indeed much more to do with the cult of ancestors and with the structuring of kinship, than with worship of the Divine through an act of Prayer. Understanding *li* only as "rites" and as a foundational element of Chinese "religion" thus erroneously corroborates the impression that the primary object and function of these performative gestures consists in the worship of divine entities.

a. Li 禮 *or when "rites" are in fact behavioral norms.*

Instead of translating *li* as "rites" as the Western sinological tradition has done for so long, it might be more useful to translate the term as *behavioral norms*. Doing so would better convey the structuring and performative social power of the codified ritual gestures of Ancient Chinese society. The intensive and extensive ritual codification of gestures and speech in official ceremonies resulted in a normalization of conduct that played an integral role in the general resorption of transcendence within Ancient Chinese society. The self-referential pervasiveness of *li* in Ancient Chinese life and its structuring/structural social significance reduced the need for a referral to a transcendent and metaphysical source of authority like God.

Despite its shortcomings, Montesquieu's analysis noticed the relative absence of a priestly class exclusively devoted to sacerdotal functions in Chinese imperial society. The French Enlightenment thinker noted instead the central role played by "scholars" and "magistrates" in the officiation and administration of *li*. The ritual performance of the ancient cult of ancestors inherited from the Zhou dynasty led to an overlap between the administrative responsibilities of government and the performative execution of codified behavioral norms. The ritual performance of ancestor worship did not emphasize the immortality of a transcendent soul. Rather, it (re)enacted the *perpetuation* of invisible-immortal-ancestral spirits, *shen* (神).[210] Through the performative administration and officiation of *li,* the *shen* spirits of the ancestors continued to effectively live *inside* this world and not *beyond* it, unlike the theological God(s) of the Western traditions.

In the paragraph that immediately follows the one cited above, Montesquieu aptly remarked that the notion of *li* was intrinsically tied to the "extremely composed Chinese manner of *writing*." Montesquieu's insight was corroborated by archeological evidence and by the works of the recently deceased sinologist Leon Vandermeersh who studied the links uniting the sinographic system of writing with the shamanistic techniques of the seers of the Shang dynasty.[211] The codification of behavioral norms in written works like the *Liji* (禮記) or "Book of Rites" was therefore not the result or the record of an injunction professed by a transcendent Voice (as with Moses receiving the tablets of the Law on Mount Sinaï): it represented instead the *trace* of *ancestral techniques* embedded in a web of symbolized processes and symbolic procedures. The hexagrams of the *Yi Jing* and the ideographic system of writing were endowed with "mantic" properties that had little to do with prophecy and much more to do with a formalized style of *examination.*

While the Western prophetic tradition emphasized the declarative power of an utterance emitted by a transcendent Voice (God telling Moses "thou shall not..." or the voice of the pithy of Delphi telling Oedipus his Fate), the Chinese writing system first developed in the Shang dynasty codified the reading of divinatory *clues* obtained through a set of structured and symbolized procedures that involved the burning and puncturing of bone shards and tortoise shells.

b. The internal coherence of behavioral norms: Xunzi's formalization of li as cosmological order.

As the system of writing derived from the oracular inscriptions became more and more formalized, an understanding of *li* as a totalizing, structuring, and structural *behavioral performance* became increasingly prevalent among the literate ruling classes. The order of *li* and of its behavioral norms was thought to reflect the spontaneous *coherence* (the other *li* 理) of the processes and procedures of the world: it served as a cosmological justification for a distinct type of political, societal, and philosophical *conformism* that effectively shut down a great deal of possible lines of philosophical inquiry. The great thinker Xunzi (3rd century BCE), one of the most formidable formalizers of *li,* offered the following cosmological appreciation of the significance of behavioral norms:

> Behavioral norms (*li*) possess three roots (禮有三本): Heaven and Earth, which are the roots of Living (生); the First Forefathers, who

are the roots of the Groups; Lords and Masters, who are the roots of stable Governance (治). Where would Life come from without Heaven and Earth? Without the Forefathers, where would we come from? How could there be stable governance without a Lord or Master?[212]

For Xunzi, behavioral norms constitute a global and uniform response to all questioning: they effectively end any debate about the origin of the world. It is impossible to probe beneath them or to exceed the framework they offer; they act as a structural *matrix* not only for society, but also for the global and continuous dynamic of Living (生) itself.

Xunzi then goes on to affirm that the authority of the ruler derives both from "Heaven" and from the continuity of "all ancestral lineages" (故王者天太祖). His writing thus *inscribes* the political authority of the sovereign in an immanent *behavioral matrix* derived from a *processual order* that composes the fabric of human and non-human Life. Xunzi's factual evocation of ancestral lineage precludes the need to resort to a transcendent, God-given right. The performative aspect of *li* therefore espouses not only the norms that regulate human conduct, but also the norms that regulate cosmological processes, like the changing of the seasons. It is in this regard that the behavior of humans reflects the behavior of Heaven on an analogical level. The structuring and structural rationale that underlies the performative behavioral norms carried along by the term *li* is unsurpassable. And yet, it is neither mystical nor ineffable but instead *self-evident*.

The self-evidence of statements like "how could there be stable governance without Lord or Master?" grounds the authoritative rule of behavioral norms in a coherent reasoning that cannot be questioned because it dissolves the need for any further inquiry. What need is there indeed to think of a figure like God that lies outside the world when the rightful execution and performance of *li* perpetuates the internal order of the world? What need is there to question the *meaning* of the world when the simple act of espousing its *coherence* (理) guarantees conformity with the rightful ordering of its processes?

196

c. "Does Heaven speak?" or the Master's distrust of speech and narrative.

Whereas the religions of the West found a strong grounding in the power of narrative and in the execution of the performative utterance of prayer, the Sages of Ancient China like Confucius bore a strong distrust of speech and of narrative:

The Master said, "I would prefer to not speak." Zi Gong said, "Master, if you do not speak, then what shall we, your disciples, have to recount?" The Master said, "Does Heaven (天) speak? The four seasons pursue their courses, and all things are continually being generated, but does Heaven (ever) say anything?"[213]

This canonical passage of the *Analects* offers a definitive assessment of the way in which speech and words, *yan* (言), remain utterly unnecessary when it comes to the generation and manifestation, *sheng* (生), of all things, *bai wu* (百物). From this cosmological perspective where Heaven manifests all things, the performativity of prayer as a "speech act" becomes useless since Heaven, the source of all generation and manifestation, unlike the biblical God or the Gods of Ancient Greece, *does not speak.*

As the *Classic of Poems* succinctly states, the motions of Heaven both "tie together", *wei* (維), and "manifest", *xian* (顯), the world: their "command," *ming* (命), is "not easy." The Poet-Sage who seeks the guidance of Heaven does not engage in an act of Prayer which renders the presence of God effective through the performativity of invocation. Instead, he performs his "deference," *jing* (敬), through the administration, officiation, and above all, "study," *xue* (學), of a set of codified gestures and prescriptions. The sinogram *jing* (敬) originally refers to a dog sitting in front of a figure of authority: it suggests the *pre-verbal* and *gestural* aspect of a *behavioral performance* which encapsulates the ethics of *jing* that the Poet-Sage deploys and transmits as he "displays" a "powerful," *de* (德), and yet deferential, mode of "conduct," *xing* (行).[214]

Far from being epic adventures full of dramatic twists and turns, replete with colorful heroes and villains, the lives of the illustrious poets, sages, and rulers of Early China like Confucius or the Duke of Zhou appear to follow an orderly flow. Even though they lived exceptional lives filled with struggle and strife, the Duke of Zhou and Confucius ultimately *resorbed* their individuality within a cultivated behavioral capacity: *deferring* to the "power" and "virtue" (德) of the infinite and continuous processes and proceedings of the Way of Heaven- *tian-dao* (天道).

5/ The *Yin*, the *Yang*, and the "Way of Heaven," or the "master-emblems" of Ancient China.

a. *"Initiating capacity," or the first trigram of the* Yi Jing

The text that perhaps most vividly marks the transition from the divinatory practices of the Shang dynasty centered around the worship of the *Shangdi* or "Lord Above" to the formalized understanding of *tian-dao* codified during and after the Zhou dynasty is without a doubt the *Yi Jing* or "Classic of Changes." The *Yi Jing* represents a striking amalgam of archaic divinatory techniques and of a more conventional style, at least in the Early Chinese context, of discursive exposition. The opening hexagram (☰) composed only of (unbroken) *Yang* marks is named *Qian* (乾): it is said to be a figuration of the *initiating capacity* that is at work in all processes. The liminal formula that opens the *Yi Jing* offers a succinct account of this "initiating capacity":

乾：元亨，利貞

Qian: Yuen heng, li zhen

"Initiating capacity: Commencing-prospering, profit(ing)-correct(ing)."[215]

Such an opening statement, as we can see, neither constructs nor dramatizes. It has no conditions nor suppositions; it ties together two consecutive movements, two concurrent steps of a *transitional process,* two instances that simultaneously *relay and renew* each other.

Rather than being a proper "sentence" or proposition, this opening statement offers a performative illustration of the *four phases* that the succession of the four seasons exemplifies. The first part of the statement matches the crystal-clear *yang* ascendent phase of the year: spring corresponds with "commencing" (元), while summer manifests "prospering" (亨). The second statement mirrors the opacity of the *yin* descendent phase of the year, autumn corresponds to the "profiting" (利) of the harvests, while winter reflects the corrective "rectitude" (貞) of retreat and restraint. The "rectitude" of winter thus represents a cautious and patient capitalization of resources that enables the renewal and commencement of spring.

*

The *Tuan Zhuan* (彖傳) commentary of the *Yi Jing*, which was compiled centuries after the original text, can arguably be seen as the ancestral bedrock that ties together the *Rujia* (儒家) "School of Scholars" that the West named "Confucianism," with the ancient divinatory practices of the Shang and early Zhou dynasties. The *Tuan Zhuan* commentary embeds the moralization of conduct that characterizes this foundational intellectual and ritual tradition of Early China within the natural order of Heaven. The commentary of the first hexagram *Qian* neatly introduces the terms *Tian* and *Dao* into the explanation of the ancient cosmologies to anchor them in a coherent understanding of the phenomenality of processes, thus rendering irrelevant any appeal to a transcendent Creator:

> How ample (*da* 大) is the initiating capacity suggested by *Qian*! Ten-thousand things (*wan wu* 萬物) find in it their initial funding(s) (*zi* 資): as such, it [*Qian*] governs Heaven (天) [...]. The Way (道) of *Qian* corresponds to modifying-transforming (*Bian-hua* 變化), each one holds upright its nature-destiny (*xing-ming* 性命). To maintain together: great harmony (*da he* 大和). From there ensues profit (利) and correctness (貞).[216]

This passage of the *Tuan Zhuan* is crucial to understand the immanent and processual order that defines the Way of Heaven. *Qian* or the "initiating capacity" represents a primal emergence that arises from latent "fund," *zi* (資) that is readily available for capitalization. *Qia* is in no way analogous to a demiurgic figure responsible for a founding act of Creation. *Qian* did not create Heaven in the way that God created the Sky, instead it governs/unifies, *tong* (統), the processes that characterize Heaven, such as the motions of clouds or rainfall.

The *Ru* scholars that formalized the divinatory practices of the Shang into the behavioral norms -*li* (禮)- of Early China established a formal parallel between the harmonious rule of men and the harmonious ordering of heavenly processes. The association of the synonymic compound *bian-hua* (變化)[217] and of *Dao* (道) with the immensely polysemic character *Qian* (乾) generates a plurality of interpretative possibilities that enlivens and sustains the *signifying potential* of the opaque oracular inscription, and of the trigram figure (☰) it names. Both graphemes are thus transformed into a utilizable set of *governmental tools* capable of evoking the concomitant order that governs the heavenly world and the earthly world. In the decidedly un-theological worldview of the *Ru* commentators, the possible significations of the ancestral divinatory practices and their practical *viability* as tools of governance were constantly assessed and *deployed*. For these learned scholars, the processes that governed and tied together Heaven were equivalent to the processes that governed and tied together the world of men. There is no distinct separation between the amplitude (大) of the world of men (人) and the amplitude of Heaven (天), all three ideograms find their root in a single and eminently human common graphic denominator: *ren* (人).

b. Governance, commensurability, and the pervasive coherence of the Dao.

The *Ru* scholars commenting the *Yi Jing* thus established a *commensurability* of non-human and human processes that served a governmental and behavioral function. Instead of engaging in theological speculation, they sought to devise efficient tools of governance and administration that could *regulate* both public and private life. Miles away from the Western representations of a distinct and infinite heavenly plane that bears no common measure with the finite order of the world, the scholars of Early China deployed the "master-emblem" *Dao* to signify the infinite *viability* of a world that neither needs nor knows an *incommensurable* "beyond." The commensurability of the Way of Heaven, *tiandao* (天道), of the Great Way, *dadao* (大道), and of the Way of Men, *rendao* (人道), finds an implicit justification in the following oft-commented formula of the *Xici* (繫辭), or *Great Commentary*, of the *Yi Jing*:

一陰一陽之謂道

Yi yin yi yang zhi wei dao

"One *Yin* one *Yang*, that is called *Dao*"

In the *Great Commentary*, the *Dao* thus becomes, not the Supreme Being that rules the world, but instead the ultimate "master-emblem" capable of absorbing under a single sign the global and continuous *alternating* of worldly phenomena; both non-human and human, both *Yin* and *Yang*. This cursory and emblematic formula is followed by two others, one which corroborates it and another which completes it, thus instituting within a single sentence the global, all-encompassing, and all-inclusive *coherence* of the *Dao*:

繼之者 善也, 成之者性也

ji zhi zhe shan ye, cheng zhi zhe xing ye

"That which continues reflects advantageous virtue, that which accomplishes reflects natural character"[218]

Moral virtue is thus conceived as the prolongation of spontaneous regulation, there is no hiatus separating human conduct from the harmonious course of the world. There is no need to evoke a transcendent God capable of harmonizing the world of men with the world of nature; precisely because there is no point of rupture, no *incommensurable breach* that separates the ethical from the cosmological, the natural from the supra-natural.

*

What separates the common usage of *Dao* in Classical Chinese literature from the expression of a form of subjective, mystical *belief* in God is indeed the pervasive *inclusivity* of this notion; the term *Dao* holds the capacity to *resorb* any breach made within the order of the sayable. The *Dao* thus does not require the jealous and commandeering Christian *belief* that demands that the infinite plurality of Ways be reduced to a single Way- Christ's Way. For Christians, the Way of Christ expresses the univocal Truth of the One God: "I am the Way and the Truth and the Life. No one comes to the Father except through Me." (John 14:16)

Finding a seemingly endless and unshakable grounding in a set of semantic parallelisms, *Dao* expresses a continuous and uninterrupted thread of thread of interweaving processes, it alludes to a concordant web of interrelated phenomena that endlessly "pass on through," *tong* (通).[219] Whereas God names the unnamable, *Dao* names the virtue of non-obstruction that enables all communication. The vocation of this term is not to indicate a destination, a finality, a point of salvation, a "guiding towards" but rather an infinite capacity to pass on by. The Way is not projected in advance, it does not represent the road or pathway to God, the *Dao* is instead accomplished as one walks (道行之而成) as the Zhuangzi so elegantly states.[220] The *Dao* does not lead to Truth, and yet its manifests Life's infinite viability (it just keeps on going) and infinite generativity (it just keeps on coming). *Dao* communicates neither the founding cause nor the ultimate meaning/destination of Life. Rather, this master-emblem of Early Chinese thought communicates how worlds arise and how they renew themselves, thus alluding to Life's infinite sustainability, to its endless capacity to nurture-nourish itself; the emptying action of the *Dao* generates the void intervals that make possible a ceaseless *passing through*.[221]

The meaning of any cosmogony is fully resorbed in the Dao's infinite capacity to absorb all things: Dao alleviates the need for any mystical or existential belief in another world of "mythical origins" since it names the Source of Living that lies within Life itself. What need would there be to invoke an external source of Life to regulate the conduct of men when the source of the regulation at the heart and root of all Life lies within this world? What need would there be for the experience of faith in a world that ceaselessly manifests its own infinite viability?

6/ Faith in God and the experience of the incommensurable: naming the Other, without falling prey to ideology or mysticism.

As we bring this chapter to a close, it becomes clear that the faith and belief in God that structured the Western understanding of the world did not unfold as such in Ancient China. The master-emblems *Tian*, *Dao* and *Yin-Yang* do not require the kind of *intimate* subjective belief that God demands of the faithful. It can be argued that the arrival and progressive diffusion of Buddhism in China at the beginning of the Common Era represents a historical turning point of exchange where scholars and rulers began to adopt a set of foreign practices and beliefs, thus developing a more intimate and subjective relation to the political that resembles the Abrahamic experience of Faith as a living leap into an "Other." The scholars of the court were nonetheless quick to resorb the alterity of Buddhism within the pre-existing ideographic system of writing derived from the ancestral oracular practices.

a. Ch'an *or how the master-emblems of the Classics harmonized Buddhist scriptures.*

Buddhism was not adopted as standalone set of beliefs that negated the moral and behavioral precepts found in the Classics. Rather, it was thought of as a *continuation* of these pre-existing traditions. The affinities tying together *Ch'an* Buddhism with texts like the *Laozi*, the *Yi Jing* and the *Zhuangzi* have indeed been oft commented throughout history: the master emblems of Ancient China like *Tian*, *Dao* and *Yin-Yang* had no issues folding themselves into Buddhism's initially foreign conceptual framework. It was in fact quite common for "translations" of Buddhist sutras to incorporate full-on citations of pre-existing Classical Chinese texts. In practice, the pervasive and inclusive ubiquitousness of *tian-dao* and of the *yin-yang* made it nearly impossible for a foreign set of beliefs and practices like Buddhism to be seen as anything else than a *variation* on a pre-existing theme. Buddhism did not become an un-integratable "Other" that requires nothing less than an act of total submission, a decisive and intimate leap of faith. Instead, its sutras and precepts became just another just another set of notes in the infinite set of harmonious scales belonging to the "piping reeds of Heaven" (*tian lai* 天籟) so poetically described in the second chapter of the *Zhuangzi*.[222]

Buddhism did not sustain nor achieve the kind of hegemonic domination held by Christianity or Islam in the Mediterranean world: its influence on government was intermittent and it was heavily contested by many scholars who deemed it incompatible with the administration and officiation of the behavioral norms outlined in the Ancient Classics, precisely because it advocated for a form of *supernatural detachment* from the world and its social customs.[223] Through the process of *translation*, supernatural elements of Buddhist asceticism which clashed with the spontaneous and self-evident "intra-natural" coherence of the cosmology and ethics of the Ancient Classics, were *harmonized* with a pre-existing social order made of codified behavioral norms and of canonized literary forms. The metaphysical allure of Buddhism was dimmed, its literary modes of expression evolved in a way that fully integrated the stylistic codes of Classical Chinese literature: the tradition of *koan* or *gong'an* literature perfectly illustrates the lasting influence of the Ancient Classics on Chinese and, more broadly, East Asian Buddhist thought.[224]

b. Translating "God" in(to) (Classical) Chinese or the rupture of the incommensurable.

In the same way that the translation process dimmed the metaphysical allure of Buddhism and the rupture that such a metaphysical faith supposes, the translation of the Western word "God" in Chinese *resorbed* much of its supposed univocal transcendence. Christian missionaries disagreed on the correct translation for God as soon as they encountered the Chinese Classics: they could not agree on whether the archaic *Shangdi* or "Lord Above" found in the *Classic of Poems* or the Jesuit priest Matteo Ricci's invention *Tianzhu* (天主) "Lord of Heaven" constituted the proper translation for the Abrahamic God.[225] To this day, a plurality of terms are used to designate God across a variety of Christian and Islamic denominations in China. And yet none quite evoke the supernatural transcendence or the metaphysical rupture unequivocally referred to as "God" in the Mediterranean world. The very fact that "God" would have to take on multiple names in China and East Asia made it all the more difficult to assert his universal Oneness.

*

The word "God" itself indeed bears no standard of common measure with other words, it represents a pivotal and incommensurable point of rupture and oblivion within Western thought. It evokes the distance and tension that separate the subjective revelations of the prophets of the First Testament from the objective demonstrations of the philosophers of Ancient Greece. Whereas the Supreme Being of the Greek philosophers can only be identified as a *supposed entity* (as an "it"), "I" can, as a singular and individuated subject, directly *address* the God of Abraham, Isaac, and Jacob as "Thou" or "You." These two representations of the divine (objective vs. subjective, demonstrated vs. revealed) share no common measure. And yet, both structure Western thought in seemingly equal measure.

*

Attempting to reconcile the two *incommensurable* polarities of demonstration and revelation contained within the word "God" appears to be an impossible task. Nonetheless, a distinctive thread of the Western philosophical canon, the "mystical" tradition, has attempted throughout the centuries to reconcile the revealed, subjective God of Faith with the demonstrated, objective God of theology. From Plotinus to Martin Buber, the "mystical" philosophers of the West sought to highlight the dramatic tension and ambiguity that separates the subjective experience of God from the objective problem of God's (non)existence. The tension and drama that animates Western mystical thinking betrays an excessive proximity to its object of inquiry:

Western mysticism presupposes the universal validity of the term "God," yet it cannot imagine the existence of a world where neither the God of Science nor the God of Revelation are needed to construct a civilization.

c. (Un)naming the Other, the pitfalls of negative theology, and the intercultural metaphysical minimal.

The Western mystical tradition cannot think without God, it can therefore only examine from within itself the presuppositions carried along by the word "God." The mystical antinomy of a God that we "cannot live with" and "cannot live without" inevitably leads to the self-deconstructive process of "negative theology" that Derrida discussed in his minor, albeit brilliant, work on mysticism.[226] For Derrida, the act in which one names God and addresses him as such represents the paradigmatic example of an instance wherein subjects constitute themselves by addressing a categorical *Other*: a being that can always be named, but never fully identified or known, a being whose Being cannot be reduced to a distinct object. In the mystical worldview, the act of naming God becomes the ultimate means of access to the Self. And yet, it also constitutes the foundational "deconstruction" of the name "God" and of the naming Self that says "I."

*

While the deconstructive approach to the word "God" -pioneered by the negative theologians and brought to its apex by Derrida- is not devoid of merit and interest, the intercultural approach to the question of God deployed in this chapter can unearth and uncover *unthought possibilities* for thinking the metaphysical in the 21st century, without veering into the stereotypical rhetoric of metaphysics, scientism, or mysticism. The recourse to the *exteriority* of Ancient China's literary, historical, and mythological traditions offered a strategic point of entry into the question of God precisely because the terms that defined the Western debate surrounding God find no exact equivalents in these texts. In this regard, the intercultural examination of the Classics of Early China not only exposed the theoretical presuppositions (ideality, transcendence) that led to the deployment of the idea of God in Western culture, it also highlighted the *resorption* of the idea of transcendent Divinity within the Chinese cultural context.

Our goal was therefore not to construct Ancient China as some "cultural Other" engrossed in mystical "immanence," but rather to uncover an *unheard* relationship to a *metaphysical* Other that lies *in between* the Western name of God and the master-emblems of the Classical Chinese corpus. In other words, the work of intercultural reflection recuses both the universalism of mysticism and rationalism, as well as an all-too-prevalent form of ideological culturalism derived from a weak understanding of the French "philosophy of difference" made famous by the likes of Derrida and Deleuze.[227] Through the careful construction of montage devices that juxtapose philological research and philosophical reasoning, it is possible to avoid the pitfalls of comparatism and its complacent enumeration of resemblances and differences. Instead of pitting cultures against each other in a comparison or, even worse, in a confrontation, the strategic operation of intercultural philosophy consists in a *reflection process* that facilitates the emergence of newfound conceptual tools that can operate in between cultural lines in a globalized context.

*

One of the key elements that emerges from this intercultural reflection is a *metaphysical* conceptualization of the *incommensurable*. The *uncovering* of an incommensurable within our world indeed suggests the *effraction* of an Other within it: a (literally) *meta-physical* Other that belongs *neither to our world, nor even to another one.* The aim of our philological and philosophical analysis of the Ancient Chinese "Way of Heaven," of the Greek understanding of the divine, and of the Abrahamic experience of faith in God was not to offer yet another contrite assessment of the Nietzschean theme of the "death of God," be it apologetical or critical. Instead, we sought to *un-cover* the *infinite breach* of an Incommensurable *rupture* that deploys itself within experience and that nonetheless overfills the very categories of experience.

*

Far from being a pathetic post-modern tragedy that revels in the inevitable dissemination of meaning that follows "the death of God," the uncovering of an Incommensurable through intercultural reflections deploys an un-ideological and un-mystical thought of the Other that can reinvigorate philosophy and diffuse a universalizing *ethics of living*. The frontal, dizzying shock of the Incommensurable forms the conceptual basis of a *metaphysical minimal*: the one that the Jesuits could not *avoid* nor shun when they reached the shores of China. Instead of providing us with a totalizing, normative, and ultimately, dogmatic approach to ethics, the concept of the incommensurable as a metaphysical minimal gives us the possibility to deploy *the fracture* contained within existence itself. Is the uncovering of the incommensurable not an invitation to leap, not *out of*, but *into* the *unheard* possibilities that its irruption reveals?

CHAPTER VIII
The incommensurable unheard(s), or the meta-physical minimal(s)

1/ The mathematical trace of the incommensurable: cracking the edifice of Reason.

The concept of the *incommensurable* offers a privileged point of entry into what can be named a *metaphysical minimal*. On the one hand, incommensurability refers to the impossibility of establishing a comparison or an equation between two distinct terms: as we have seen, Chinese script (in its classical form) is *incommensurable* with alphabetic script. A metaphysical minimal, on the other hand, refers to an *excess* that is internal to experience and thus does not reach "beyond" experience. In other words, the experience of a metaphysical minimal represents an instance wherein the constitutive frameworks of experience (the subject/object relationship, the categories of space/time) are *cracked open* by the *irruption* of an *incommensurable*.

a. The incommensurable: a concept with mathematical origins.

The philosophical approach to the concept of the incommensurable finds its grounding in mathematical reflection. In mathematics, "irrational" numbers like $\sqrt{2}$ are said to be incommensurable with "rational" numbers like 2 because their *ratio* ($\sqrt{2}/2$) produces an infinite "irrational" number (0.86602540378 etc.). Numbers like $\sqrt{2}$ or π thus share no *common measure* (mathematical notion of *commensu-*

rability) with numbers like 2. A line of fracture separates finite "rational" numbers from *infinite* "irrational" ones and thus makes them incommensurable to one another: "rational" numbers cannot *resorb* the crack that separates them from the "irrational" ones. Nonetheless, numbers like $\sqrt{2}$ or π remain *effective* despite being incommensurable with "rational" ones; their capacity to exceed commensurability does not make them any less *real*. The endless succession of their operation reveals an *internal infinite* that is neither exterior to nor "beyond" mathematics: the infinite computational processes and series that the number π forms *crack open* the common measure which justifies numbers and that they themselves justify.

The existence of "irrational" numbers both *stands outside* the common measure (*ratio*) of finite computations (2+2=4) and the ranking (*ordo*) derived from them (1<2<3). Ever so real and yet forever *resistant* to the carefully constructed order of a world (*cosmos*) conceived as a rational system, the incommensurability of "rational" and "irrational" computations which cracks open the harmony of Numbers from within has been an object of both fascination, distrust, and anguish since the Ancient Greeks.

*

It is no secret that the discovery of mathematical incommensurability was a taboo matter for the Ancient Greeks. According to the scant and fragmentary sources we possess, the Pythagorean philosopher Hippasus of Metapontum, whom Aristotle associates with Heraclitus as a thinker of "primordial fire,"[228] suffered a tragic fate after having *encountered* the incommensurable. Although it is impossible to precisely reconstruct what exactly happened to this individual who lived over 2500 years ago, various sources weave the legend of a man who was either banned, sentenced to death, or led to suicide by his fellow Pythagorean peers for having divulged the troubling existence of incommensurable irrational numbers to the greater public. Hippasus' discovery of the demonstrable existence of irrational numbers within geometric computational processes *ruptured* the rational order of mathematics that the Pythagoreans held to be sacred. His story, however legendary it may be, proves that the encounter with the incommensurable supposes a *collision* with a real and undeniable pothole of *(un)knowing* that we *necessarily* run into and that we would nonetheless rather just ignore, glide over, or dismiss.

The existence of the incommensurable proves that thought and thinking are not the product of a "natural" desire for knowledge as classical philosophy would have it; they are instead the consequences of a *constraint* born out of a confrontation with *the real*. This constraint leads to an *encounter* with an *unthinkable* that nonetheless imposes itself on thought and corners it into thinking. The absence of a measure (*metron*) that would directly tie together irrational numbers and rational numbers forces us to recognize the existence of a *without common measure* (*a-sum-metria* in Greek) within the ratios and orders of measure itself.

b. The number pi and the crack(s) of Reason.

The existence of incommensurable para-meters, of mutually exclusive and yet co-existent/co-operative frameworks of measure which discreetly *crack* the edifice of knowledge *from within* has long constituted philosophy's seed fund of "wonderment" (*thaumazein*). The incommensurable lies at the source of philosophical reflection. And yet, it also constitutes philosophy's own self-professed limit and avowal of ignorance.[229] The admittedly forced and forceful discovery of mathematical incommensurability doesn't abolish or discredit the rational order of numbers, nor does it call upon another order or a form of counter-rationality. The incommensurable does not suppose a system, nor does it set the foundation of an alternative approach to logic: what makes it so troublesome is that it definitively *cracks open* the order of reason, even if that crack can be understood on a, if not rational, then at least conscious basis after the fact. The crack of the incommensurable doesn't recuse the overall coherence of numbers and of their sequencing but it insidiously erodes their assurance and security. The breach that the number *pi* opens within commensurability is fractional, infinitesimal, and yet, as such, it *cannot be integrated* into the order of rational numbers.

The distance that separates *pi* from rational numbers can never be fully bridged, the hiatus that subsists *in between* the two orders of numbers renders ineffective any attempt to mathematically equate them. This hiatus can be indefinitely reduced, and yet it remains forever *irreducible* because of a structural principle of *necessity* that paradoxically *defies* structure itself, thus exposing the *gaping hole* that lies within its hollow core. The breach within the continuity and compactness of the order of numbers that the incommensurable makes manifest is at once discrete, unsuspected, and easily glossed over. It remains nonetheless abyssal: an infinite is discovered within the interstices of its creases. As they expose unbridgeable voids that cannot be *assimilated* by or within any common standard of measure, the cracks of the incommensurable reveal gaping spaces that are to remain forever opened and unfillable, like the void that forever subsists *in between* God and Adam's fingers in Michelangelo's fresco at the Sistine Chapel in Rome.

2/ The universality of the incommensurable: the (unheard) politics of wandering "outside the square."

If we are to admit that the incommensurable's mathematical existence opens up -and also uncovers- a form of universality, it becomes legitimate to ask ourselves what status the "incommensurable" holds in non-Western thought traditions.

a. The incommensurable and the ethics of interculturality.

Probing the incommensurable's capacity to act as a universalizing philosophical tool does not necessarily entail the facilities and pitfalls of comparatism, nor does it represent a "spiritual" attempt to forge an artificial and ecumenical "perennial philosophy" attached to a constructed, and therefore mythical, concept of a "universal human nature." Invoking the universality of the incommensurable could in fact be conceived as a political means of resistance against the dynamics of alienation and uniformization that pervade the world. For example, one could effectively argue that the People's Republic of China's ongoing human rights abuses in Xinjiang province and Tibet constitutes a violent shunning of the *incommensurability* of Uighur, Han Chinese, and Tibetan culture. Condemning the PRC's brutal policies *in the name of* the incommensurable does not constitute an appeal to the Western concept of human rights, a concept that the PRC all too eagerly dismisses as being an imported tool of colonial dominance. It constitutes instead a statement of fact: cultures, and more specifically languages, are not wholly commensurable with one another. Attempting to completely eradicate a language or a culture by *commensurabilizing* it into another one in the name of a nationalistic ideal of "harmony" constitutes a blatant denial of the *hiatus* that subsists *in between* cultures and makes them incommensurable with one another. Unlike the universality of subjectivity or individuality upon which human rights are founded, both of which appear to be highly predicated upon the historical advent of Modernity in Europe,[230] the mathematical universality uncovered by the incommensurable suggests the following question: can one encounter a universalizing thought of the incommensurable in Classical Chinese literature, that is to say can a non-ontological and non-essentializing mode of thinking also offer us a conception of "what is not of this world and yet not from another one"?

b. The inkling of the incommensurable in the Zhuangzi.

It is clear enough at this point that Ancient China became largely indifferent to the incommensurable Other that the Hebraic tradition focused its attention upon; it is also obvious that the approach to mathematics that its civilization developed varied significantly from the mathematical forms of the Greeks.[231] Nonetheless, there is an anecdote in the 6th chapter of the *Zhuangzi* which, in an indirect and *oblique* manner, points towards an *existential incommensurable* that surfaces in the universal human experience of grief and loss.

In this fictitious and mocking anecdote, we find an ironic portrait of a dumbfounded Confucius who regrets having sent one of his disciples to pay his respects to the followers of an illustrious Sage who just died. Confucius' disciple Zigong comes back from this mission confused and outraged; he does not understand why the Sage's disciples blatantly disregarded the behavioral norms and official prescriptions (*li* 禮) that codify grieving: instead of wallowing in silence, they were merrily chanting! The disciples of the deceased Sage even went as far as to mock Zigong when he asked them whether such singing constituted ritually appropriate behavior. Upon his return, the outraged disciple asks his Master:

> 'What men are these? The decencies of conduct are nothing to them, they treat the very bones of their bodies as outside (外) them. They sing with the corpse right there at their feet, and not a change in the look on their faces. I have no words to name them. What men are these?' 'They are the sort that roams (遊) outside (外) the square (方) [of the world],' said Confucius. 'I am the sort that roams (游) inside (內) the square [of the world]. Outside and inside are not equatable with one another and do not touch each other (外內不相及), to send you to mourn was stupid (陋) on my part. They are at the stage of being fellow men with the maker of things, and go roaming in the single breath that breathes through heaven and earth. (而遊乎天地之一氣)"[232]

The writing of the *Zhuangzi* pins down the incommensurability of the "inside" (內) of the "square" or of the "conventions" (方) of the world that Confucius "roams" (游) in and of the "outside" (外) the square or of the conventions of the world that the disciples of the deceased master roam (遊) in. The inscription of the text bears a subtle nuance that denotes the incommensurability of the two distinct forms of roaming that Confucius identifies (conventional vs. unconventional roaming, roaming inside vs. roaming outside); and yet the distinction he makes is not constructed in the form of argument or as an affirmation. Rather, it is pointed out as a mere statement of fact which is evidenced by the simple observation that Confucius' roaming is written 游 and theirs is written 遊. Confucius' avowal of his stupidity, narrow-mindedness or "squareness" (陋) seems to betray the following, unspoken, line of questioning: how could I be so stupid and narrow-minded so as to imagine that I could put on equal footing *what cannot be equated*? How could I not see that their roaming and mine do not "touch each other"?

*

The language found in the *Zhuangzi* is not articulated in terms of Being (as is the mathematical incommensurable of the Greeks) or within the context of a deployed idea of God (as is the incommensurable Other of the Bible). Instead, it offers the ironic portrait of a ridiculed Confucius made to look like a "square" and deploys a thought of intertwining breaths and fluxes that animate the world- the thought of *Qi* (氣). The coy image of a befuddled Confucius offers an implicit and allusive portrait of an unidentifiable and indeterminate Sage who evolves in concert with the "single breath" (一氣) which lies at the source of the continuous engendering and transforming of the world. And yet, this source of the world is not made into another world either: it does not hold a definable and identifiable status (a form of predicable "being") upon which it founds its Truth.

There is indeed a rupture, a hiatus, that separates the two no-longer-communicating dimensions that Confucius' character alludes to. And yet this "outside" or "beyond" (*wai* 外) dimension that the Singing Sages rove in and point towards does not find a properly theological or metaphysical consistency that can be distinctly dissociated from this world; it cannot be parked in an ordered construction that lies in an identifiable and predicable "beyond" this world. The "outside" direction that they *hint towards* is suggestive, these Sages offer no solutions nor destinations. Instead, they give us an *inkling* that allows us to grasp, for the briefest of moments, the literal "ex-istence" or "standing outside" of a *possibility*: "roaming *outside* the square of the world," all the while remaining, at the same time, wholly *within* the "square of the world." Their story discretely highlights a *wayside* of the world which lies outside its well-trodden roads, and yet wholly *within* its spheres of confluence: the anecdote offers a suggestive illustration of a form of tacit adventuring that does not reach "beyond" this world and instead reaches *beneath* its sights and sounds.

*

The *Zhuangzi* thinks of an "outside" this world and yet refrains from ontologizing it (as the Greeks did when they constructed the mathematical incommensurable into a "being" and object of wonderment) and from deifying it (the supreme Otherness or Outsidedness of the Kingdom of God as in John 18:36 "My kingdom is not of this world- *emè basileia estin ouk ek toutou cosmou.*"). The roaming of the singing sages suggests a "retreat" from the world which leads to a disengagement from its habitual norms and customs, it implies a *clearing* of its limitations from the "outside." And yet, it does not represent a *credo* nor a religious *conversion*.

The *Zhuangzi* conceives of its own discourse and speech as manifestations of the incommensurable, without making this incommensurable the expression of a Message and without pinning it down into a logically demonstrable assertion: its "words" are deliberately "empty and foreign," its expressions "vast to the point of infinity," its "statements possess neither limit nor border." The statements of the *Zhuangzi* are said to be "mad" and "wayward:" how could one indeed let the incommensurable spring forth in speech and in writing without appearing to be crazed and bewildered? Because the world ("*Tian Xia* 天下" or "what lies beneath heaven") is both "muddied and bogged," it is logical that the roving Sage cannot "communicate" with it in "consistent terms." Even though "he comes and goes alone and in concert with the refined spirit of Heaven and Earth," he nonetheless harbors "no disdain" towards the "myriad beings" that populate the world.[233]

*

The writings of that fellow human named Zhuang Zhou who lived nearly 2,400 hundred years ago in Ancient China thus leave a signed and stylized mark that *points towards* what is "not of this world," what lies "outside" of it, and what effectively *ruptures* its norms and conventions. Nonetheless, the style of the *Zhuangzi* never rejects "this world" as a pure form of illusory appearance, nor does it ever invoke "another world" in which one would be freed from the confines of this one (absence of any concept of salvation). The idiosyncratic and incommensurable stylistic traits of the *Zhuangzi* were never to become mainstream in Chinese literary culture as it evolved throughout the ages, even if they remain, to this day, markers of literary excellence in China and beyond. The text's un-integratable singularities, its antiquated, obscure and yet penetrating formulations, constitute a semantic barrier that both prevented its ideological recuperation by imperial power while facilitating its subterranean, silent, and diffuse transmission amongst a limited yet dedicated readership.

Unlike the figure of Confucius who remains integral to the ideological construction of the modern Chinese Empire as it spreads its global influence, the figure of the dreamer and ironist Zhuang Zhou, that strange and wayward fellow who left behind a set of *incommensurable* and endlessly *savorable* texts, has been largely washed away by the waves of History. The stylistic irreverence of the *Zhuangzi* has been progressively covered up by the authoritarian and traditionalist legacy of the autocratic ideology that shaped imperial rule for nearly two-thousand years and which continues to influence the formulaic and allusive rhetoric of the People's Republic of China to this day. Even so, the text continues to deploy *unheard possibilities*: it *manifests*, through the factual display of its own incommensurability and un-integratability within any ordered discourse or ideology, a *force of resistance* which roves *on the wayside* of convened and policed patterns of speaking and writing, *outside* of the mechanisms of propaganda, be they insidious or blatant.

*

The *Zhuangzi* thus *hints towards* the basic fact that there *exists*, within experience, within "this world," an Incommensurable that ruptures the convention of speech, discourse and convenance *from within;* all the while pointing towards an *outside* "this world" that makes "us," as humans, *ex-ist*, that is to say- stand outside- the order of the "myriad beings" that roam "within the square" of commensurability and predictability of "this world."

3/ Living Incommensurables: *jouissance*, the intimate, and death.

Saying that the Incommensurable traverses experience and ruptures it from within does not constitute a thesis or an argument. When one thing is said to be incommensurable with another one, there is no argument being made about whether one of those two things is superior to the other. The sentence "*a* is incommensurable with *x*" is a minimal yet maximal observation that lies *on the wayside* of any ideology or predetermined stance: it is a discrete yet potent assessment of a factual situation.

The assessing and stating of the incommensurable cannot be constructed as a value or as a judgment: it is neither an assertion that professes a form of truth endowed with a positive content, nor is it even a proposition that ties a predicate to a subject. The assessment that states "*a* is incommensurable with *x*" lies both beneath and prior any constituted position; as such, it cannot be subjected to criticism or argumentation.

In this regard, the incommensurable does not constitute a "foundation" for (a) metaphysics but rather an instance of *departure* that initiates the motion of thought. The detection of the *incommensurabilities* that fracture the common measure of experience *from within* reveals a plurality of *tipping points* that resist systematization and rationalization. On an experiential and existential level, there are three forms of *shifting* that can be singled out as revelatory instances of the Incommensurable that tears through the fabric of "our" human experience: *jouissance*, the intimate, and death.

a. The incommensurability of jouissance and pleasure: a translation problem.

The common and frequently used French word *jouissance* (pronounced joo-ee-suns) points towards two levels of the incommensurable, one linguistic and the other existential. The word is defined in the French dictionary as a term that denotes "a pleasure that is fully tasted" and as a legal term that refers to ownership; it is, on the one hand, intimately *tied* to the liminal and intimate experience of the *orgasm,* and, on the other hand, bound to the legal apparatus of property-rights.

*

As such, the term *jouissance* holds no exact equivalent in English, it can be approximately translated by terms like "enjoyment," which does not seize the intensity of the French word, or more esoterically by a term like "ecstasy," which carries along with it a "spiritual" connotation that is at odds with the crude materiality that the legal usage of the term *jouissance* suggests in its reference to "ownership." On a purely linguistic level, translating the term *jouissance* into English reveals an *un-resorbable hiatus* that subsists *in between* two languages, it exposes the incommensurability of one language to another. The word *jouissance* points towards the incommensurable singularities that compose any given language and thus *separate* it from other ones.

In the same way that "2" bears no common measure with " $\sqrt{2}$," *jouissance* holds no equivalent with any word in the English language. The singularity of a language can only be reflected by and through an *encounter* with another language, an encounter which reveals the incommensurable and infinite lines of *fracture* separating the two of them. The encounter with a hitherto unbeknownst language and the real shock of incomprehension that it supposes produces a *constraint* that induces a speculative and exploratory process of *mediation, (de) limitation,* and, most obviously, *translation.*[234] Translating the French word *jouissance* into English thus exposes a linguistic breach of incommensurability that *fractures* any totalizing conception of language; one which would presuppose the existence of a shared "natural language" that is common to, if not all animate beings, then assuredly all human beings.

b. Jouissance and the sexual: a psychoanalytic approach.

The linguistic fracture that the word *jouissance* reveals also points towards an *existential fracture* that underlies the so-called "peak experiences" of life. The French dictionary renders *jouissance* as a superlative synonym of "pleasure" and yet, as Freud hinted at in *Beyond the Pleasure Principle* and as Lacan shouted it in his seminars in the early 1970s, there is a sexual dimension which lies within the experience of pleasure itself that is vertiginously *excessive*. When it comes to sexuality, the subjective, rational, and self-interested focus of the pleasure-seeking principle (*eros*), which habitually orders the processes of the conscious mind (the "I"), is *exceeded*; this excess of the sexual thus reveals a crackled surface of contact (the "That") shaped by repetitive impulsions (drives) that leap in, around, and *in between* the abyssal breaches that puncture it.

Whereas the pleasure principle of the "I" structures the conscious ordering of libidinal drives (*trieben*), the tipping-point experience of *jouissance* represents or repeats that precise instance of pleasure which punctures pleasure *from within*, thus *de-structuring* the order of consciousness. As it un-lodges the conscious subject's rational(ized) understanding of what constitutes "pleasure," *jouissance* hints towards a speculative and mythological image, the much discussed Freudian "death-drive" (*Thanatos*).[235]

After having acknowledged the obvious links that tie the sex drives ("*Sexualtriebe oder Eros*") to the pursuit of pleasure, Freud recognizes the "difficulties" (*schwieriegkeiten*) associated with the recognition of a second class of drives that are also indubitably bound to the sexual (as evidenced by sadism or masochism), but that seem to counter-balance the self-preserving drive (*selbsterhaltungstrieb*) of the *Eros* principle without ever fully negating it:

> "On a theoretical ground, we supposed the existence of a *death-drive* on the basis of evidenced biological considerations, its proposed task is to lead organic living back into an inanimate state; all the while *Eros* pursues its target, life. Through an ever-widening concentration of particles, [Eros] disperses living substance so that it [life] can complicate, and also, naturally, maintain itself."[236]

In this crucial, dense, and notoriously ambiguous sentence, Freud highlights the paradoxical nature of his theoretical hypothesis of the "death-drives." For Freud, these drives evolve *on the wayside* of the pleasure-seeking impulses that both "maintain" (*zu erhalten*) and "complicate" (*zu komplizieren*) the fabrication of "organic living" (*Organische lebende*). The "death-drives" thus "lead back" (*zurück-zuführen*) living and "life" (*das Leben*) into the primordial "inanimate state" (*leblosen Zustand*) -i.e. non-life or death- from which all drives seem to proceed. Writing like the true and yet unassuming poet that he was, Freud plays with the sounds of the German language, combining various terms that incorporate the radical "*leb-*," which refers to life in both a scientific and existential capacity, with a combination of verbal and nominal forms that include the prepositional, adjectival, and adverbial particle "*zu-*," which denotes directionality. The sonorous and poetic effect that emanates from his purportedly scientific text creates a destabilizing and dizzying *effect* that suggestively points towards the *incommensurable* trajectories of the two drives, *Eros* and *Thanatos*.

Much like the incommensurable existence of irrational numbers cracks open the internal order of rational numbers and stands outside their order without formally negating it, the speculative existence of a "death-drive" stands outside, shatters, and "scatters" (*zersprengten*) the conscious order of pleasure and its logic of self-preservation, without ever impeding its logic and order. On the contrary, as *Eros* "pursues" *(verfolgt)* its "target" (*Ziel*) -i.e.the sustenance of life- through an "ever-widening concentration" (*durch immer weitergreifende Zusammenfassung*) of "particle-gathering" that condenses "living substance" (*lebenden Substanz*), it becomes irrevocably *tied* to *Thanatos* as the latter "disperses" (other possible translation of *zerpsrengten*) Eros' "living substance," thus leading life back into non-life. In other words, the pursuit of "peak-experiences" of pleasure -i.e. the pursuit of *jouissance*- paradoxically both preserves and destroys life; it points towards that dimension of human existence which literally exists or *stands outside* the predictable processes that characterize the observable life of non-human organisms.

*

What Lacan picked up on and harped on in his seminars as he thematized Freud's theory of the "death-drive" under the distinctly French auspice of *jouissance* is that the pursuit and obtainment of sexual pleasure and of "peak-experiences" marks a singular moment of *existing* in any given human life. From a psychoanalytic perspective, existential instances of *jouissance* corresponds to moments of *standing out(side)* where *Eros* and *Thanatos*, living and dying, *interpenetrate* each other and thus produce an *intimate* bond that both straddles and cracks the boundaries that delineate the common measures of sociability and finitude.

c. The incommensurability of the intimate and the social.

When we become *intimate* with someone, the moments that we share together, the moments where it's "just the two of us" as Bill Withers beautifully sings, are moments that *stand out* from the moments we live with others; what we say or live with our intimate partner shares *no common* measure with what we say or live with others. Like a pocket that isolates us from common relationships, like a tent under which we find shelter or like a fire that we tend to, the intimate signals its *waysidedness* as soon as it is initiated. When I enter in an intimate relationship with the Other (with You), I cease to harbor ulterior motives and I no longer project plans onto You. By doing so, I've extracted the Other from the relationships of power and interest that more or less always define the common measures of society.

The verification that there is an incommensurability of one to the other (the intimate vs. the social) is within reach. While society requires me to maintain a level of conversation, in the intimate I can remain in silence with the Other- or with You- without ever feeling bothered: silence then becomes a vector of the intimate, perhaps even more so than speech. Furthermore, when I am speaking intimately with the Other or with You, I may have "nothing" to say or I may just communicate those little "nothings" that do not mean anything; I no longer have to "communicate": speech and silence are rendered equivalent, their opposition is undone. In the melting-pot of the intimate, cautions melt away and aims disappear. The intimate is thus incommensurable with the relationships that make the world, it exists or *stands outside* them, even though it is *lived* in "this world" and not in another one.

The intimate reveals an *imperishable (no)thing* that exists *within* life. Baudelaire, a great thinker and poet of the intimate, writes in *The Balcony*:

"We so often said *imperishable* things,

the nights illuminated by the ardor of the coal."[237]

Living would in fact remain vain for us if we did not have deep within us the profound sentiment that the intimate, in its bottomless depth, opens a beneath- and not a "Beyond"- death itself. Is it not possible to say that it is the individual or the personal that perishes? Is the intimate not the very "imperishable" that Baudelaire alludes to? One could, in sum, reiterate what Levinas says about interiority, albeit in a more justified fashion for the intimate: the intimate moment "establishes a different order from the historical time in which totality is constituted" and it "is no longer absorbed in universal time"[238]; or, the space that the intimate moment occupies within the time of universal history does not "account" for its reality. Even great civilizations are reduced to nothing, leaving behind mere ruins and traces. Yet when the intimate is accessed, time is fractured and overflowed to the point where the intimate cannot be resorbed in the time of the world and thus does not die with it or within it. Does the same not hold true for the *moment* of death? Isn't the thought of our own death the most intimate thought we can entertain? As is the thought of our own *jouissance*? The very moment of death contradicts death by opening an Incommensurable within it.

d. Death, jouissance, and the incommensurable.

It is true that *jouissance* and death answer each other. Not so much because they are both experiences of the extreme and of the limit which represents the two instances in which experience is undone, one (*jouissance*) prefiguring and profiling the other (death). It is instead *jouissance* and death's capacity to *crack open* and *overflow* the fabric experience that ties them to the irreducible incommensurability of singular human existence. The irreducible singularity of a human living his *jouissance* and the irreducible singularity of a human who witnesses dying hints towards a most intimate point within the subject that is no longer contained by the subject; towards a moment when the subject is no longer a subject, becoming nothing more than an "object" from the perspective of others, something, as opposed to somebody, that can only be buried or burned. The incommensurable moment of death is not so much death as an organic "phenomenon," a phenomenon that is easily integrated within the naturalistic understanding of organic living renewing itself in death. It is not even the "episode" of death which occurs, like in an Ancient Greek drama, only "in passing" and suggests a return to Source, a shift into mystery or the advent of another, re-incarnated, life.

Ideology's efforts concentrate on reintegrating the rupture that death supposes within a predetermined framework of meaning that attempts to inscribe its incommensurability within the common measure of this world (naturalism) or within the common measure of another one (metaphysics). Yet ideology cannot fully contain or resorb this incommensurable *event* of death which fractures for the briefest of moments the commensurability of the world. There is indeed no common measure which renders the moments Before and the moments After death commensurable to one another; the two moments follow each other and yet they do not "reach" towards each other or towards us as Lucretius says.[239] A breach of incommensurability is opened *in between* Life and Death when the gaze suddenly no longer gazes, when the breath fades into a final rasp, and when the body becomes inert and stiff, the incommensurable *revealed* before our eyes falls prey to the *shunning* and *avoiding* of reintegration, belief, and consolation; or, it just dissolves itself into the forgetfulness of the world.

4/ Shunning and avoiding, or the fate of the Incommensurable.

The incommensurability of the event of death can only madden us if we pay too much attention to it and if we get suckered into it: gazing into the gaze-less eye which has suddenly become fixed and emptied projects us into a vertiginous, bottomless, and dizzying breach of uncertainty and unspeakability. The rupture of the event of death is not only a rupture of continuity, it is also a rupture of commensurability where two entities (the living being vs. the dead being) approach each other and nearly touch each other without ever being able to actually enter into contact and thus merge into a whole. The infinite crack that separates them cannot be bridged or filled.

a. Death or the advent of avoiding and shunning of the incommensurable.

And yet, life and death are not incompatible or mutually exclusive: on the contrary, they are correlated, one supposes the other. The problem isn't that they bear no relationship to each other and are thus incomparable, the problem is that, in the event of death itself, there is no single unit of measure that allows us to equate the Before with the After.

The event of death leaves a mark that leads to a systematic dynamic of *avoiding* and *shunning*. We do everything in our power to avoid thinking about the incommensurability of death when we run into it head-on or stumble upon it accidentally: I begin avoiding the thought of the death of others and loved ones before beginning to avoid thinking about "my" death. The possession that thinking of "my" death supposes points towards a most paradoxical tip of incommensurability since, when "my" death occurs, "I" no longer exist: once "I" am dead, "I" no longer am.

Avoiding thinking about one's own death is the great avoidance that characterizes the "story of our lives": we all pretend and act "as if" we won't ever die. We shun and silence the event of death as we *tune out* the *un-heard* reverberations that emerge in the wake of death.

Shutting closed the eyes of the dead body represents the first attempt to silence and shun the unbearable incommensurability of the lifeless gaze and its perpetually open eyes.

*

Society can only silence and shun the incommensurable that the Event of death indecently exposed. The first words that are spoken as we exit the cemetery, the first comments that we make about those who are either present or absent, organize in chorus the great societal act of shunning. Everyone knows that these words bear no common measure with what just happened and that their sole purpose is to haphazardly lodge, as best as they can, this without-common-measure that just occurred into some kind of measure. Even though we "know" that these words possess neither meaning nor value, we cling onto them, stack them upon each other and densify them in a process of tacit and complicit accordance: we use them to attempt to fill up the suddenly irreducible crack that has just been opened, trying our best to link up the un-linkable and mend the un-mendable. These empty words that we say to avoid saying are meant to break silence, they are by no means hypocritical, disinterested, indifferent or forced; nor are they just banal ways of saying that "life must go on." Instead, they represent an avowal that what has just happened definitively bears *no common measure* with the measure of the livable and of the bearable.

It is true that in past times the rituals surrounding death -all human societies have of course crafted a diverse array of rituals surrounding the event of death throughout time- in fact nurtured and nourished a capacity to integrate the event of death into a framework of measure. Ancestral rituals integrated the event of death within a framework of salvation and/or cycling; death was *resorbed* within a collective ceremony that renewed and strengthened the sense of kinship. As such, the disappearance of ancestral rituals today can only expose us even more to the cold bleakness and nudity of the great shunning of death's incommensurability- an inescapable *real* that we all reluctantly deal with, at some point or another in our lives...

b. Suicide, the incommensurable and the unheard.

The incommensurability of the event of death with the life that surrounds it is made most apparent in the case of suicide. When it is not committed under constraint, the act of suicide constitutes a blatant opening of an Incommensurable within the world. We will never be able to fully account for a suicide, we can never fully *integrate* it within our frameworks of understanding. We will never manage to densify and fill up the gaping *crack* that it opens in the world with explanations and rationalizations. Much like intimate convictions and feelings, the most *intimate* decision of suicide is impermeable to rational arguments. We can invoke and amass as many causes and reasons as we want to explain a suicide, yet they will always fall short of making sense of the gesture that goes along with killing oneself; this gesture remains not so much incomprehensible, but rather unapproachable: an *un-resorbable hiatus* will always subsist and thus separate suicide from the order of the reasonable. *Leaping into* the logic of suicide- a logic which wanders *on the wayside* of the constitutive logic of life within this world, the tenacious tendency to "persevere in one's being"- becomes a necessary moment of any serious philosophical confrontation with the Incommensurable.

*

The incommensurable that the act of suicide opens cannot be closed or shut down: we can only *shun* its event and subsequently *avoid* talking about it; or only talk about it in hushed tones and in discrete asides: what is it that we collectively fear to name in the event of (a) suicide if not the Incommensurable? If the question of suicide suddenly comes up in conversation, we will all of a sudden attempt to bashfully bury it up, doing our best to forget about it in order to move on with our conversation and with our lives.

Yet prior to that hurried motion of silencing, lies a voided moment of silence: spoken words, for an instant, no longer connect with each other in their customary fashion. As a collective, we agree to side-step or wander around the suicidal fracture. Instead, we prefer to leave its un-easing reverberations *unheard*. Organized religions (is it not indeed true of all religions and is it not their common justification?) push to an extreme this enterprise of shunning and re-integrating suicide by publicly condemning it or by praising it under the auspice of martyrdom. After all, organized religions often functioned as great ideological integration-machines that choked the incommensurable out of existence and obfuscated its uncanniness. As they attempted to cover up the incommensurable with the timeless and noisy veil of metaphysics and with the social constructs derived from it, organized religions and absolute beliefs nonetheless failed to eradicate an ineradicable *metaphysical minimal* that subsists within existence and experience even though it remains *unheard*.

5/ The (un)heard and the (un)accountable "thing in and of itself," or the inkling of a metaphysical minimal.

a. Gazing at a dead body or the incommensurable experience of the unheard.

There are indeed moments when the *perceptual* lying right in front of us -i.e., what we are currently perceiving- can no longer be contained by the subjective parameters of perception: when I am watching a dead corpse in a funeral parlor, "my" subjective experience of the colors, of the skin, and of the sight of the lifeless face in front of me -i.e., "my" subjective experience of the perceptual "objects" I am gazing at- is exceeded and overloaded. Words cannot aptly seize the *unheard* which surfaces in this moment and *cracks it open*, from within. The unheard in this case signals both what *can* still be heard, the hitherto unheard *possibility* of life's continuation, and what *cannot* be heard, a silenced and un-integratable unheard, a literal *impossibility*: death's infinite breach of incommensurability both exceeds and overloads the "commensurabilized" parameters of perception.

*

What can be said of the perceptual holds true for the affective: gazing at the dead body reveals something within us that can no longer be contained by affection; our capacity to experience emotion on a subjective level becomes submerged. The affects within us surge and can no longer be contained, a bottomless breach that is neither psychological nor reactive, nor even "internal" is opened: the bottomless breach of grief and loss is not only intensive and experienced on a subjective level, it resonates and reverberates well beyond "me." The experience of grief and loss *hints towards* an *ancestral link* that binds us to a distant collective: the "us" that "we" use when speaking of "our" shared heritage- the *human*.

The pain of losing loved ones paradoxically reveals "our" inter-relatedness with "them": as the living links bonding "us" to "them" are severed, *unheard* reminiscences, vibrations and affects linger around and continue to float about in "our" world, the world of the living, while others disappear into "their" world, the world of the dead. If anything, death possesses the striking capacity to *amplify* the unheard: as it *(un)arises* within the fields of consciousness and existence, it *reveals* an indefinite plurality of *unheard (im)possibilities.*

b. The unheard as an encounter with the Other.

We'd have to poke our own eyes out, clog up our souls, or obstruct our own spirits to not hear this *un-heard crack* that Death reveals *within* the world. When we *encounter* Death and *un-hear* the crackling of its reverberations, we effectively brush up against an *Other*: an Exterior or a *(no)thing* that cannot, for the briefest and yet most significant of moments, be integrated into any human framework or parameter.

It is tempting for us to dodge the unheard in one manner or another; we most often do our best to forget about it and/or bury it in denial. One of the most convenient solutions that we have found to deal with the *(no)thing* than the unheard displaces both within and outside us is to forge the rationalizing category of the "supra-sensible" or "super-natural." This rationalizing path of convenience has of course been the one privileged by metaphysics throughout the ages. Historically, Western metaphysics parked the lacking and yet *metaphysical* excess of the unheard high up in the tower of Being. As philosophy became ever more determined, and ultimately disillusioned, in its search to find a pure Being separated from the appearing and manifesting forms of Things, it engaged in an obsessive search and/or dismissal of a hypothetical "other world" (the platonic "world of forms"; Kant's "noumenal realm"). The constructions of metaphysics have yielded little fruits for those of us who fail to comply with the urge to dismiss and dispel the unheard, those of us who are instead drawn to its *(no)thingness*.

*

The *(no)thing* that the unheard uncovers is neither exceptional nor astounding. We are led to it, even outside of the dramatic circumstances in which death arises. The unheard maintains us on the threshold of the *(un)assignable*. It does so without announcing a rupture with the ordinary, without being cut off from appearances and their inherent *semblance*. Attuning to the unheard and tending one's ears towards it lies *on the wayside* of metaphysics' maximalist pretenses: it involves instead a discrete *attuning* to the subtle processes which *un-cover* a moment of *de-fencing* and *de-categorizing* where the boundaries separating the "physical," the "intellectual," and the "emotional" become imperceptible. This discrete moment of de-fencing and de-categorizing is not a declamation or proclamation: the unheard indeed *arises* in the most unassuming ways, it is *un-covered* in the most quotidian and most banal of situations- a singular face that detaches itself from a crowd, or even a cloud seen wandering about the sky.

c. The unheard as a metaphysical minimal.

The unheard designates a raw metaphysical *minimal*. "Minimal" signifies here that we cannot do anything less than recognize (literally *re-cognize*) the *remnant* that the unheard brings into our world as a *(no)thing* that was accidentally stumbled upon one morning or evening.

*

Much like the "moral minimals" that Adorno foraged in his *Minima Moralia*,[240] we can *encounter* "metaphysical minimals" at the most immediate levels of experience. Sprouting up freely like mushrooms and lying beneath the construction of any idealist or pragmatist system of morality, Adorno's "moral minimals" should not be dismissed as trivial or anecdotal. Having not been enshrined in a constructed discourse which delineates proper and improper morality, they suggestively *hint towards* an *effective* form of *ethical living* that does not reach towards the "beyond" of metaphysics. Adorno's "moral minimals" do not dissociate themselves from the *real* in any way, shape, or form.

*

Conceiving of the unheard as this metaphysical minimal maintains the metaphysical in an initial and *evocative* state. The *evocation* of the unheard *overflows* the constitutive frameworks of experience; it does not refer us to an "other(ed) thing" and does not call upon an "other experience," let alone "another world." The unheard creates a tensive effect: the metaphysical (which can now be referred to in a neutral or partitive form) that it uncovers is neither hypothetical nor "hyperbolical" like the age-old constructs of metaphysics.[241] And yet, despite everything being done socially to skew, distort, and evacuate it, the *overflowing* of the unheard *remains*, as such, *in-eradicable*.

*

The purpose of sociability is indeed to lodge *the* metaphysical within a niche and wash away its virulence to bury it into oblivion. Nonetheless, the metaphysical unheard shows up everywhere in experience, at the *ground level*.

*

As the unheard de-countenances our capacity of apprehension and takes us out of habitual perceptual and mental frameworks, it offers us *access* to an "other." The form of "otherness" or "alterity" that the unheard *uncovers* does not represent an "Other (symbolic) order" or an "Other (metaphysical) world."While society tries to cast *the* metaphysical into oblivion, metaphysics on the other hand betrayed the unheard every time that it puffed itself up into a constructed discourse endowed with positive content, or into a field of inquiry separated from all others. Whenever metaphysics encountered this Outside, this incommensurable and un-resorbable unheard, it conveniently stowed it in an Elsewhere. Metaphysics' "elsewhere" thus became yet another *inside*, simply because its purpose was to lodge the incommensurability of the unheard within a predetermined order of measure and meaning.

6/ Wandering on the wayside of the spectacular and the extraordinary, catching glimpses of the unheard as it un-appears.

The unheard is indeed neither spectacular nor extraordinary: surfacing and *arising* in the most ordinary of moments, for the briefest of instants, it is glimpsed at as one wanders *on the wayside* of habitual frameworks of perception and understanding. And yet, it remains grounded in the ordinariness of daily life. Because the unheard is encountered in the most quotidian situations (clouds moving across the sky, a face detaching itself from a crowd), it is also what we no longer notice, what we tiredly gloss over as we get on with our lives. The unheard is typically left *on the wayside* of our preoccupations; it goes on about unnoticed until it abruptly surfaces, quickly hides itself, and subsequently generates an uncanny blend of *lassitude* and *vertigo*.

Yet if the unheard is indeed the only real that we can encounter, then can it, as such, ever disappear? Will it not always be there, in the background? Will the ceaseless cycling and fading of faces, winds, and clouds not perpetuate itself regardless of whether we will still be around to see it? Does the real(ness) of the unheard, both tedious and shocking, not represent both the fullness and the limitedness of contingent experience? Isn't the unheard a *revelator*, not of disappearance, but rather of *un-appearance*?

a. Swann's Way and the concept of un-appearing.

Turning to literature offers a welcome point of entry into these philosophical questions which are as much existential as they are technical. When Proust's character Swann kisses for the first time Odette, the woman who will then become his lover and later his wife, we are told that he "holds her face, for an instant, at a short distance, in between his two hands." Is this gesture not, as a common and wholly reasonable belief would hold, an effort on the libertine lover's behalf to savor more fully "his" accession to the object of "his" lustful desire? Perhaps this gesture can be attributed instead to a more essential reason, a secret fear that has yet to be elucidated, a reason that would have more to do with apprehension than with satisfaction: is something not *lost* in this moment of attainment? The rationale that this gesture betrays cannot be conveniently attributed to a purely psychological motif: what it discreetly touches upon -on an existential level- belongs to *the* metaphysical.

Swann's gesture highlights that, in this very moment, he foresees - or already feels- that his then-nascent relationship with Odette is bound to *fade* into the *lassitude* which defines every day relating. Odette's face as it offers itself to his lips will no longer sufficiently detach itself, it will no longer appear to him and will thus cease to emerge: lacking the *waysidedness* that characterized the shock of the initial encounter with the Other, the *unheard* that Odette's face carried along with it will from now on be recovered by the mundaneness of habitual cohabitation, buried under a menacing form of proximity. At the end of his analysis, Proust offers the following strange, abrupt, and hardly translatable sentence which nonetheless leaves no doubts hanging: "Perhaps Swann was even attaching on Odette's not-yet-possessed, not yet even kissed face, as he was seeing it for the very last time, that look (*regard*) with which, on a day of departure, we express how we would want to take with us a landscape that we are to forever leave behind us."[242]

*

What does "leaving" mean, when it is on the contrary proximity that will impose itself from now on? What does it mean when a face that is about to become familiar carries along with it the *loss* of a "landscape," in all its immensity; a landscape that is, in fact, about to be swallowed up and forever forgotten? This face which becomes familiar does not disappear, it instead *un-appears*.

*

To disappear is to retreat from presence, to sink into absence and to no longer be visible- like the sun which hides, at night, in the horizon. To *un-appear*, on the other hand, is to retreat from appearance, to lose one's potential of emergence: what un-appears is fully and continuously visible. What *un-appears* is folded back into *an un-heard* and *un-seen* that can be neither *grasped* nor even perceived. As we gaze at the sun, as it *sprawls* and stalls in the sky, we grow weary of looking at it and can no longer cast our eyes upon it; the sun has not disappeared, but rather *un-appeared*.

*

The verb "to appear" indeed possesses these two opposites or "antonyms:" "to disappear," a recorded and lexicalized term, which declares the obviousness of experience; the other, "to un-appear," its secret, or better yet discreet and hitherto unexplored opposite, a neologism which paradoxically touches upon our singular *existential capacity,* understood here as our literal capacity to *stand out*.

234

*

The two opposites of appearing designate an effacing of perception. And yet, in one case, this effacement of perception results from the removal of presence (in death, the face disappears), while in the other case perception effaces itself because *presence installs itself within its own presence.* As it makes itself at home, presence undoes its own appearing; once presence is *installed,* it is no longer menaced of disappearance or removal. On the contrary, presence does not cease to *sprawl* and *(in)stall* itself.

*

One might as well say that in this case it is presence's capacity to *cease to disappear* which makes it *un-appear.* On a beach when the sun has found its towering position in the sky and fixates itself at a seemingly unmovable point, when the colors have started to settle in (the "blue" of the sea, the "ocher" of the sand), the presence of what we name a "beach" begins to *sprawl* as it *(in)stalls* itself; in broad daylight, before our own eyes, a "beach" progressively *un-appears.*

*

The mundaneness of gazing at the sun on a beach suggests that the unheard can be found *within* the most ordinary moments of our existence, the ones that are the most sprawled out and most obvious, as opposed to the most fleeting and hidden. And yet, as such, we cannot normally access it within the constituted frameworks of our experience; it thus seems to be exceptional within our very experience, which is why we then wrongly confuse the unheard with the extraordinary. Because presence un-appears as it sprawls and installs itself before us, it signals the fatality of its "(not)being" and "(no) thingness." The unheard can therefore only begin to be heard when the ever-stalling and ever-wearying sprawl of Being *cracks* itself *open*: when presence suddenly *overflows,* no longer coincides with "itself," no longer remains sprawled and (in)stalled, it suddenly becomes *salient* once more and makes an irruption into our lives as it *un-covers* itself.

*

The unheard springs forth when the sprawl and stall of presence covering itself up *cracks open* and when, in the slightest of breaches, appearance and appearing can *arise* once more. It is thus only possible to catch glimpses of the unheard or to briefly intercept it: it can only be perceived *in passing,* precisely because the unheard dissimulates itself in and through its own sprawl. The unheard can therefore only be lightly *brushed up against*; it reflects a soft *efflorescence,* its *arising* within ordinary experience can only be approached at the *moment of emergence* or in the *instance of retreat.* Seeping both *through and in between* the cracks of continuity, the unheard half-opens a breach within the opacity of *existence*.

b. The unheard and the ethics of existing.

And yet, it is not only the unheard within the world which calls upon this *un-covering*; incessantly, on a daily basis; it is, first and foremost, more intimately and more crucially, our life itself which calls upon it. The fact that life, and firstly life *within us*, calls upon this un-covering is in fact, the -not so much secret but instead discrete- principle of ethics.

Because life repeats itself, because it sinks and stalls within its durations, because we have forever been installed in life, and firstly life within us, life itself *un-appears*. Life indeed covers up life, or rather life bogs itself down for the simple reason that we continue to live. Locking itself up, sinking into itself, stalling itself in its coincidence with itself, life is no longer saliant; it no longer emerges, ceases to *soar*, and becomes instead *sprawled* and *(in)stalled*.

*

To begin to effectively *exist* will precisely consist in this *un-co-*

vering of life. Rather it will consist in beginning to hear what remains *unheard* within life itself- the rest (the "moral" life) will thus only be a mere consequence of this un-covering. Within the un-covering of life one can clearly distinguish what separates the unheard from the unknown. If the unknown within life is what the future holds for us and is thus *what we cannot know* (whether we will succeed in our ventures, when we will die, etc.), the unheard within life corresponds to that *in and of itself of life-* or that "life in and of itself"- that *we cannot access* because we do not cease to reduce it, primarily by way of assimilation and rationalization. And yet, when this life suddenly becomes endangered after an accident or an illness, when we unexpectedly "get away with it," the bogged down life begins to *crack open* and lets us, underneath its covers, from within its bottomless breaches, *glimpse* at what *remains unheard,* within our life, *this life.*

*

In front of the death of an Other, the unheard within life brushes up against us. Also, to prevent such an un-covering from reweaving and reforming itself into silence, we will have to make this un-heard within life *crack its way* into speech and form; so that we can *begin to hear*, and thus *finally say,* the *unheard.*

7/ On the wayside of the heard and said: attuning to the (unheard) productions of metaphor.

In order to hear and thus say the unheard, it is necessary to wander *on the wayside* of what has *already been heard and said.*The heard and said satisfy themselves with their own self-evident and self-coinciding obviousness. Saying what has *yet to be heard* within the confines of what language has already constituted as being "said" "sayable" is at once exceedingly difficult, utterly necessary, and, above all, eminently *possible.* As we shall see, a philosophical and intercultural conceptualization of *metaphor* in fact possesses the power to *transport* us *out of* the "heard and said" and *into* the unheard. .

> *a. Metaphor and the invention of the unheard: more than a "figure of speech."*

If poets and those who follow their suit (writers, visual artists, and musicians) have always been spokespeople of the unheard and its metaphors throughout history and across cultures, then it is assuredly because, throughout their diverse practices, they have meticulously cultivated a capacity to wander *on the wayside* of what is *already heard and said* within (a) language, be it poetic, dramaturgic, pictorial, or musical. Poetic activity reflects a singularly *human* capacity to *invent* ways of *hearing and saying the unheard* that stand both *outside* and yet wholly *within* the convened conventions of language, speech, and performance. Regardless of the Place or the Era, it is obvious that the (de)constructive process of *metaphorization* has long constituted the intercultural (and even at times transcultural) *sediment* of all poetic and esthetic traditions.

*

Metaphor is much more than a "figure of speech" within language, even if it is supposed to be the "queen" of such figures. Metaphor indeed corresponds to that point *within* language where language *frees itself* from the principle of its closed identity and from its sterile adequation. Metaphor opens a perspective within what appeared to be walled and enclosed; it enables the emergence of the unheard within speech. The word "metaphor" in Ancient Greek evokes "transport" ("relocation"); metaphor thus *transports* us into the foreign or into "another," it corresponds to the *transference* of meaning. Aristotle even states that metaphor consists in the application of an "improper noun"- or more precisely of a noun that relates to the order of the "other" or the foreign (*allotrios*)- to another noun. For the Greek philosopher, metaphor's singular capacity to "carry around" (*epiphora*) meaning is at once deeply significant and, above all, *effective*.[243]

*

Classical rhetoric has always fostered a tendency to diminish this fundamental aspect of "otherness" or "foreignness" that metaphor introduces within language, even though it is precisely this aspect of metaphor which offers the greatest possibilities for thinking. Classical rhetoric indeed relegated metaphor within the category of "figures of speech" and turned it into a decorative and embellishing ornament. European Rhetoric approached metaphor solely from the perspective of "resemblance" and thus conceiving of it only under the legitimizing perspectives of "conformity" and "analogy," it folded the "foreignness" of metaphor back into the order of the Same.

Classical European thought, thinking as it did within the terms of "Sameness" and "Identity" (the very terms of ontology), did not recognize the introduction- or even better, the intrusion of the Other within the Same- that metaphor produces. In other words, European Classicism disregarded the *labor of the Other* that profiles itself with the usage of metaphor; it betrayed metaphor's *unheard potential* as it neatly stowed it away in the convenient and (pre)convened category of "figures of speech." Although Classicism often praised metaphor as being the most "beautiful" and "laughing" of said "figures," it only evaluated and judged metaphors in relationship to their adequation and to their adapted or appropriate character. Classicism thus neglected the effective and *operative* displacement or relocation that the *poetic usage* of metaphor (literally) *produces*.

Perhaps our tendency to so often gloss over the power of metaphor is itself the product of this historic disregard for metaphor? Do we not expect so little out of metaphor because we tend to disregard the power of its *waysidedness*? Is it not this *disturbance* that metaphors bring about in the order and confines of language that at once troubles and *enlivens* us? Do we not avoid and shun metaphor because it lets the "other" or the foreign crawl, by way of effraction, into the (pre)determinations of language?

*

Classical European thought aligns metaphor with comparison, as if the former was only a shortened and more elliptical version of the latter. And yet, isn't there an *incommensurable hiatus* that subsists when one states: "This man is strong like a lion" as opposed to "This man is a lion"? It would be uncouth to avoid the meticulous inspection of the distance that separates these two "figures of speech." In a comparison, the two terms both conserve their proper and integral signification- "man" remains "man" and the "lion" remains a "lion"- both terms preserve their very "being" or their identity; no semantic incompatibility is perceived, the contextual isotopy is maintained. Metaphor, on the other hand, "transports" the meaning of one term into the other, without transition, and in such an abrupt fashion that there is indeed a *rupture* of coherence: one term is *cracked open* by the irruption of the other, its identity is rattled and shaken- *metaphor does not integrate the other.* Whereas comparison assimilates the other and neutralizes its alterity, metaphor preserves the other as other and maintains its foreignness; that is why metaphor is "alive" as the French philosopher Paul Ricoeur once wrote,[244] it works against the *sprawling* of meaning and instead condensates it.

b. Language as metaphor: the "real" and the enigmatic "thing in and of itself."

Is the essence of language itself not metaphorical? Is metaphor not so much more than just a "figure of speech" and instead what makes language itself *possible*? Nietzsche certainly had this intuition even though he viewed this metaphoric nature of language as a symptom of facticity. If transposition is indeed the initial function of language, then such a transposition would in fact bar our access to truth: beginning with the initial "nervous excitation" that marks our encounter with the "real" (that enigmatic X) and that transfers/ transforms "it" into an image, a sound, a representation, there is only a continuous process of *metaphorization* according to the German philosopher. For Nietzsche, the process of metaphorization further estranges us from a primordial and original form of knowledge that could grant "us" access to the "things themselves." Humans nonetheless hide this sedimented trajectory -from one order into another- from themselves: "we" naively believe- and thus gregariously lie to ourselves- about our capacity to touch, by way of speech, what would be a primal and unequivocal form of "truth."

240

Language does not say the truth (on an ontological level) because it always transports and transposes us into an "Other." For Nietzsche, truth is merely the outcome (the disguise) of a process of metaphorization that eludes us; "Representation" with words (*Vorstellung*) is just the result of a continuous "displacement" that never ceases to "dissimulate" the "in and of itself" of things. Nietzsche essentially tells us the following: we think we can know things "in and of themselves" when, in fact, we only possess metaphors for these things.[245]

*

In order to no longer think of metaphor as a deviation or as lie, as Nietzsche did, and to instead envision it as a *resource*, it is necessary to examine inside out this *"in and of itself"* of metaphor that he alludes to. Doing so will allow us to unblock metaphor's potential and uncover its "un-heard."

*

In other words, we must examine the ways in which the *in and of itself* of the unheard and of metaphor designate two sides of the same coin: the flipping of one side of the coin to the other represents the shift of the Classical age into Modernity. The consummation of this shift from Classicism into Modernity establishes the effective substitution of metaphysics and of its ontological language (presaged by Kant and brought to its apex by Nietzsche) with a form of *poetic language* (Rimbaud, Mallarmé). The treason of the classical and ontological "in and of itself" that results from language's forced process of *metaphorization* as it is denounced by Nietzsche, is, also, that very process which makes metaphor itself *the privileged means of access to the unheard*. Understood in this manner, the unheard can now, as a concept, substitute itself to the ontological understanding of the thing "in and of itself."

*

Metaphor's capacity to transport us into the other is indeed an ambivalent function that can be twisted and turned. As Kant and Nietzsche critically highlighted, metaphor's *transporting-function* can be assimilatory; it can all too easily accommodate the unknown of the "in and of itself" within the framework of our subjective – or anthropomorphic- "representations" (*Vorstellungen*), thus leading us to the inevitable loss of this "in and of itself." And yet, the transporting-function of metaphor can also be *dis-assimilatory*; when metaphors wander *on the wayside* of the Same and of Sameness, they *reveal* an "other" -an *alterity*- that *rattles* the mute identity of "Sameness."

c. Covering vs. un-covering or the "transportive" functions of metaphor.

It is necessary to thread even more precisely this fine line which separates the two sides of metaphor: the side which *covers up* the "(not) in and of itself" of "being" and the side which *un-covers* and thus *reveals* the unheard. More specifically, it is necessary to examine the distance which separates the verb "to reveal" from the verb "to unveil." The extreme proximity of these two verbs can lead to confusion, both are indeed related to the Latin "*velum*" which means "veil," and yet it is essential to dispel their illusory synonymy.

*

To *unveil* is to remove the veil that hides an unknown which lies behind it- unveiling is the fantasized gesture of metaphysics.

To *reveal,* on the other hand, consists in bringing to light what is already present: revealing consists in bringing to light that presence which does not appear because of being's own capacity to cover itself up as it sprawls, stalls, and gets bogged down in its adequation with itself and as it ultimately *un-appears* before our own eyes. "Mystery" can therefore be unveiled, but the unheard is *revealed.*

*

The vocation of metaphor is thus to bring forth the *revealing-uncovering* of the unheard: metaphor's capacity to reveal stems from the fact that it is- such is the strength of its paradox- a *mediation of the immediate*. Direct description, unfolding as it does within its own adequation, remains in a relationship of reference that consists in identifying, labeling and categorizing: it only says the *sprawl* of being. Alternatively, comparison is a mediation that admits to being a mediation, it is pegged and held by its "like…" or its "as ifs," and thus remains a parallel, refined, and yet external, representation of the world. Because metaphor instead *transports* directly into an "other," it possesses the ability to make the here and now emerge in its *soaring capacity*. Metaphor thus revealing intensity and newness before they become normalized, abstracted, convened upon, and relegated into the "well-known" realm of experience.

In a direct description, there is no "other" and sameness prevails. In a comparison, the other is assimilated to the same. In a metaphor, the other is transported into the same; and yet, it also preserves its "otherness." Instead of regulating, accommodating, and deactivating otherness or alterity, as is the case in a comparison which maintains its two elements in a *relationship* with each other, metaphor *opens up* a distance with sameness *within* the order of the same. It *produces* an *encounter* that is felt like a shock and an event.

*

Metaphor thus liberates this *unheard encounter* with otherness or alterity from the reified "in and of itself" that description brings forth with its *covering up*. Because metaphor maintains the other as other, in its tension as an "other," refusing to assimilate otherness into the order of sameness, it breaks into the order of the same and thus *cracks open* its sterile identity. Metaphor *overflows* the sameness of experience getting bogged down in its obviousness and repetition; as it opens itself up to a *yet-to-be-heard*, metaphor reveals an Other or an alterity that exists both wholly *within* and yet entirely *outside* the parameters of experience.

d. Shitao's metaphor(s) or when (the) mountain(s) inhabit(s) (the) sea(s).

The proper function of metaphor is therefore to *transport* into an "other," to overflow the essence of the metaphorized "thing in and of itself," and to undo its stated determination as an identifiable "being." This functional and "alterative" property of metaphor can be more easily, and thus more radically, thought of as one ventures outside of the confines of the Western categories of Being, essence, and determination; that is to say, *on the wayside* of the language of ontology.

*

The 17th-18th century painter and Buddhist monk Shitao offers us a point of entry into this "alterative" understanding of metaphor when he tells the aspiring painter to: "paint the waves of the sea *by way* of the mountains of the earth" and "paint the mountains of the earth *by way* of the waves of the sea."[246] The wandering poet-artist justifies this apparently strange suggestion by affirming that doing so allows "the mountain itself to thus inhabit the sea" (亦山之自居于海); all the while making "the sea itself capable of inhabiting the mountain" (海能自居于山). "The mountain and the sea," indeed, "inhabit each other in this way" when one paints the *unheard* that lies both *within and outside* them. "Attaining this [inhabitation effect] concerning the sea, and yet losing it concerning the mountain; or attaining this effect concerning the mountain and losing it concerning the sea, such is the *receiving-acceptance* (受) of a narrow-minded man." "In my own *receiving-acceptance*" (我之受也), Shitao proudly tells us, "The mountain indeed instantly goes towards and up against the sea; the sea indeed instantly goes towards and up against the mountains (山即海也, 海即山也). In the conclusion of this passage of his treatises, he elliptically states: "it is on a mountain(s)-sea(s) mode that I know [the world] (山海而知)." On a "mountain(s)-sea(s) mode" implies that the poet-painter not only perceives the mountain as a mountain, in terms of its ascribed identity; indeed, he also perceives it "like the sea," or better yet *through* the sea. In doing so, he opens up the mountain to the *unheard* within the mountain, *by way* of the sea.

*

Following the logic of Shitao's metaphorizing language on such a literal level facilitates the excavation of a discrete and yet crucial teaching that imperceptibly underscores the decisions we make in our daily lives. The term *shou* (受) translated here as "receiving-acceptance" evokes both the idea of receiving and withstanding, it suggests both receiving a gift and enduring hardships. Shitao thus crucially points out that his metaphorical "mountain(s)-sea(s) mode of knowing" allows him to both "receive" the gifts and good tidings of life and "accept" its griefs and losses. His metaphorizing approach to speaking, writing, and painting, *transports* mountains and seas *into* and yet also *out of* each other; it *nurtures* and *nourishes* a capacity to live *on the wayside* of convention and habit. Shitao's art demonstrates the singular, ethical, and *existential* force of a "life truly lived," one that has wholly invested itself in metaphorical productions. Metaphors indeed give us the capacity to *stand outside* the geographical and historical determinations that have conditioned and alienated human life throughout Time and Space.

*

Could metaphor become, within language itself, the trace of an *ethical vocation* that does not dissociate itself from the world and instead, from within the inside of the world, unfences the self as it bogs itself down in the sterility of its identity and locks itself up within its own *in and of itself*? Is metaphor not what opens us up to an "other" and lets us be overflowed by its otherness, this otherness of an Other which does not lie in a "beyond this world" but instead in the immediacy of "our" world? Is metaphor not the *gateless point of entry* into a "life truly lived," a life which *resists* being bogged down and which instead attunes to living's potentially infinite *soaring-capacity*?

CHAPTER IX
Truly living or "life truly lived"

1/ Living the "true life" or truly living: a philosophical conundrum.

Living the "true life," "life truly lived," or *truly living*-is such a theme not the supreme promise of the Western philosophical tradition, its ultimate goal?

*

Beginning with Plato, the question of the "true life" (*alethès bios*) emerges as one of the fundamental preoccupations of philosophy. In the influential *Theaetetus* dialogue, Socrates establishes a distinction between those who are attracted to philosophy and those who dismiss it; he draws a firm line that separates those who gravitate towards truth and those who fall prey to fallacy.[247] For the Greek philosopher, seekers of truth can produce a form of "harmonious speech" that aptly praises "the true life of gods and blessed men." In doing so, the seekers of truth elevate their lives to a status of truthfulness that reflects the inherent perfection of the divine. Conversely, those who dismiss philosophy and the pursuit of truth are condemned to be drawn to the "utmost wretchedness" of the godless, blinded as they are by their "utmost foolishness." Socrates' radical bipartition of life into "true" and "fake," philosophical and non-philosophical, has the merit of being clear: the question of the "true life" is the philosophical question *par excellence*.

*a. "The true life is absent" or "life does not live:" two rema-
nences of an old tune.*

Although Socrates affirms that his distinction between the philosophical and non-philosophical life constitutes a digression, the theme
of the "true life" persisted well into 19th and 20th century philosophy:
it became a genuine leitmotiv of the Western intellectual landscape,
even in its most *negative* formulations.

*

Arthur Rimbaud's sentence *"la vraie vie est absente"* or "the
true life is absent" inverts the Platonist assumption that links together
truth and presence.[248] Rimbaud's sibylline formula suggests that the
only "truth" that can be found in life lies not in presence, as Socrates
and Plato would have desired, but rather in *absence*.

*

For Rimbaud, the "true life" thus can never be found, it only exists as an evanescent mirage that reveals itself as it *passes by*. While
Socrates had dreamed that the "true life" could represent the essence
of meaningful living and thus embody a pure presence capable of reflecting the pristine excellence of the divine, Rimbaud's poetic characterization of the "true life" as a pure absence reflects the impossible, and yet endlessly *real* melancholy of a conception of truth bound
to *ephemerality*. Rimbaud's lapidary aphorism suggests that the only
"truth" to be found in living is its inherent impermanence. If "the true
life is absent" as Rimbaud suggests, then we are only living insofar as
we are making ourselves absent, as we *pass on* from life into death.

*

Written during his forced exile in the United States during
WWII, Theodor Adorno's *Minima Moralia* picked up on Rimbaud's
twist on the Socratic theme of "the true life." Adorno indeed inscribes
himself both in the continuity of Rimbaud's disillusioned poetics and

of Socrates' philosophical project. He opens his text with the following liminary inscription borrowed from the Austrian writer Ferdinand Kürnberger: "*Das Leben lebt nicht*" or "life does not live." Later on, in the eighteenth aphorism entitled *Refuge for the Homeless*, Adorno concludes with the following sentence: "*Es gibt kein richtiges Leben im falsches*" or "There is no right life in a false one."[249]

On the one hand, Adorno's liminary inscription stays true to Rimbaud's radical assessment regarding the "true life:" revealed only through absence and passing, the "true life" *does not live*. On the other hand, the second sentence fully reinstates the value of the Socratic ideal of a "true life" distinguished from a "false life." From Socrates and Plato to Rimbaud and Adorno, from the 4th century BCE to the second half of the 20th century, the theme of the "true life" thus seems to simultaneously represent the apex of philosophical reflection and its utmost limitation. It is at once the thread that traverses the entirety of the Western thought and the *rut* that brings it to a standstill.

Re-thinking the possibilities contained within the Western notion of the "true life" thus appears to be a privileged avenue to rethink the role of philosophy within the globalized context of the 21st century. If *truly living* and "life truly lived" have the potential to become polemical concepts, a set of *fighting tools* fit to address urgent political issues like socio-economic inequality, authoritarianism, and climate change, then it is necessary to question the assumptions that govern the concepts of "truth" and "living."

b. Neither humanist nor anti-humanist, neither knowledge nor wisdom.

A renewed philosophical understanding of *truly living* and of "life truly lived" cannot be yet another invocation of "humanist values" predicated upon a representation of universal Human Nature. Such an invocation would merely reinstate paradigmatic categories of Western thought like "truth," "being" and "human nature;" as if the thorough deconstruction of these categories had not already been acted upon in the 1960s and 1970s by the likes of Foucault, Derrida, and Deleuze.

*

Finding a decentered, operative, and intercultural understanding of living requires a re-examination of one of Western philosophy's most central premises: the *differing* equivalence of knowledge (*episteme*) and wisdom (*sophia*) first outlined by Socrates in the *Theaetetus*:

—— Socrates:

And so, the wise are wise by way of wisdom (*sophia*).

—— Theaetetus:

Yes.

—— Socrates:

And does this differ (*diapherei*) at all from knowledge (*episteme*)?

—— Theaetetus:

Does what differ?

—— Socrates:

Wisdom. Or does the knowledge they possess not make them wise?

—— Theaetetus:

Of course, it does.

—— Socrates:

Then wisdom and knowledge are identical (*tauton*), aren't they?

—— Theaetetus:

They are indeed.

—— Socrates:

Well, I must now say that I am at an impasse (*aporo*) because I cannot sufficiently grasp (*labein*) through my own efforts or encounter (*tugchanei*) at any given time for myself what knowledge really is.[250]

The importance of this passage cannot be understated. It represents a critical junction in the history of Western thought, a point where "knowledge" (*episteme*) and "wisdom" (*sophia*) were rendered *equal and yet differing* under the auspice of a single verb: being (*to on*). Although Socrates readily argues that *episteme* and *sophia* are "identical" (*tauton*), he admits that he is at an "impasse" (*aporo*) because he cannot "grasp" (*labein*) or "encounter" (*tugchanei*) the "being" (*to on*) of knowledge. Even though he can encounter wise men who possess wisdom, and thus knowledge, it is in fact *impossible* for him to seize the essence, or the "being," of knowledge: he *cannot know* what knowledge truly "is."

*

Any knowledge of being moving forward would therefore not be akin to being *as such* but rather to a *representation* of being; there could be no knowledge or truth as such, but rather only representations of knowledge and truth. A continuous thread in Greek thought runs from Parmenides to Plato and all the way down to Aristotle: truth and knowledge correspond to *non-contradictory* representations of being. In the philosophical tradition inherited from the Greeks, the generality of the concept subsumes the contradictory singularities of experience under a unique, non-contradictory, and therefore logically "true" representation. The general concept of "being" thus subsumes all the singular instances of "being" (i.e all "beings") that compose it, however contradictory these various instances may be. The conceptual, and thus general, understanding of "being" therefore remains free of the individual determinations that constitute the singular and contradictory instances of "beings."

*

In Western philosophy's regime of truth, representation, and non-contradiction, the concept of *living* is of little interest. The ambiguous and inherent *contradictions* that its concept supposes are obvious: the most obvious one being that it is impossible, on a purely onto-logical level, to distinguish living from dying. Living and dying

251

"are," *de facto*, part of the same process.

As a concept, living expresses nothing more and nothing less than a *pure contradiction*. It is therefore not surprising that Western philosophy would wholly disregard it for nearly two millennia. If living can only be understood by way of contradiction, then what use would it hold in the context of a philosophical quest that seeks to determine a univocal and non-contradictory concept of the "true life"? Following Aristotle, the concepts of being and representation thus appeared to be surer pathways to establish a non-contradictory standard of truth. They served as a scientific (or more literally, *epistemic*) index capable of measuring the (possible) conformity of the "true life" with the (impossible) truth of knowledge.

*

The concept of *living* was thus largely left aside by Western philosophy and was instead recuperated by Christianity, only to be neutralized by God's Supreme and indivisible Oneness: "I am the Path (*hodos*), the Truth (*aletheia*) and the Life (*zoe*)" (John 14:16). It is interesting to note that the term commonly translated as "life" in the Gospel of John is not the term *"bios"* used by Plato in the *Theaetetus* to describe the "true life of the gods and of blessed men." While *bios* specifically suggests the lifespan of a human, the far more general term *zoe* designates life in its totality. The philosophical concept of the "true life" (*alethes bios*) and its explicit focus on human singularity were thus subsumed under the all-encompassing universal "truth" (*aletheia*) of the Christian religion. All life (*zoe*) was to be bound to the only possible source of "truth": God. *Living* thus became a mere consequence of God's Truth in the Christian paradigm. Thinking of a form of "life truly lived" that *differs* from Christ's universalizing "Path" (*hodos*) is senseless; John 14:6 states once more: "No one comes unto the Father except through me." What relevance could the philosophical question of living hold when the Life of Christ represented the only truth worth knowing, the single roadway and sole access point that led to the God responsible for the Creation of all Life?

2/ "Life truly lived," mediation, and meditation: a literary and intercultural perspective.

If the philosophical theme of the "true life" and the problematic definition of *living* that it supposes have been all too obscured by religious or scientific discourse, then how can the *ethical* stakes carried along by these tired refrains be approached once more with a "beginner's mind"[251]? How can we find an understanding of living that simultaneously bears the *general strength* of philosophical discourse and also displays a minute attention to *contradiction*?

How can we take into account the *differing* representations of living that human cultures have sowed and dispersed throughout Time and Space? Is it possible to simultaneously *acknowledge* the singularity of cultural contexts and of their particular representations of living, all the while also *exceeding* these very representations? Aren't *all* cultures capable of *tapping into* the *infinite resources* of living? At the dawn of the 21st century, a genuine *philosophy of living* must *construct* an intercultural, and above all, *non-ontological* concept of living. If we are to tackle the timeless question of "life truly lived," then doing so remains an *ethical necessity*.

a. "The only life that is truly lived is literature" or the necessity of vision as mediation.

Literary writing, and the modern novel in particular, offers a concrete point of entry into the thorny question of "life truly lived." Marcel Proust was indeed one of the first to explicitly approach the philosophical theme of the "true life" through the lens of autobiographical fiction. In the last tome of his magnum opus *In Search of Lost Time*, Proust's narrator writes:

> "The true life, life finally uncovered and (en)lightened, therefore the only life that is truly lived, is *literature*. This life, in a sense, inhabits in all instants all men, as well as artists. Yet they do not see it, because they do not seek to (en)lighten life. Their past is thus filled with countless *clichés* -or "negatives"- that remain useless because their intelligence has not "developed" them. [...]; for style in the case of the writer and color in the case of the painter are not a matter of

technique but rather of *vision*. Style is the *revelation* of what would otherwise be *impossible* through direct and conscious means, a revelation of the qualitative *difference* of the manner in which the world *appears* to us; a *difference* that, were it not for art, would remain each and one's own eternal secret. Only through art can we *exit* ourselves, it allows us to know what another sees in this universe that is not our own and whose *landscapes* would have remained as unbeknownst to us as the ones that might exist on the moon. Thanks to art, instead of seeing one world, our own, we see it multiply itself; there are as many worlds at our disposal as there are original artists, they are more *different* from one another than the ones that roll in the infinite and, many centuries after the fire from which they emanated becomes extinct, their special ray still beams towards us, whether they are called Rembrandt or Vermeer.[252]"

Proust's narrator offers precious insights for our questions on "life truly lived" when he highlights the *correlative relationship* that binds the "uncovered and (en)lightened" *experiential truth* of life to the *metaphoric constructs* of "literature," "style," "color," and "art." The narrator's indication that "literature" is equivalent to "the only life that is truly lived" showcases both the artificiality of what is constructed as truthful *and* the necessary "intelligence" required to *transform* inert things into "uncovered and (en)lightened" *living*. In the same way that a process of "intelligence" transforms unused photographic negatives, *"clichés,"* into "developed" images, in the same way that "style" transforms writing into literature, experiential processes of (en)*lightening* and (en)*livening* transform *living*. These processes are not a matter of reproducible "technique," they are instead the *existential markers* of an *always singular* "vision."

*

Proust clearly states that the processes of (en)*lightening* and (en)*livening* that transform non-life into life aren't just the apanage of artists and writers, they instead "inhabit in all instants all men." And yet, it is impossible for all men, including artists and writers, to perceive the deferring, differing, and revealing mechanisms of "qualitative difference" as they "appear" to *all* of "us" without a *mediation*. The singularity of a writer's style and of a painter's palette are the result of both "direct and conscious" and, more importantly, "unbeknownst" or unconscious, processes of *un-covering*. These processes *reveal* the *mediating activity* of his singular "vision." Similarly, the singular "vision" of any non-artist un-covers and, above all, *mediates* his concrete experience of *living*.

"Vision" needs to be understood here in its broadest sense as a reference to an individual's unique capacity to *interpenetrate* the fabric of the world *via* the *mediating activity* of his sensory perception. The mediating activity of the writer's style, of the painter's palette, or of lay person's senses leads to the "revelation" of "landscapes" that would otherwise remain "unbeknownst" to all of us that are not him. Were it not for *mediation*, these *living landscapes* would "remain each and one's own eternal secret."

b. The Gateless Barrier of Living Zen, or the Way of meditation: introducing the Wu Men Guan.

Thousands of miles away and approximately 700 years before Proust's lifetime, a wandering *Ch'an* Buddhist monk living in Song-dynasty China named Wumen Huikai offered another precious literary evocation of "life truly lived"; it does not seem like a stretch to say that its "special ray still beams upon us." Indeed, Wumen's literary writing captures the multi-faceted, ambiguous, and above all, *mediated* processes of *(en)lightening* and *(en)livening* capable of leading *all* of us to "the only life that is truly lived."

While *Ch'an* or Zen Buddhism is of course famous for being the "way of meditation" (the character *Ch'an* 禪 is indeed most often translated as "meditation"), it is perhaps less common to think of *Ch'an* as a literary "way of mediation." And yet, literary writing and its *mediating activity* play an important role in the *Ch'an* tradition of the *gong'an* or *koan*. The *gong'an* tradition revolves around short and enigmatic anecdotes, dialogues, and statements designed to pull the practitioner into a deep state of interrogation. The two characters for *gong'an* (公案) signify "public case"; initially, the tradition referred to a certain kind of judicial, almost clinical, type of investigative "case study." *Gong'an* were assembled in a set of "collections" whose core function was to assemble the "public" deeds and sayings of the old Masters so that aspiring *Ch'an* practitioners could study them.

During the Song dynasty period, the *gong'an* tradition became more explicitly influenced by Classical Chinese literary culture and it became common practice to incorporate poetic verse into the *gong'an* collections.[253] Wumen Huikai was undoubtedly a master of this nascent poetic tradition that consciously incorporated the stylistic codes of Classical Chinese literature in an effort to reach out to wider audience amongst the members of the literate classes: he wrote many poems in the traditional 4-character style of verse found in the most canonical text of the Classical Chinese literary tradition, the ancient *Classic of Poems* or *Shijing*.[254]

*

In the opening verse of his *gong'an* collection entitled *Gateless Barrier* (無門關), *Wumen Guan* in Chinese or *mumonkan* in Japanese, Wumen writes:

大道無門　　On the great gateless Way,

千差有路　　there a thousand differing roads.

透得此關　　As you penetrate and reach this passage-point,

乾坤獨步　　you initiate (heaven) and receive (earth), walking alone.

As usual in the *Ch'an* tradition, the compact, allusive, and evasive formulations of the Masters require thorough commentary and explanation! The poetic forms of the *gong'an* are purposely opaque and often requires sub-texts meant to supplement the original verse. Our "gateway supplement" into the opening verses of the *Wumen Guan* will be the American Zen teacher Robert Aitken's less literal translation of the stanza:

256

The Great Way has no gate;

there are a thousand different paths;

once you pass through the barrier,

you walk the universe alone.

In an effort to further explicate the dense passage and detail its significance, Aitken also offers a poem attributed to Wumen. Although this poem is widely known and distributed, there is good reason to believe that it is apocryphal since it is not included in the original text of the *Wumen Guan*. The poem is only referred to in a 1957 Japanese edition of this text, so Aitken was likely exposed to it during his extensive study with Masters of Japanese Zen. Here is the original Japanese verse of the apocryphal poem accompanied by Aitken's translation:

青天白日一声の雷。

Seitenhakujitsu issei no kaminari

A thunderclap under the clear blue sky;

大地の群れ眼豁開す。

Daichi no mure manako kakkai su

All beings on earth open their eyes;

万象森羅斉しく稽首す。

Shinraban shô hito shiku keishu su

Everything under heaven bows together;

須弥誖跳して三台を舞う

Shumi hôtto shite san-dai o mau

Mount Sumeru leaps up and dances.

Both the sibylline opening verse of the *Wumen Guan* and the apocryphal poem that accompanies it perfectly display the ways in which dense poetic formulations can *capture* the singular *moments* where *living* becomes *(en)lightened* and *(en)livened*. These "differing (差)," and "thousandfold" (千) moments are just as startling and "penetrating" (透) as the booming "tone of thunder" (声の雷) ripping through a "clear blue sky" (青天白日). Such moments *un-cover* heaven's "initiating-capacity" (乾) and earth's "receiving-capacity" (坤), they "open" (開)" the "emptied eyes" (眼豁) of all the "forests" (森) and of their "nets" (羅) of spider-webs who simultaneously "bow their necks" (稽首) in a "coordinated" (齐) motion as the sound of thunder *resonates*. The *irruption* of thunder into the world un-covers the singular "leaping" (跳) and "dancing" (舞) motions of the three "towering" (台) plateaus of the Sacred Mountain.

*

Although the processes of *(en)lightening* and *(en)livening* can be experienced and transcribed in words, they do not represent a *goal* or a *destination*. Instead, (en)lightening and (en)livening represent instead a "passage-point (關)" that, once crossed, reveals only the "solitary" (獨) pace of the wanderer's "step" (步). The form of *living* that *Ch'an* meditation and the literary *mediation* of the *gong'an* un-cover thus isn't a generic tradition or a reproducible formula ascribable to a single Master. *Ch'an* or Zen cannot be reduced to a single technique or a single "art," however (en)lightened and (en)livened that "art" may be.

The *Ch'an* or Zen *mediation-meditation* -or *medi(t)ation*- that uncovers living thus belongs to *no one,* and yet, to *all*. It is both Zen and not-Zen, or, in more Western terms, "art" and "not-art." The *singular* poetic images of a "great gateless Way" (大道無門), and of the shuffling feet of a lone wayward wanderer *attuned* to the *unheard reverberations* that resonate alongside the "tone" (声) of a "single" (一) roaring thunderclap allows *all of us,* regardless of our cultural baggage, to "penetrate" (透) the singular *fabric* of a world and *vision* belonging to an individual who lived over 700 years ago. If we elliptically circle back to Proust's eloquent formulation, we can assuredly assert the following: these poetic images of *mediation-meditation* give us the means to "know what another sees in this universe that is not identical with our own universe, a universe whose landscapes would have remained for us as unbeknownst as the ones that might exist on the moon."

c. From language to language(s): translation or the generative transformations of un-covering.

Although juxtaposing Proust and the *Gateless Barrier* might at a first glance seem odd and contrived, both texts showcase a set of *intercultural depictions* that highlight a form of *living* that is both *(en)livened* and *(en)lightened* by two specific kinds of *mediation-meditation*: reading and writing. Proust's novel and Wumen's poetry both *capture* a *commitment to living* that is at once timeless and placeless: both texts reach *beneath and beyond* the singularities of the *human language(s)* that they were written in.

*

The geo-historic *translation* process that is required to *un-cover* the *literal potential* held within these texts is never the product of a uniform algorithmic formula that would somehow restitute the "true" or accurate meaning of any given language or sentence. Instead, philosophical translation is a process of *generative transformation* that un-covers a plurality of meanings that might have otherwise remained *unheard*. Intercultural philosophy therefore does not offer a uniform protocol for *truly living* or "life truly lived," nor does it propose a universal mediation or meditation designed to address the global problem of *alienation*. And yet, an intercultural *philosophy of living* can *(en)lighten* and *(en)liven* the *fabric of thought* through the *translation* and *production* of *concepts*.

The translation and production of philosophical concepts cannot be tied to an ascribable form of "cultural" identity, even though all concepts of course have their own singular cultural *itineraries*. Concepts travel across borders and circulate *in between* cultures, translation is what makes this traveling and circulation *possible*. When we engage with concepts through translation, we realize that the various notions and terms we use as concepts, that is to say the words we use to help us *abstract ourselves* from the world and from its History, are in fact heavily dependent upon a virtually infinite plurality of spoken, written, and performed *languages*. The concepts that translation *produces* are not fixed entities endowed with a permanent meaning. Rather, they are *living concepts* whose primary function is *mediation-meditation*. The mediation-meditation of concepts can help us both "penetrate" the "passage-points" of the world and its cultures as Wumen writes, while also allowing us to "*exit* ourselves" and the world, as Proust says. The concepts of intercultural philosophy thus allow us to both *see through* and *exit* the quotidian alienation of the world.

*

Far from being a form of "spiritual bypassing,"[255] the intercultural and philosophical approach to the question of living recuses any facile marketization of so-called "spirituality." Unfortunately, the marketization of spiritual traditions has conquered bookstores throughout the world and lured countless sincere readers and seekers into a tepid New Age *mélange* of "East" and "West." This unfortunate cross-cultural blend confuses more than clarifies the already opaque and ambiguous question of *living* and of "life truly lived." While the philosophical style of writing displayed in this book may lack the immediacy of mass-market books referring to Zen like Eckhart Tolle's *The Power of Now,* it is important to point out that this kind of "easy-reading" has egregiously capitalized on millenary forms of *mediation-meditation* only to render them into uniform and lifeless *commodities* that perpetuate the very alienation they seek to remedy. More than ever, one must challenge the all-too prevalent commodification of spirituality and thought that dominates the marketplace of (un)happiness and its Instagram-ready laundry-lists of injunctive "to-dos." Philosophy can expose the astounding pretentiousness of these lists and injunctions which offer illusory "one-size-fits-all" solutions to life's most insoluble existential difficulties: pain, longing, desire, loss, and (self)realization. In doing so, philosophical reflection can enrich the *experiential terrain* of *living* and of "life truly lived" through the *production* of *living concepts*.

3/ Truly living vs. fake living or the lasting (de)merits of a primordial philosophical cleavage.

The philosophical problem of the "life truly lived" and the conceptual exploration of the terrain of living that results from it are anchored in subjective questions that are as much existential as they are *experiential*: is the life I'm living somehow *fake*? Am I *truly living*? Am I not *missing out* on "the true life of gods and blessed men" praised by Socrates? Am I just wasting away in a virtualized *semblance* of life? Am I becoming *covered up* by the "thickness and impermeability of conventional knowledge" which occults "the reality that we might very well die without having ever known, and which is quite simply our life," if we are to quote Proust's narrator once more?

What these existential questions reveal is that *truly living* and "life truly lived" are neither given nor equivalent to a static and identifiable representation of the "true" or "ideal" life. *Truly living* thus isn't a metaphysical quest for another world or another reality that somehow bears more truth than the one we live in; it is not a search for some absolute, ontological definition of what "living" truly "is."

a. Emerging and soaring vs. stalling and dwindling.

The undeniable *emergence* of a process of *(en)lightening* and *(en)livening* that suddenly cracks us open and *un-covers* an *un-heard* dimension of living, as described by Proust's narrator or by the *Wumen Guan* is as certain as the process wherein life becomes depleted, covered up, and shriveled. The motion of living thus appears to be cleaved in two: *bogged down* on the one hand in a *stalling* that leads to the *shunning* of living and to the *dwindling* of life; open on the other hand to a *soaring* which *un-covers* the (en)lightening and (en)livening *unheard possibilities* of "life truly lived."

In this regard, the intercultural philosophy of living developed here reiterates the age-old Platonist or Buddhist theme that splits living into two cleaved *polarities*: *truly living* vs. *fake living*; weighted, dimmed and (dis)illusioned living (*samsara*) vs. (en)lightened and emancipated living (*nirvana*). This cleavage of living into two distinct forms raises the question of the *ethical choice* that underscores the shift from *fake living* into *truly living*. This choice is not a moral judgment that distinguishes a "good life" from a "bad life," nor is it a valuation that distinguishes "successful living" from "failed living." The ethical choice that *truly living* requires thus isn't a mere "lifestyle choice." If we are to follow Plato and the Buddhists, and thus posit that living is cleaved in two, then it becomes necessary to distinguish "ordinary living" from *waysided living*.

No life is "normal" and all life is singular. Everyone is led to wander *on the wayside* of the ordinary at some point or another. Wandering on the wayside leads us to a *tipping point* that *opens* our lives to *unheard possibilities* that are revealed to us in a *hiatus* whose irruption into our world is as undeniable as it is potentially distressing. The kind of bewildered wandering that uncovers the gaping hiatus of *existence* thus isn't a reiteration of the age-old philosophical theme of the "examined life." Instead, it designates a point of *opening-overflowing* that exceeds the constitutive frameworks of experience. The ethical choice of "life truly lived" thus represents a *leap* into the *un-covering of the un-heard*.

b. Retracting-living vs. expanding-living, detaching vs. (dis) engaging.

The active choice of *truly living* implies an *attention* to the two following dynamics of living: *retracting* and *expanding*. Whereas *retracting-living* falls into the normalcy, repetition, and alienation of busyness and its standardized tasks, *expanding-living* gains *perspec-*

tive through a process of *extraction* and *abstraction*. Extracting and abstracting enable the *construction* of a vantage point that exceeds the parameters of spectatorship. Whereas spectatorship implies an attitude of passive detachment, extracting and abstracting are the result of a series of *operations* that enact simultaneous processes of *(dis)engagement*. Philosophical concepts are the privileged tools for such operations of extraction, abstraction, and (dis)engagement: their measured and, above all, *reflective* usage in an intercultural context provides an *ethical underscoring* which colors the always singular and virtually infinite *fabrication* of "life truly lived;" *in between* and *across* cultural spheres of influence. Much like a film score accompanies the creation of emotions in cinema, conceptuality and abstraction provide a philosophical *accompaniment* to living: they offer a supportive assistance that is not necessary, but rather, *effective*.

*

Even though conceptual devices and abstractions support the ethical and artful fabrication of "life truly lived," they can also easily fall prey to an all-too-familiar preachy rhetoric of *conversion*. The religious and/or dogmatic rhetoric of conversion has always professed the metaphysical and/or moral superiority of a life that lies *beyond* this life. The experiential *overflowing* that *un-covers* the *unheard possibilities* of *life lived on the wayside* is distinct from the kind of metaphysical overturning championed by Nietzschean philosophers like Deleuze. Indeed, the Deleuzian overturning of metaphysics supposes an onto-logic of reversal: Being is substituted with Becoming, The One is substituted with the Multiple, the Identical is substituted with the Different, the True is substituted with the Fake.[256] *Truly living* and "life truly lived," on the other hand, suppose an *existential availability* that literally *stands outside* any onto-logical perspective; they are the *realization* of an *unheard presence* that is not onto-logical, but rather *dia-logical*.[257]

Neither here nor there, neither cultural nor universal, neither being nor not-being, forever *in between* places, cultures, and things, the intercultural *dia-logue* of "life truly lived" and of *truly living* can only be thought of as a paradoxical, Derridean *double-bind*.[258] The realization of "life truly lived" involves both *exiting* our world and further *penetrating* it: on the one hand, it implies being bound to the *incommensurability* of our unique, singular vision; on the other hand, it is bound to the active mediation-mediation of our vision which allows us to *share* our perspective with others. What this means is that *truly living* is not a matter of escapism: it is not a path of *avoidance* where abstraction and concepts become far-fetched justifications that enable a conversion to a "lifestyle" predicated upon a given or identifiable understanding of the world, let alone its supposed "beyond."

In this regard, Parmenides' assertion that the path of philosophy lies "outside the beaten path of men (*ap anthropon ektos tou patou estiv*)"[259] remains relevant if we do not overreach for a metaphysical interpretation. Wandering *on the wayside* of the "beaten path of men" supposes a capacity to distance oneself from the regime of human opinions, however (un)enlightened or (in)correct they may be. The tension that cleaves living into *truly living* and *fake living*, fake life and "life truly lived," does not require an ethical stance which assigns value to different "modes of being." Instead, it involves an ethical *leap* into a *situation* of *un-knowing* which favors an *opening* to aspects of *truly living* that would otherwise remain *un-heard*.

*

Truly living bears no common measure with a power of *judgment* capable of rendering a definitive epistemological verdict that leads to an unconditional understanding of "truth." A *philosophy of living* does not constitute an objective understanding of the "truest" conception of life, nor does it correspond to a subjective comprehension of what one thinks is "truthful." Such an objective and/or subjective preconception would cover up the *unheard* possibilities of "life truly lived" that elude both subjective and objective (pre)determination and representation. "Life truly lived" does not represent a form of living illuminated by an external source of truth, it does not result from an external *projection* that institutes a hierarchy where truth is deemed superior to life.

264

Truly living does not entail an aspirational quest predicated upon goodwill. "Life truly lived" is neither a perfect or idealized life founded upon Being, Truth, or God (metaphysics), nor is it a life predicated upon the forever elusive search of an unattainable external object like happiness or fulfillment (Aristotle's Ethics or Freud in *Civilization and its discontents*). It is not even Life intensified to dizzying peaks of self-affirmation (Nietzsche's *Zarathustra* and Deleuze and Guattari's "body-without-organs" in *A Thousand Plateaus*). Neither idealist nor romantic, neither spiritualist nor vitalist, the *philosophy of living* recuses any dramatic *overturning* of philosophical paradigms: idealism vs. materialism, spiritualism vs. organicism, desire as a structural lack vs. desire as an immanent production. It is not a confrontational approach to debate where defeating the adversary becomes the objective, but rather a *dissident style* that explores *the wayside(s)* of predetermined positions and axioms.

4/ Neither doctrine nor ideology: cutting through the fakeness of discourse, un-covering the liminal traces of mediated-meditated wounds.

a. The pitfalls of method and technique or Ju-zhi's Firm Finger.

"Life truly lived" washes over the secretions of "-isms," the moment of rupture that characterizes the shift from *fake living* into *truly living* cannot be ascribed to an ideology or to a canonized form of doctrine or teaching. There is no set "method" that outlines the steps needed to uncover *fake living* and bring about *truly living*. And yet, the points of rupture where the facticity of (fake) life is uncovered and where the hitherto *unheard possibilities* of "life truly lived" begin to emerge are all-too-subject to ideological and doctrinal recuperations. The millennial history of organized religions illustrates the calcification effect wherein the absolute singularity of a "life truly lived" (Moses, Buddha, Christ, Muhammad) is quickly subsumed by the ever-increasing powers of semblance, fake-life, and of their infinite discursive machinations of alienation, repression, and oppres-sion. *Ch'an* or Zen Buddhism is in this regard no different from any other religion or "-ism": its teachings have also become the object of dogmatic adherence and obedience throughout the ages.

Nonetheless, precisely because of their poetic and *visionary* in-clinations, textual elements of the *gong'an* tradition of *Ch'an* manage to *exist* or "stand outside" the alienating logic of dogma. If it is read outside the prism of traditional Buddhist interpretations, but instead through a philosophical and intercultural lens, the third *gong'an* of the *Wu-men Guan* – "Together-Callous' Firm Finger (俱胝堅指)"-can indeed be understood as such an example of the literary genre's *capacity* to in fact *resist* ideology and its dogmas. The text's sub-tle word play, grounded as it is in *evasive allusions,* wanders *on the wayside* of orthodoxy; it openly challenges the idea that "enlighten-ing-enlightenment," or more prosaically, "realization" (悟),[260] can be reduced to a single teaching, rule, or "meditation" (禪). The opaque economy of its poetic style resists both translation and interpretation, largely because it leverages to great effect Classical Chinese's lack of verbal tenses, declination, and punctuation.

Although there are many existing translations of this famous *gong'an,* it seems essential to *re-translate* and *re-literalize* the text in its entirety if we are to truly *engage* with it in a philosophical and intercultural perspective. Most translations of the text *cover up* the text's *poetic capacity* with pre-existing doctrinal and historical in-terpretations of Buddhism.[261] Rather than offering a translation that attempts to lodge the text's intentionally opaque features into a pre-existing cultural, historical, or metaphysical frame of reference, it will prove at once more difficult and more *useful* to pay the utmost attention to each specific character and associate it with a translitera-tion and translation that is as literal as possible. In doing so, we will attempt to *un-cover* the *unheard possibilities* that Wu-men's *gong'an* still contains, nearly 800 years after it was first published:

266

三

San

3

俱胝堅指

Ju-zhi jian zhi

Together-Callous' Firm Finger

俱胝和尚

Ju-zhi he-shang

Head-monk Together-Callous,

凡有詰問

Fan-you jie wen

interrogated and asked about Every-thing,

唯舉一指

Wei ju yi zhi

just raises one finger.

後有童子

Hou you tong-zi

Later, there is (a) Servant-Boy.

因外人問

Yin wai-ren jie

And so, a foreigner asks him:

和尚說何法要

He-shang shuo he fa yao

"What's the Head-monk's most important rule?"

童子亦豎指頭

Tong-zi yi shu zhi-tou

Servant-Boy also props up a finger-tip.

胝聞

Zhi wen

Callous hears,

遂以刃斷其指

Sui yi ren duan qi zhi

and subsequently severs that finger with a blade.

童子負痛號哭而去

Tong-zi fu tong hao ku er qu

Servant-Boy is burdened, saddened, branded, and tearful; and so, he leaves.

胝復召之

Zhi fu shao zhi

Callous repeatedly summons him,

童子迴首

Tong-zi hui shou

Servant-Boy's head turns,

胝卻豎起指

Zhi que shu qi zhi

Callous still props up an elevated finger,

童子忽然領悟

Tong-zi hu ran ling wu

Servant-Boy is suddenly-spontaneously led to enlighten-ing,

胝將順世

Zhi jiang shun shi

Callous transmits the obedience of the world.

謂眾曰

Wei zhong yue

He calls the crowd and says:

吾得天龍一指頭禪

Wu de Tian-long yi zhi-tou ch'an

"I obtained the one-finger-tip meditation from Heavenly
Dragon,

一生受用不盡

Yi sheng shou yong bu jin

one life cannot deplete its accepted usage."

言訖示滅

Yan qi zhi mie

Words of conclusion manifest annihilation.

無門曰

Wu-men yue

No-Gate says:

俱胝並童子悟處

Ju-zhi bing Tong-zi wu chu

Together-Callous and Servant-Boy both locate enlighten-
ing,

不在指頭上

Bu zai zhi-tou shang

it does not lie in the finger-tip above.

若向者裏見得

Ruo xiang zhe li jian de

If you see and obtain this from within,

天龍同俱胝並童子

Tian-long tong Ju-zhi bing Tong-zi

Heavenly-Dragon together with both All-Callous and Servant-Boy,

與自己一串穿卻

Yu zi-ji yi chuan chuan que

and you yourself, are still pierced by one thread.

頌曰

Song yue

The ode says*:*

俱胝鈍置老天龍

Ju-zhi dun zhi lao Tian-long

Together-Callous's bluntness establishes old Heaven-ly-Dragon.

利刃單提勘小童

Li ren chan di kan xiao tong

A blade's profit alone handholds and investigates little servants.

巨靈 擡手無多子

Ju ling tai shou wu duo zi

Enormous spirits raising hands do not have many children.

分破華山千萬重

Fen po Hua-shan qian wan zhong

Separated (and) broken, Mount Brilliant's gravity is ten-thousandfold (and) innumerable.

*

The characters of the *Wu-men Guan* continue to destabilize readers and translators centuries after they were first written down because their allusive, evasive, and evocative *interplay* exceeds the parameters of reflection and signification. What is so remarkable about the various translations of the *gong'an* is their more or less concerted attempt to *cover up* the texts' *un-heard senselessness* with pre-existing meaning, when, precisely, *there is none*. Whereas the literal translation of the four-character idiom (*yan qi zhi mie* 言訖示滅) that concludes the anecdote allusively evokes "words of conclusion" that "manifest annihilation," Aitken prefers "with this he entered into his eternal rest," while Ding-Hwa translates "after saying this, he entered Nirvana;" Shibayama, more soberly, renders it as "when he had finished saying this, he died."

The Japanese Zen master's translation and interpretation of the *gong'an*'s absurdity is at once the most economical and the most profound. Although Shibayama is of course commenting on this text from his own perspective as a Zen master, his remarks powerfully insist on the ambiguity of the story and on the *content-lessness* of the one-finger meditation: "Callous' finger and his young attendant's finger are the same finger. Still, there is a fundamental difference. While Callous' finger was Zen itself, the universe itself, the attendant's finger was just an imitation without the fact of his own experience. It was a *fake* with no life, and therefore should be cut off." Even though Shibayama's religious interpretation of the text maintains it in a doctrinal perspective where the "Zen of One Finger is the Truth pervading the whole universe,"[262] he nonetheless recognizes that the story exhibits a perplexing degree of *foolishness*: "Callous and Heavenly-Dragon are making fools of everybody. [...] to make the boy attain *satori* (悟) by cutting off his finger- how absurd! Even to hear it pollutes the ear."[263] What is key in Shibayama's interpretation is not so much that the story expresses the "Truth pervading the whole universe." Rather, it is that the "absurd" senselessness of the tale *cuts through* the *facticity* of dogmatic "imitation" and thus enables the *"satori"* or "realization" (悟) of "life truly lived." In other words, the distant echoes and reflections of *(non)sense* that emanate from the text *un-cover* the gaping cracks where language's impossible attempt at communicating oneness (一) simultaneously reveals and conceals itself. The anecdote, its exegesis, and its poetic accompaniment function like a blade that *cuts through* doctrinarian interpretations that attempt to dilute the uncanny force of the text and recover it under the single ideological umbrella of an "-ism," Buddhism first and foremost.

*

The combination of the three modes of discourse (narrative, exegetic, and poetic) exposes the fundamental *ambiguity* of "life truly lived": impossible without mediation-meditation's (endless) *un-covering-(en)lightening capacity,* and yet also impossibly mediated and meditated *by and through* language's (ceaseless) *re-covering-shunning capacity.* The juxtaposition of three distinct literary registers that characterizes the form of the *Wu-men Guan* destabilizes and fractures the univocal signifying potential of the texts: it depicts the inherent lines of cleavage and division that run through "life truly lived," as well as the ceaseless ideological recuperations that *truly living* elicits.

Much like Master Callous' bloody one-finger meditation cleaves and divides, the different and differing texts portray the *arising* of unheard questions and reflections. This arising marks a shift in perspective where the un-covering of *fake living* and of its illusory doctrines opens up a field of mediating and meditative *awareness* that wanders on *the wayside* of the conventions of discourse, facticity, and semblance. The awareness that these centuries-old semiotic forms draw into focus reflects and reverberates the dense and contradictory fabric of *truly living* and of "life truly lived": "separated (分)," "broken (破)," and "heavy (重);" and yet also "(up)lifted (擡)," "threaded (串)," "resplendent (華)" and "realized (悟)." Instead of providing ready-made answers to life's thousandfold existential questions about the nature of "All-Existence" (凡有) and the "realization" (悟) of "life truly lived," the *dissenting irony* of Wu-men's singular writing style *cuts through* the ages: it exposes the "blunted foolishness (鈍)" any reader or commentator's pretense to reduce the signification of the story to a single meditation, teaching, or saying.

*

At a first glance the *gong'an* can be interpreted as an apologetic and yet puzzling teachable moment that justifies the methodic usage of violence as a form of meditation. And yet, the slow *decanting* and *savoring* that its (re)reading and (re)translating requires uncovers a plurality of interweaving and interpenetrating lines of signification that force the reader and the translator to *encounter* the text on a level that is at once experiential, metaphorical, and *effective*. In other words, the text both mimics and deconstructs the *raising* and *slicing* gestures that it describes. Wumen's writing uses elaborate wordplay to dispel the falsely equivocal meanings of terms that refer to "(up)raising (舉)" and "(up)holding (提)" and "(up)lifting (擡)," a series of processes that are executed, assisted, and mediated by a "firm (堅)" usage of the "human hand (手)" and by the "tip (頭)" of its "fingers (指)." The interplay of allusive mimicry and evasive irony colors the *signifying effect* of the text so that its semiotic surface becomes opaque, reflective, and *resonant* like the cratered surfaces of Pierre Soulages' black and white paintings.[264]

The definitive signification of the *gong'an* can never be wholly un-covered: even though it will always remain unclear, it remains nonetheless "brilliant" (華) like a muddled pool of water or a towering mountain reflecting the sunlight. Was the little boy enlightened because the master's punishment showed him the stupidity of mimicry? Or on the contrary, was the young attendant enlightened because his screams and tears un-covered the master's own stupidity? Is it Heavenly Dragon's one-finger meditation that is idiotic or is it Callous' assertion that he never exhausted the usage of this meditation that is foolish and uncouth?

b. On the wound as inkling.

Even though no single answer to these questions can ever be found, (re)reading and (re)translating the *Wu-Men Guan* today continues to generate and *un-cover* a seemingly infinite plurality of singular reflections and echoes. As long as it is (re)read and (re)translated by wanderers open to the exploration of its *liminal margins,* the text enables the *reverberation* of dense, opaque, and yet reflective waves of intercultural and philosophical *resonance.* Such marginal waves of resonance lie *on the wayside* of ordinary language's *shunning-capacity,* they circumvent organized discourse's norms.

An intercultural and philosophical (re)reading and (re)translating of the *Wu-men Guan* does not *un-cover* a "true" meaning that could have been "lost in translation." Rather, it *reflects* and *echoes* a virtually endless series of *evanescent inklings*. These inklings point towards an *indicial* instance of rupture and severance that *cuts through* the facticity of semblance and *fake living*. The image of the bloodied *encounter* of the little boy crying his heart out and of the Master reaching out to him with his raised finger simultaneously evokes and manifests the primacy of a *memorialized wound*. The memorialization and memorization of indicial wounds point towards shunned and avoided *threshold-events* of *incommensurable* suffering and helplessness. Wound-events require mediation and meditation to be covered up, ideologized, and ultimately de-vitalized; even so, they can only be *un-covered* through an intercultural and philosophical process of *mediation-mediation* or *medi(t)ation*.

c. Marxism-Leninism and Neuro-psychologism or the bypassing of the "existential."

Discourse, religion, and ideology have always served as the premier un-covering and re-covering devices meant to soothe fractured human hearts, their core purpose has always been to mend the un-mendable: the *incommensurability* of death, loss, and suffering. In this regard, the atheistic ideologies of the 20th century like revolutionary Marxism-Leninism and neuro-psychologism are no different from the ancestral religions of the pre-modern world: they have merely objectified or "subjectified" the uncovering-recovering processes that mediate, meditate, and ultimately cleave *living* into antinomic poles (oppression vs. emancipation, health vs. illness, fake living vs. truly living). Even though Marxist-Leninist critique and neuro-psychological analysis still manage to un-cover the reified and alienated facticity of fake life and of its struggles (labor, psychopathology), they accord little attention to the *neither subjective nor objective* instances of *dis-alienation* where life becomes *(en)lightened* and *(en)livened*.

Because of their propensity to either excessively objectify -Marxist-Leninist critique- or excessively subjectify -neuropsychological analysis- the fabric of experience, both discourses veer into an ideo-

274

logical explanation of the world that *re-covers* the *incommensurable cracks* that *fracture* it *from within*. They provide modelized solutions (communism, neuro-biological balancing) designed to achieve pre-determined goals (an emancipated society, a "happified" individual life). In doing so, these ideologies perpetuate an Ends/Means logic that obfuscates and *re-covers* the cracked lines of flight that *cut through* and *sever* the fabric of living; the very lines of flight that the incommensurably *singular* experiences of death, suffering, and realization *un-cover*.

*

In the language of existential philosophy, these experiences which overflow the parameters of experience throw us "out of Being" and thus make us "ex-ist" or *stand out*. The discourse-machines of revolutionary Marxism-Leninism and marketized neuro-psychology most often presuppose a predetermined form of universal "natural law" and/or "human nature," as well as a teleological and universalist conceptions of complex phenomena like "happiness," "illness," "oppression," and "emancipation." Because of these presuppositions, they cover up the suspended thoughts and breaths of "life truly lived." As they wander on *the wayside* of dogmatic adherence and obedience, the thoughts and breaths of a "live truly lived" *leap into* the incommensurability of death, *jouissance* and the intimate. In doing so, they uncover *unheard possibilities* capable of producing an *opening medi(t)ation* that exists both *within and outside* this world.

5/ Breathing, resisting, thinking: refusing fake life in the name of "life truly lived."

The experiential paradox of "life truly lived" finds its paradigmatic expression in the knot that ties together four existential coordinates: metaphorization, mediation, meditation, and *breath(ing)*.

The immediacy of "life truly lived" can indeed be accessed through a metaphoric *breath(ing)-medi(t)ation* that assumes and reflects the contradictory *fabric of living*: *breath(ing)* is at once re-covering and un-covering, filling and emptying, generating and depleting. Ordinarily covered up by the activity of the thinking mind or by the silent permanence of unconscious vital processes, the cultivated *awareness of breath(ing)* produces a paradoxically immediate *fabric* that simultaneously mediates, meditates, and metaphorizes our experience of the world. It is this *fabric of breath(ing)* that allows us to *weave together* the *contradiction of living* into a web of mediations, meditations, and metaphors; a web that we can be purposefully *cut through* so that we can readily "stand outside" it, and begin to *finally live*.

a. Breath(ing) as metaphor(izing).

The mediating and/or meditating *metaphorizing activity* that cultivates *awareness of breath(ing)* therefore holds the potential to uncover the existential *fabric of living*: it fosters a capacity to "stand outside" both the dissociative dynamics of mental processes and the entropic dynamics of vital processes. The cultivation of a metaphoric *awareness of breath(ing)* does not supersede mental or vital processes, it instead leads to a shift in perspective where the immediacy of these processes is *un-covered*. It is a *ground(ing)-medi(t)ation* that *metaphorizes* the *interplay* of two polarities: breathing vs. thinking, vital vs. existential, necessary vs. contingent, unified vs. dissociated. These oscillations circulate both *through* and *within* the vacant, opaque, and depthless surfaces of *living*. In the same way that the breath moves in and out the vital organs, emptying them on the exhalation and filling them on the inhalation, mediating, meditating, and, above all, *metaphorizing* both empty and fill the thinking mind.

Media(t)ion and *breath(ing)* thus *actualize* a singularly *human* capacity: nurturing-nourishing the *evasiveness* of *living*, which literally *stands* (exists) *outside* the pre-determined mental and vital fields of constitutive and constituted experience. Never losing sight of the constitutive frameworks that (pre)determine experience, never deliberately annihilating or overturning them, a mediated, meditated, and metaphorized *awareness of breath(ing)* nonetheless wanders on the *wayside* of any pre-xisting experience, simply because it *manifests* the absolute singularity or "oneness" (—) of "life truly lived." The mediated, meditated, and metaphorized *awareness of breath(ing)* maintains the determinacy of experience in perspective. In doing so, it engages with in an indeterminate and ever-broadening *field of awareness and reflects upon* the elementary and yet inaccessible contradictions that cleave *living* into two opposing directions: a *soaring* pole of *expanding-awareness* and a *sprawling* pole of *retracting-for-getfulness*.

*

The *(en)lightening* and *(en)livening* emergence of "life truly lived" can thus be *initiated* with nothing more, and/or nothing less, than a mediated, meditated, and metaphorized *awareness of breath(ing)* or *breath(ing)-awareness*. That such a *medi(t)ation* would be capable of *un-covering* the *fake living* that obfuscates our lives and turns them into stereotypical caricatures seems both straightforward and demanding. As soon as the un-covering operation of the *awareness of breath(ing)* is initiated, it requires a constant activity so that it is not drawn out of focus or forgotten. Without this effort to *sustain* the un-covering operation of *breath(ing)-awareness*, the semblance of fake life instills itself once more and resumes its operation of obfuscation, reification, and alienation. Because living is inherently ambiguous, cleaved, contradictory, and paradoxical, the exploration of living that "life truly lived" supposes and the *medi(t)ation* of *breath(ing)-awareness* that it requires are themselves full of ambiguities, cleavages, contradictions, and paradoxes: living needs to be *re-covered* by the *sprawl* of semblance and yet the initial *soaring* of "life truly lived" requires the *un-covering* of semblance. Even the simplest and most *minimal* of activities, *breath(ing)-awareness*, is fraught with contradictions that cannot escape the re-covering of mediation, meditation, and metaphorization.

*

In this regard, Adorno's phrase "life does not live" rings truer than ever because it fully assumes the paradoxical nature of living: if "life truly lived" wanders *on the wayside* of the entropic dynamic of life falling back into death, then can it even be *accessed*? If the emergence of "life truly lived" exceeds the frameworks of experience, then how can one really experience it? The all-too-easy *"carpe diem,"* "say yes to life," "just be Zen about it," or "just breathe it out" tropes of "positive thinking" that flood the marketplace of (un) happiness cover up the inherent ambiguity of living: they falsely suggest that "life truly lived" is easily accessed and always within reach. These ready-made assertions dissimulate the strong "NO" of *refusal* that lies at the heart of an oblique operation of *un-covering*.

b. The unheard force of the neg-active.

If such a thing as "life truly lived" exists, that is to say if *truly living* can verily *stand outside* fake-living, then it assuredly does not exist or stand out in some positive capacity. The shift into "life truly lived" is first and foremost determined by an *un-covering* of fake life and of its *resignation*. The uncovering of fake life is a negative activity, a *neg-active* force which manifests itself as a resounding and resonant "NO." It is a refusal of resignation, of its tacit appraisal of the entropic retraction of possibilities that characterizes the motion of life collapsing back into non-life. Refusing fake life in the name of "life truly lived" implies *resisting* the defeatist, *bogged down*, and *avoidant* affects summed up by the popular sayings "well… that's life… *c'est la vie…* what can you do about it…" The bogged down and resigned life finds itself stuck in a rut and stripped of all *initiating capacity*; caught in a web of adherences that paralyzes it, life lived in resignation cannot access the *soaring* that is *un-covered* by the *encounter* with the *un-heard* and the *incommensurable* of "life truly lived."

*

In Marxist terms, the resigned life is both alienated and reified: at once estranged from itself and turned into a commodity, its liveliness is subsumed and consumed by an ever-increasing proliferation of processes that cover it up with semblance and objectification. The four processes -stalling, resigning, alienating, reifying- that distill facticity into living and thus *cover up* the *unheard possibilities* of "life truly lived" form a self-perpetuating macabre square dance of disenchantment. And yet, *in between* the dense threads of fake-living woven together by these four poles of (dis)illusion lies a liminal, incommensurable, and neg-active *voiding function* that *resists* the belittling avoidance of common measure and common sense. As it negates and uncovers the facticity of fake living, the voiding neg-activity of *resistance* uncovers a point of respite, cracking, and *re-opening* that un-resigns, un-sticks, un-alienates, and un-reifies our lives.

*

"Life truly lived" thus cannot be tied to any inherently "positive" representations, it cannot be reduced to the embodiment or enactment of a pre-existing ideal or value, nor can it be ascribed to an identifiable technique, lifestyle, or ideology. Understood in a philosophical and intercultural sense, "life truly lived" is instead a neg-active *force of resistance* that un-covers the *semblance* that insidiously infiltrates itself in the quotidian of our lives. In this regard, a mediated, meditated, and metaphorized *breath(ing)-awareness* cultivates a *voiding function* from which "life truly lived" can proceed and emerge; it is in no way a "breathing technique" that can be learned and mastered like a craft or a skill. A mediated, meditated, and metaphorized *breath(ing)-awareness* does not constitute a negation of the mind nor of the body, it does not establish the superiority of a spiritual or philosophical "true life" that supposedly supersedes material fake-life. Rather, it is a *neg-active decision* that consists in engaging in a head-on *confrontation* with the ceaseless activity of the mind and body through a deliberate and paradoxical form of *in-activity*. The ethical decision that underpins a mediated, meditated, and metaphorized *breath(ing)-awareness* is a negation of the fake-living and, above all, *fake-thinking* that covers up and bogs down the *soaring expanse* of "life truly lived."

*

The forces of fake-living and fake-thinking that permeate and infiltrate our lives have only become more powerful with the advent of the digital age. Resisting the facticity of digitalization and social media *in the name of* "life truly lived" and *truly living* emerges as one of the premier *ethical (neg)actions* of our time. The concepts of "life truly lived" and of *truly living* as they have been articulated in this chapter could indeed form the basis of a *neither culturalist nor universalist* intercultural and philosophical *ethics of living;* an ethics that arms us with effective and operational *neg-active medi(t)ations.*

*

An intercultural and philosophical approach to *truly living* and "life truly lived" does not compare and contrast culturally determined modes of thinking and living. Instead, it *reflects (upon)* their *unthought* singularities and thus *produces* philosophical *medi(t)ating devices.* The intercultural and philosophical concepts of *truly living* and *breath(ing)-awareness* can indeed *resonate* with a timeless and placeless *signifying-effect:* the one that *passes through* a virtually infinite plurality of (en)lightening and (en)livening *liminal margins*; margins whose memorialized and memorized *wound-events* still possess the *capacity* to *cut through* the simulacrum of commodified fake-thought and fake-living. If one were to invent a name for these marginal instances of dis-alienation that cut through the fake and thus *re-open the possibility* of "life truly lived," one could call them: *de-coincidences.*

CHAPTER X
Re-opening possibilities: de-coincidence, an *ars operandi*.

1/ Tomorrow's lost ideals.

It has become impossible to draw up a plan or a *model form* of the ideal City or State. In order to build a *model*, one has to be able to *isolate*. The astounding complexity and interconnectedness of today's world makes it nearly impossible to isolate any given thing or phenomenon: our models are more and more algorithmic, they correspond to partial technical optimizations and are increasingly the purview of a highly specialized workforce. Drawing a model of a common Good that we can all aspire to seems to have become a task that we are incapable of accomplishing. More and more so, we seem to have adopted the punk slogan NO FUTURE: we have ceased to *believe* in a more radiant *tomorrow*.

Climate change, extreme weather events, pandemics, and protracted wars, all of which seem to define the early 21st century, have made it even more difficult for us to construct a stable image of the future, let alone a meaningful political model. We are tempted to retreat into the present and its "here and now:" the ideology of "presentism" has never been stronger as we become increasingly disconnected from our History, and depressed at the perspective of an apocalyptic Future.

*

And yet, *something else* can be done to counter the gloominess of our times. This "something else" does not consist in *projecting* an "ideal" model onto the chaos of our world, nor does it consist in *denouncing* the wretchedness of the world; the world and its noisy clamor drowns out the isolated voices of denunciation. Instead, we can *detect* the *blockages* that obstruct the present, so as to better "crack" them open. When we crack open the blockages which keep the present in its apparent state of "stuckness," we begin to "de-coincide," that is to say: *re-open possibilities*.

*

What is it that blocks a situation and keeps it stuck within the walls of its confines, if not a form of complacent *adequacy*? Is it not such a form of *self-satisfied adequacy* that we continue to *adhere* to which leads to the *bogging down* of a previously open situation in our individual and collective lives?

If we scrutinize these *forms of self-adequacy* that *bog themselves down* in their own conformity in all the terrains of our experience, we begin to see how they insidiously infiltrate daily living. Following this moment of attentive *detection*, we can remain on the lookout for those discreet instances where the (self)sterilizing impulsions of (self) adequacy can be *untied.* It is the only way to loosen up a self-hindering situation which previously appeared to be at a standstill. The installed *coincidences* of life (the way we met, how I ended up doing what I do, who I spend my time with); along with all the familiar "we must accept all things as they are" moral tropes of commonplace, coincidental wisdom can indeed be *cracked open.* If we pay sufficient attention to the moments and instances where these coincidences of life and thought suddenly no longer *hold*, we are able to "exist" or *stand outside* the *tipping points* that shape and shift, not only our individual lives, but also the course of History.

These tipping points of our individual and collective lives call us back to the drawing board: they *re-open a future* at a moment when any representation of "the future" seemed impossible. Shaking up established ways of thinking and *re-opening possibilities* cannot be done without a certain degree of invention; that is why it made sense to invent a new name – *de-coincidence* – for these instances of tipping, cracking, and opening which make the "yet-to-come" of *a* future *possible*.

*

While the concept of a "coincidence" as we use it in everyday life evokes a fortuitous event, it also refers to a specific notion in geometry. When two geometric figures (two lines for example) intersect perfectly, so that it is impossible to distinguish one from the other, they are said to "coincide" with each other. From a geometric point of view, the point of de-coincidence corresponds to this precise and discreet point where these two figures which seemed to merge into one another no longer overlap nor assimilate into a single object. The point of de-coincidence indeed corresponds to this tiny point of *shifting* where what seemed to be fixed and determined becomes once again moving and, above all, *indeterminate*. When two geometric figures no longer coincide with each other, the *distance* that opens up *in between* them creates a *vacancy* whose existence had remained unsuspected until now- a pure *possibility* that, up until then, had remained *unheard*.

*

"De-coinciding" consequently consists in re-introducing movement where there is no longer any. *De-coincidence* proceeds by way of a *deviation*, it distrusts the quiet and adhesive overlapping and assimilation of coincidence: it grants us *access* to *the unheard of the possible*. Discreet, barely even perceptible, its *work* remains nonetheless, if not efficient, then at least *effective*.

2/ Coincidence is death.

Commonplace wisdom wants us to believe that the adequacy of coincidence, as such, is positive. When we deem that something or a situation is "adequate" or "positive," we imply that this situation or thing is "sufficient," that it is not subject to lack or incompletion. And yet, as soon as adequacy installs itself in its self-sufficient characteristics, it ceases to be questionable and freezes itself in a form of complacent conformity. In other words, the "adequate" possesses an uncanny ability to adhere to its own adequacy as it becomes "glued" or *blocked* within its own adhesive confines. Once adequacy has been positively identified and settled upon (a manager, a leader or a healer stating that his "positive results" demonstrates the "adequacy" of his methods, for example), it becomes gradually and imperceptibly more inert as it transforms itself into *positivity.*

Understood from this perspective, positivity corresponds in fact to the *negative within the positive*: it corresponds to that point where the positive *secretly shifts into its contrary*; that point where it turns itself into a force of *obstruction* that prevents any situation from evolving. Positivity prevents the deployment of a future because of its own self-adequate complacency.

*

Our own individual lives, as well as our collective History, revolve around a truth that we remain all-too-oblivious to: the sprawled-out, self-destructive positivity of a perpetually adequate world where everything "fits in its right place." The self-adequacy of a world where everything is "well adapted" can suddenly shift, without warning, into *a negative that we do not see*; a negative where "fitting in its right place" becomes synonymous with the adhesive, lackluster, and alienating repetition of uniformity and sameness. This "homeostatic" positive is nothing more and nothing less than *death.* When everything is "in its right place" and "fits together," when there is no longer any space for any other possibilities, we are *effectively dead.*

As we put our trust in the displayed legitimacy of positivity, we no longer question it; we cease to work on the *unheard possibilities* that the relentless, and yet silent, sprawl of positivity adhesively *covers up*. The contemporary phenomenon of "toxic positivity" spread across social media platforms by vapid "influencers" and the ineptitude of the "positive psychology" that inspires them offers the perfect example of what happens when the positive is over-emphasized: it becomes a nefarious negative that prevents all thought and evolution.[265]

*

Thankfully, it is possible to *crack open* any situation or discourse that becomes bogged down in its own self-adequacy. Once the veneer of positivity has been cracked, one can wander *on the wayside* of the coherent and coinciding interior of self-adequacy's inescapable, if not natural, tendency: to transform itself into a negative inertness bound to succumb to its own lethargy.

De-coincidence therefore refers to acts and pathways where self-adequacy's inevitable drive towards inertness is *deviated* from its initial course. This neologism is intended to *(re)open the possible* in language, in thought, and in living: it highlights how the *way out* of a blocked situation most often proceeds directly *from within* the situation itself; how an unbearable situation of complete coincidence can be led to de-coincide *from within,* so that it can unbind itself as it opens itself up to the *unheard* that it still contains.

*

Both religion and science offer concrete examples to illustrate the relevance of the concept of de-coincidence. In the religious context, the story of Genesis represents a striking example: nothing could happen within the perfect self-adequacy of the Garden of Eden. This equilibrium of heavenly adequacy had to be cracked open (the serpent, the apple, the error…): it was necessary to introduce a *de-coincidence*, which in this case took the form of a disobedience, so that a new possibility for humanity, a possibility born out of an *initiative,* could emerge.

*

The scientific theory of Evolution can also illustrate the concept of de-coincidence: "humans" first became *human* when they began to wander *on the wayside* of the initial coincidences of animal life: breathing, eating, sleeping, feeling, moving; coincidences that bind humans to the "order of nature." Bipedal posture and the autonomation of facial and hand muscles led to the invention of a detachable and, above all, *transmittable* tool that paleoanthropologists call a "chopper." From the chopper ensued the exponential development of *human technique,* which progressively became unrelated to biological determinations like brain size and motricity.[266] Even though our physical brains and basic neurobiological cognitive operations have evolved very little in over fifty-thousand years, our techniques and technologies have continued to develop at an increasingly rapid rate. With the advent of the transmittable tool, technical operations ceased to be solely correlated to biological determinants: they began to make us progressively *de-coincide* from the natural order and the animal world as they ushered in an *unforeseen possibility-* the *human.*

3/ De-coincidence at work.

At the most basic level, it is safe to assert that *living* is de-coinciding. Living indeed consists in continuously untying the coincidences that my life leads to. The coincidences of my life -the things I "settle for": a job, a relationship, a group of friends- can potentially bog it down; it is only when I untie the coincidental aspects of my life and *de-coincide* from them that I, effectively, *begin to live.*

Re-opening possibilities: de-coincidence, an *ars operandi*

*

I am only alive today insofar as I am de-coinciding from the norms and adequacy that yesterday installed into my life. If I do not pay heed to the insidious alienation of self-adequate repetition drilling itself into daily life, the coincidences of yesterday's living can all-too-easily fixate themselves and become static; they lead me back to a form *of "non-life"- Death.*

*

De-coincidence finds another strong illustration in the domain of art: an artist is only an artist insofar as he is willing to de-coincide from the art that has already been made and has been recognized as "art." If we look at an exceptional artist like Leonardo Da Vinci, it is clear that what makes his paintings so "outstanding" is precisely the way in which they *stand outside* the established norms of the context that birthed them. When the Renaissance polymath began to incorporate the calculations and operations of the emerging sciences of physics and anatomy into his creative process, he invented *unheard* ways of drawing and painting the world and ushered in a new era for the Arts and Sciences: his incredible usage of light and darkness (*chiaroscuro*) and the efflorescent smokiness of his brush marks (*sfumato*) truly *de-coincides* from anything that had been previously depicted.[267] If we think of a more contemporary example in culture, we can also invoke Jimi Hendrix and his undeniably *de-coincidant* usage of the electric guitar: Hendrix's singular style blended rock, blues, and pop in previously *unheard* ways; his performance of the *Star Spangled* Banner at Woodstock redefined the significance of America's national anthem for an entire generation.

*

The same holds true in the domain of thought: I am only thinking insofar as I am de-coinciding from what has already been thought;

I am only thinking when I wander *on the wayside* of what has been constructed as "adequate thinking" sealed in the form of (a) "truth." Descartes in this regard offers a fantastic example of what a de-coincident thinker looks like. For nearly 400 years, scholastic Christian theology stifled philosophical inquiry in Europe and imposed a dogmatic interpretation of Aristotle's metaphysics: God was the source of all knowledge and certainty because He was the center of the Universe.

Unconvinced by the speculative doctrines of scholastic Christian theology that derived all knowledge and certainty from God, Descartes' philosophy instead made the thinking Self -the "I"- the source of all certainty. In a novel thought-experiment where the philosopher imagined himself to be under the influence of a "malignant genie," he began to doubt the very existence of his own body. After positing that his body and his sensory experience could in fact be the product of an ill-intentioned deception, Descartes nonetheless ascertained the following with his famous "I think, therefore I am" sentence: even if my body is an illusion attributable to "malignant genie," I still *know* that my thinking mind (*esprit*) exists; even if the "malignant genie" is tricking me, I *know* that I am still *thinking* about him tricking me. Descartes' novel thought-experiment and his re-interpretation of the traditional mind-body-soul divide ushered in a radical shift in human thought, a de-coincidence that would change science, the arts, and the world itself for centuries to come. God was no longer the source of all knowledge; instead, knowledge could be achieved through the individual experience of *consciousness*.[268]

*

Psychotherapy can also be understood as a mode of de-coincidence. In psychotherapy, the patient is installed in his symptom, he is adhering and coinciding with the coherence of the image of "self" that he has constructed for himself. The paradox of the patient's position is that he is holding onto this form of psychic coincidence even though it is making him suffer. It is of course insufficient on the therapist's behalf to simply "call out" the patient's propensity towards self-coincidence; nor is it possible to *overturn* this rock-solid psychic position that finds so many ways of justifying itself. The therapist can only operate indirectly, from the side, in an oblique manner, to subtly incite the patient to *un-adhere* to what has become his own form of self-conformity. To do so, the therapist needs to detect a *crack* in a psychic configuration that most often finds its origins in a traumatic experience. Once this detection work has been accomplished, it is then possible to begin to *crack open* the blockage that is holding back the patient: doing so leads him to *de-coincide* from the habits and thoughts that he had both comfortably and intolerably walled himself in.

4/ Ethics of de-coincidence.

De-coincidence does not matter simply because we became humans by de-coinciding from our animal nature and found within ourselves a capacity to *invent* "the human." It doesn't only matter because "living" involves de-coinciding from a previously existing state of homeostasis. *Truly living* amounts to untying the coincidence in which the Self or the "I" binds itself into a determined "character" or "type;" it entails a capacity to "stand outside" one's Self or "I."

*

De-coincidence is doubly ethical: in relationship to oneself and in relationship to Others. It involves untying the adequation-adaptation in which the "I" entraps itself so as to deploy life in its capacity of *existence,* a capacity which literally *stands outside* what has become stuck and inert. It also involves de-coinciding from the Self and the "I" because it is only in doing so that I can access Others and effectively *encounter* them, rather than only crossing their paths, rubbing shoulders with them or, even worse, assimilating them to myself. If I am coinciding with myself, if I am not *over-flowing* the boundaries of my Self, I cannot *accost* Others.

*

There is perhaps no better example to illustrate the ethics of de-coincidence than marriage: is marriage not the most perfect form of coincidence that we can find in our existence? And yet, when marriage installs itself in its coincidence it becomes deathly; the super-coincidence of marriage leads to the establishment of a *relationship* whose very positivity can only degenerate if we do not know how to shift ourselves away from it and untie ourselves from it. The case of marriage illustrates the ethics of de-coincidence because it shows how the concept allows us to simultaneously envision our capacity to stand outside of the perspective of the Self and the Other; outside My perspective and Your perspective.

5/ Coincidence is ideological.

When an idea becomes coincident, it becomes ideological. A coincident idea first spreads because it appears to be both adequate and adapted; it then installs itself in its positivity, secretes adherence, and ultimately generates the impression that it is "obvious." Coincident ideas spread collectively and are no longer called into question: they generate a form of self-satisfied "good consciousness." The collective assimilation of a coincident idea results in a form of unsuspected, if not unconscious, "obedience." Obedience lies beneath subordination. One can disobey and refuse subordination: when I *choose* to disobey an order, I can become insubordinate. Yet obedience, in its most subtle and tacit forms, is no longer reflected upon: I am obedient without even knowing that I am.

*

One should also distinguish the collective and the common. The *common* is produced and promoted; its object is *sharing* and participation; in that regard, it acts as a foundation for the political. The *collective*, on the other hand, is just an additive. It elicits adhesion or rather adherence (things "gel together" in the collective), yet it does not lead to sharing. Adherence is suffered; it is the lowest level of participation and it is also the supreme degree of a form of cohesion that is no longer reflected upon.

*

Isn't ideological *coincidence* an increasingly pervasive phenomenon? Does it not uncannily differ from the (religious) *beliefs* that used to be so widespread? A major fact accompanies this shift from the phenomenon of (religious) belief to the phenomenon of ideological coincidences: if the latter have become so important nowadays, it is because the *media*, and in particular *digital media*, have become their most important producers and vectors.

*

The media's mode of functioning elaborates and produces coincident terms and themes. These terms and themes then impose themselves as they secrete obviousness, to the point where they generate the kind of obedience which escapes reflection. The "mediacracy" erects the framework of the ideological thematizations in which widespread opinions and debates manifest themselves. Since there is no transcendent authority, no imposed dogma, no (at least in the global West) overt propaganda, we are led to believe that the diversity of media expresses the "voice of the people." But is this voice truly the voice of the citizens themselves?

*

The pervasive *effect* of ideological coincidence is produced both by the montage of select events and by their constant rehashing. The media supply the information market by answering the ideological expectation that they themselves elicited. The media only discuss "talking points" which are already being discussed: this pre-selection effect leads to a snowball reaction where the number of discussions surrounding the media's favored "talking points" begins to artificially swell; the pre-determined importance of the media's favored themes installs them in the comfort of their own "coincidentality." At a certain point, these "talking points" appear to impose themselves and seem self-justified in their importance; all other topics and discussions are condemned to silence.

*

The informational surveys, investigations, and inquiries that we are too often "fed" as "news" and which populate our digital "feeds" in fact already contain the answers to the very "provocative questions" that their alluring titles claim to tackle. The media has already prefabricated the framing elements that individuals then use to produce "content" on social media platforms. We are led to believe that we are "free" to use social media to express ourselves in an original fashion so that we can eventually become "influential." We have turned ourselves into randomized and globalized individuals that use pre-hashed and pre-digested graphic, linguistic, and pictorial tropes to express our most personal and private whims and fancies. Without even knowing it, we *buy into* an ideological *media machine* that both "(em)powers" us and subjugates us as it silently consumes our thoughts and lives. Such is the *closed circuit* of coincidence: we think we are probing concrete and real aspects of life when we consume "informational" media produced by "influencers" or "experts;" and yet, we all corroborate the grand Coincidence that the media have indefinitely spread throughout society.

6/ Political resources of de-coincidence.

De-coincidence avoids the great traditional gesture of the lofty and idealized art of *modeling*. Instead, it focuses on the careful detection, at the ground level, of what begins to coincide and "get stuck;" it is an art of *cracking open*. The elements that lead to a crack, or "de-coincidence factors," are discrete, they operate at a processual level and rely upon the *deployment* that they engage within a specific situation. Most of the time, we barely notice them. And yet, they remain *operative*, from the get-go. "Cracks make caves collapse" as the Russian dissident Alexander Solzhenitsyn once famously said. Caves are not overthrown, nor are they denounced, "called out," let alone "canceled." And yet, when they are sufficiently cracked, they collapse. Rosa Parks' discreet *refusal* of segregation in 1955 constitutes the perfect example of a political act of *de-coincidence*: it was an *unheard gesture* that became one of the foundational *cracks* which would *initiate* the Civil Rights Movement.

*

Because the framework of de-coincidence does not rely upon (ideological) modeling and (ideal) models, it unties the *theory-practice* relationship. The following questions often comes up when discussing de-coincidence: "ok, so I get the theory, but what's the *praxis*? How do you *apply* it?" What these questions precisely miss is the fact that there is no "praxis" or "application" of the "theory" because de-coincidence can only be conceived of *from within* the situation in which it is introducing a shift. De-coincidence only exists insofar as it effectuates itself: it's *real* precisely because it is *already working*.

Since it is not conceived of in terms of theory and praxis, de-coincidence does not have to be tied to a "principle." Because its work consists in *un-tying*, it does not need to be thought of in terms of a pre-existing model. De-coincidence does not have to propose an "end" which would correspond with the realization of the "ideal model," it does not need a goal or a finality. The "possible" that de-coincidence re-opens is not a pre-determined "end." If an artist begins their work or production with "principles" and "goals," it will rarely result in interesting art and will most often produce formulaic or stereotypical forms that reflect the ideological and coincidental preferences of the time and place in which the artwork was being produced. An artist's work and artistic craft truly become "art" when they de-coincide from the art that has already been produced; when they wander *on the wayside* of the self-adequacy of installed forms: without planning to do so and without adhering to pre-determined models, true artists *open possibilities* for art that, up until then, remained *unheard.*

*

There is no plan or proposition which can precede de-coincidence. As soon as I trigger a de-coincidence, I am *operating*; unlike theory losing its splendor once confronted with practice, de-coincidence cannot "miss the mark" or "go wrong." De-coincidence is a concept that is always already *at work,* it cannot be dissociated from a given, concrete situation. As soon as de-coincidence begins operating, an effect is engaged. De-coincidence in this regard works well within an ecological logic: as soon as I choose to take my bike or walk instead of taking my car, I am de-coinciding and doing something for the climate.

*

De-coincidence is a *unitarian* concept: it can be understood as being relevant to all domains. And yet, its unfolding is *plural*: it is as diverse and complex as all situations and configurations tend to be. In addition, since de-coincidences are always singular and localized, since they are *situated* to begin with, they do not structure an ensemble or a "set:" they do not form a system and do not reformulate an ideological framework. As a result of this, de-coincidences do not fit in within any hierarchies: de-coincidence is a fundamentally egalitarian and democratic concept. Everyone possesses the initiative and the capacity to de-coincide based on where they are at in life: these initiatives and capacities follow *no order nor commandment.*

7/ De-coincidence, a *modus operandi*.

De-coincidence cannot be conceived of in an abstract and programmatic manner that can be formulated into "rules": there is no "method" of de-coincidence. Just because de-coincidence is conceptualized as a process does not mean that there is a "recipe" for de-coinciding. De-coincidence is not a formula and there is no "manual" of de-coincidence that could be mechanically printed, let alone applied: it resists application and yet it can be *transmitted*. Neither rule nor recipe, de-coincidence can be thought of as an "art of operating"- an *ars operandi*.

*

To "operate" can be heard and understood in two distinct ways: the first meaning refers to a productive and concerted intervention whose results both validate and justify the intervention. The second meaning refers to the more surgical dimension of an operation: removing a blockage that has the potential to become deadly.

*

This second meaning of "operating" can easily be transposed to an ideological context. What has been called the Galilean "revolution" offers a strong example of how de-coincidence operates at a surgical level in the ideological context. In Galileo's time there were two main ideological coincidences: on the one hand, Aristotelian physics; on the other hand, religious beliefs. What is striking is that Galileo did not begin his "revolution" by proclaiming that he had "overturned" Aristotle's physics or Christianity: he did not engage in a global and systematic "critique" of both modes of thinking. Instead, he took his distance from the dominant views of his time through a series of successive *small steps*: as he wandered *on the wayside* of received ideas, as he probed their coincidences from within, he was able to discreetly *crack them open* and ultimately make them irrelevant.

Unsatisfied with the limits of Aristotelian physics and with its inability to quantify movement, Galileo invented a new way of mathematizing movement that was not a direct recusal of Aristotle's ideas but that nonetheless rendered them useless. Galileo deemed that Aristotle's general method of demonstration was correct. And yet, he nonetheless understood that *mathematical modelization,* as opposed to the direct observation, held far greater potential when it came to the *realization* of the stated aim of Aristotelian physics: the quantification of movement. This is what allowed him to say: "we are bringing an absolutely new science to this most ancient of topics." As he de-coincided from the old way of approaching physics, he also *opened up possibilities* for a new science that would change the conditions of life on Earth: modern physics.[269]

8/ Destiny of de-coincidence.

The operativity of de-coincidence, at least in its early stages, is poorly thought of and rarely welcomed: de-coincidence is not "marketable." Coincidence, on the other hand, is eminently marketable. Even more so, coincidence *simulating* de-coincidence (*pseudo* or *fake* de-coincidence) is the most marketable of all. The most striking examples of pseudo de-coincidences masquerading as a de-coincidence can be found in the many populist stump speeches that claim to go "against the stream." Politicians like Donald Trump who claim to "drain the swamp," all the while fostering institutionalized corruption; crackpot "news" anchors like Alex Jones or Tucker Carlson who claim to "resist mainstream media," all the while amplifying the toxicity of the media's effect on society, are perfect examples of such nefarious pseudo de-coincidences.

*

Not only is de-coincidence un-marketable, it also represents a "hefty cost" for those who de-coincide- the "de-coinciders." De-coincidence can indeed elicit incomprehension, to the point where it can threaten the life and legacy of the "de-coinciders." If we turn to the example of Socrates, it is easy to see how his de-coinciding ways, however good-humored and unassuming they may have been, led him to be put on trial and ultimately sentenced to death. Socrates' dissenting use of irony *cracked open* the ideology of his time, it challenged received ideas about politics, religion, and social customs; it pointed out their self-adequate and self-coinciding tendencies.[270] Socrates' de-coincident desire to open up the soon-to-be crumbling world of his fellow Athenians to *unheard* ways of thinking and, above all, *living,* is what led him to be judged with suspicion and contempt. If "coincidence is death," then coincidence also inevitably judges and sentences to death, out of spite, those who attempt to crack it open: Galileo also "paid the price" for de-coinciding from Aristotelian physics when he was put on trial.

9/ De-coincidence and philosophy.

Philosophy, in its inception, celebrated Coincidence: when things perfectly overlap and when adequacy reigns, the mind is satisfied. Thomas Aquinas' scholastic philosophy beautifully summarizes pre-modern thought's celebration of adequacy and coincidence: "*Veritas est adaequatio rei et intellectus*" or "Truth is the adequation of the thing and of the intellect."[271] Classical thought indeed offered many *coincidental zones* for its thinkers to land on: the structure of Being (Plato), the order of God (theology) and/or Nature (the Stoics). These "master coincidences" of Classical thought were thought of in relationship to the ideal of "Happiness," which was then projected as a model destination for all human Life.

*

And yet, there is something that cannot possibly coincide with itself- life. Life does not coincide with life. Life is a de-coincident *over-flowing*, that is why (and how) it "lives." Is it not the erection of coincidence as the ideal of the mind and the founding truth on the basis of "self-evidence" that led philosophy to *repress life*? Does consciousness truly arise by way of a self-coincidence? Didn't European intellectualism neglect *living consciousness*'s singular activity-its capacity to *realize*? Is it not wandering *on the wayside* of the *coincident logic* of the mind which leads to the *emergence* and *realization* of consciousness?

*

We could in fact oppose consciousness and the mind: the mind aims for coincidence, whereas consciousness operates by way of de-coincidence. In this sense, art is not a mental product, it instead reflects the activity of *living consciousness*; psychotherapy is not a "treatment of the mind," it is instead the *realization* of a living consciousness that forms the most *intimate* sub-stratum of our waking and sleeping lives.

*

Even at the most basic level of my everyday experience and *perception*, a true coincidence between the world and myself is impossible. I am not the "owner" of my own vision: the act of seeing escapes "me" since it is always being shaped by the singularity of a seen object, which then becomes a forever incomplete "thing." The great philosopher of perception Maurice Merleau-Ponty perfectly summed up the way in which perception itself is de-coincident: "my body already acts like the stage director of my perception; it *shatters the illusion of a coincidence of my perception with things themselves.*"[272]

*

I cannot even coincide with myself since I am distended by Time: my access to the Present is always submerged by the Past and projected into the Future; the distention of Time constantly transports me out of myself. Any "identity" that I deem to be "mine" cannot coincide with the reality of who I am; whatever representation I may construct of myself will always be subject to modification. Similarly, I can never fully coincide with another since our individual experiences will never perfectly intersect or overlap.

The impossibility of self-coincidence or of a complete coincidence with another is not an incapacity of our experience. Instead, it is what allows us to promote it as an *experience*: it is because I don't coincide with others that I can be drawn to them; it is because I don't coincide with the world that I can be "open" to the world; it is because I don't coincide with myself that I am pushed to live my life.

*

Even though classical philosophy founded itself upon coincidence and made it its depositary of truth, modern thought did everything it could to free itself from coincidence: the interplay of the world (*Weltspiel*) substituted itself to the primacy of coincidence. In a similar fashion, classical painting justified its mode of representation by invoking coincidence with nature (likeness), whereas a modern painter like Picasso untied and even shattered the supposed coincidence of naturalistic representation and likeness.

The concept of de-coincidence does not only help us delimit two distinct eras in the history of thought. It also questions philosophy's own capacity to renew itself and raises the following question: to what degree has philosophy, in all eras, managed to find a way out of its installed self-adequacy? In other words, how has philosophy been capable of de-coinciding from itself in an effort to "think differently"?

10/ Revolution, innovation, or "re-possibilization."

When there is a blockage, the figure of speech that is typically invoked is *overturning*. In politics, the overturning of the established order is most often named "Revolution."

*

And yet, isn't the motive of a revolutionary overturning just an opportune "miracle" if we pay close attention to the course of History? The inversion that overturning implies means that there is always a risk that a revolution or overturning will lead us back to a reversed, and therefore similar, situation. Overturning keeps us entrapped in the very dialectical logic that the revolution sought to overthrow (Master vs. Slave, Perpetrator vs. Victim, Woke vs. Karen).

*

Over the course of History, the overthrowing of a monarch most often ushers in a new form of authoritarian rule: it isn't because we have overturned or overthrown a form of despotic power that we become free from it (Napoleon's First Empire after the French Revolution; Stalin's totalitarian regime of Terror after the Russian Revolution; Mao's rise to power after the Chinese Revolution). If a process of de-coincidence is not sufficiently engaged, if there is no distance established with the previous ruling order, any Revolution will in fact only lead to a form of conservative restauration.

*

Overturning is spectacular, but is it really that *effective*? De-coinciding is discrete, but it is operative from the get-go. De-coincidence belongs to a perspective that differs from overturning: as it wanders *on the wayside* of established ways, it effectively separates itself from them and thus spawns an *elsewhere*. Cracking open what is blocked, de-coincidence *re-opens possibilities* within an immobilized situation; in other words, it *re-possibilizes* the situation. De-coinciding from what I have already lived *re-possibilizes* my life. Change does not occur in two distinct stages as Revolution would have it: there is no destruction *then* reconstruction, no negative actions *then* positive actions. The simple fact of de-coinciding leads to the *re-opening of the possible*: because I am de-coinciding from the art that has already been made, I am simultaneously *re-possibilizing* the present of art.

*

Even though "innovation" has been promoted as the solution to all our problems (particularly climate change), the theme of innovation itself has become coincident: we would like to believe that innovation's capacity to "usher in the new" would be sufficient to address the woes of the present and precipitate us into the future. But can there be an "innovation" without a prior de-coincidence? Can newness emerge within thought itself? The previously evoked example of Descartes' de-coincidence is striking in this regard: as he de-coincided from the Christian philosophy of his time which put God at the center of the universe, he found a way of placing the cognizing activity of the Self at the center of the construction of a rational order. In doing so, he ushered in a new era of scientific and technological innovation. In other words, it is because Descartes de-coincided from established ways of thinking that he was able to innovate, not the other way around.

11/ A new kind of political commitment.

Is it possible to take a position *from the get-go* and to *commit* to political action, however urgent the need to act may be? Activism is only possible because of a prior instance of de-coincidence that *re-possibilizes* a blocked situation. De-coincidence is *at work*, from its onset; it establishes a *distance* with the situation that we are confronted with: de-coincidence allows us to detach ourselves from the situation because it *cracks open* what had made the present congeal into a form of unacceptability.

Without de-coincidence, activism remains fragile, easily reversible, and even forced at times. Political action understood as de-coincidence is not a way of avoiding to take a stand or of diluting the significance of said stance: on the contrary, it is the only way of making the stance or position effective insofar as it inscribes the advance of a political position in a *process*.

*

One should be careful to distinguish exorbitance (which leads to vain gesticulation and posturing) and *radicality*: understood in its literal sense, radicality is what brings us back to the *root*. If a position of disobedience does not inscribe itself in a radical labor of de-coincidence focused on cracking open the broader ideological subservience and obedience which maintains the *status quo*, then such an act of disobedience runs the risk of being anecdotal or sacrificial; it becomes all too easy to cover it up or to thwart it.

*

De-coincidence aims to re-think the Marxist concept of *alienation* to make it more suited for contemporary forms of political activism. In the past, alienating forces could be named: Capital, the Boss, or "the Man" operated in plain sight, it was possible to face them head on in order to strike back. The great Labor movements of the 19th and 20th century which led to paid time-off and universal healthcare (in Europe) resulted from such a direct confrontation of the laboring classes with the overt alienating operations of Capital and of its powers.

Nowadays, the alienating power is no longer isolatable nor discernable; it is a web of conditionings and network in which we are caught, largely on an unconscious level; there is no single person or function against which we can directly rail or immediately revolt ourselves. Alienation has become faceless, placeless, and un-targetable (I am just as complicit as You when it comes to 21st century alienation: I have a smartphone, use Instagram, and am also "plugged into" the great Machine or "Matrix," just like anyone else). The only thing I can do to resist alienation is to *crack it open*, however small, unassuming, or *unheard* that first crack may be. How could I ever face head-on what has become faceless?

Since *cracking open* shoots straight to the coherent and cohesive core of Coincidence and unties the latter through a process of un-adhering, de-coincidence is what allows me to dissociate myself from my own alienation. De-coincidence tears through alienation, it is a form of *dis-alienation*.

*

The concept of de-coincidence should be understood as a *fighting concept* capable of re-invigorating political initiative within philosophy. In previous generations of intellectuals and philosophers, philosophy and politics were merely juxtaposed: on the one hand, there was philosophical work; on the other hand, thre was political activism, which most often took the form of adhering to a Party or promoting a "cause." Juxtaposing the political and the philosophical and treating these two fields as independent, rather than intertwined, often yielded disastrous results for some of the 20th century's greatest philosophers: Martin Heidegger's adherence to National Socialism and Michel Foucault's ecstatic coverage of the Iranian Revolution are but two of the most infamous examples.

The concept of de-coincidence itself reflects a kind of political and philosophical *commitment;* it even deploys within itself a capacity that results from the *universalizing* potential of the concept. De-coincidence's universalizing deployment can be indefinitely shared, across languages and cultures, all the while acknowledging the singularities and pluralities of cultures. *Re-cognizing* the singularity of cultures helps us de-coincide from the all-too-easy recourse to the myth of a universal "human nature."

*

In the fight against the ambient and diffuse alienation that threatens us, there are perhaps many of us; and yet, there will never be enough of us. That is why the concept of de-coincidence has led us to form not an organization but an *association*. Cracks are led to meet each other; they reinforce their mutual *cracking-capacity* as they move from one field to another: various initiatives of de-coincidence can support each other and thus *co-operate*.

De-coincidence does not rally interests: the kind of *co-operative association* that results from it forms shifting interconnections rather than permanent bonds. Such a co-operative association of de-coincidences does not suppose a community of opinions, nor does it proclaim a set of "shared values;" it requires no slogans and does not need to be professed nor preached. The concept of de-coincidence does not serve as a single banner meant to assemble a range of points of view or beliefs. Instead, it promotes the *co-operative association* of infinitely diverse forms of *cracking open* that reinstate initiative and movement in blocked situations and configurations. It is this cracking open which allows *unheard thinking* to circulate once more. The world consumes coincidence and that is what makes it the world: de-coincidence cannot be consumed, it has no application, and yet, it can be *transmitted*.

CODA
De-coincidence, (a)live transmission(s): encounter(s) with an-Other

As I bring this book to a close, it seems opportune to reflect upon the concept that its final word suggests: *transmission*. My aim in writing this book was indeed to *transmit* the singular resources that François Jullien's thought offers for the world today. To stay true to the pedagogical intent of this book, it makes sense to end it with a story that illustrates my *intimate experience* of de-coincidence:

In the autumn of 2018, I crossed the walls of a place that had, until then, only existed in my (un)consciousness as a myth and as a mysterious echo- the psychiatric hospital.

In a small asylum nestled at the top of a hill of a gentrified neighborhood in LA, I began my work as a "mental health social worker." I was only a mere intern at the time, but the position became a salaried and unionized job at the end of my studies.

The encounter *with J. happened during the first weeks of the internship. It resulted from the suggestion of my supervisor who knew of my keen interest in the traditional therapeutic techniques of breath and resonance born in Ancient Asia. She sensed the* situation's *potential* and thought that there was "something to be done" to help, even if just a little bit, this individual living in immense psychic, social, and vital precariousness.

Since the ancestral techniques of breath and resonance folded themselves without difficulty into the then fashionable discourses of "mindfulness," she willfully encouraged me to go encounter *this very ill human named J.*

*

J. was a 45-year-old man who had first been diagnosed with schizophrenia over twenty years ago. In addition to his psychiatric diagnosis, he displayed a plethora of medical complications, including kidney and liver problems, most likely correlated to the high doses of neuroleptics he had been taking for years, and to his regular and prolonged use of crystal meth. J. said he had been a boxer in the past and, according to a fellow psychologist at the hospital, he sometimes imagined himself to be a famous soccer player named "Lampa." J. had been confined to the hospital for several months when I met him and he did not come out until six months later: his physiological condition and the medical support it required made it very difficult for the social services team to find a suitable place for him to stay. The reason for J.'s involuntary internment was related to auditory hallucinations; voices telling him to kill his mother and to kill himself.

As I entered the foul-smelling enclosure of the "adult unit" of the hospital for the first time, I found myself face to face with a prostrate man whose head gravitated fatally towards the ground; a man pacing in the only place where the patients were free to roam, a long and narrow corridor guarded by those who were then designated as "mental health workers."

Observed by their sullen gazes, we (both) stood there. He advanced; his head turned towards the ground, our furtive eyes barely met. We then headed to the "bubble room" of the adult sector, a room enclosed by another: the "nursing station."

A window separated the two rooms and allowed the medical personnel to constantly observe what was happening in the controllable space of the "bubble room." In this room, the patients were perfectly locked up, observed, and isolated. They did not have the keys giving them access to their "living quarters" and even less so the keys giving them the ability to leave the hospital.

The institution video-monitored the "bubble room" 24 hours a day, 7 days a week, recording the actions of both patients and caregivers. It was a strategic place of retreat for hospital staff when the violence of the patients would become unbearable; it was also a permanent monitoring device that conditioned the therapeutic encounter. In fact, the first encounters between caregivers and patients almost always took place in this room dedicated to a form of scientific observation that objectified and reified both the disease of the patients and the work of the caregivers.

Amid the violent and intermittent crashes of the doors closing and opening, drenched in the acrid and malodorous air of the hospital's "adult unit," J. and I encountered each other, there, in that "bubble room," face to face.

At the time, the only weapon in my therapeutic arsenal was a second-hand gong *bought on Craigslist and an invitation to become, for a* moment, *monitors of a* breath(ing) *at once indeterminate and indistinct; the one that Classical Chinese texts name* Qi (氣).

*

Faced with this panting man who was dozing off on a chair, almost ready to fall to the ground, I began to ring the gong, gently; I invited us to observe the movements of sound and breath that crossed the body of space that we shared together, *in that* moment. *I distinguished the filling of the* inspiration *from the emptying of the* expiration, *linking the first to the contraction of the muscles and the second to their relaxation, accompanying the floating sounds of the gong with the intermittent sound of my voice. This* moment *lasted about ten minutes, maybe less.*

Today, it seems almost insignificant or meaningless, as if it had become overwhelmed by the adhesiveness of discourse and submerged by the machinations of power. However, the speech that flowed from the resonance of the gong and from the rhythmicity that structured this moment still suggestively point(ed) towards a possibility: *the* emergence *of a phenomenon, of an* apparition, *and of a* movement *of daily life that is both simple and complex- two eyes meeting each other, two smiles etching themselves, two bodies propping themselves up, there, together, in between "Heaven and Earth," as the Ancient Chinese texts say.*

Following up on the active instance of words that were both empty of content and full of emotion, his eyes locked into mine, J. let out a thunderous: "THAT WAS GOOD !!!" In that very moment, it seemed clear that there would be, there in the "bubble room," in such a(n) (in)hospitable environment, a semblance of viability for the therapeutic activity of the gong.

*

We practiced the therapeutic ritual of the gong weekly for almost 6 months. One day, J. arrived looking particularly unwell, his breath(ing) even more haphazard than in past sessions. According to the hospital staff, his auditory hallucinations had become once again very present; he was beginning to despair of this endless internment in the asylum. That day, literally out of breath, he asked that we stop the ritual halfway; I honored his request. The following week, the ritual resumed: his smile returned, perhaps because by then his mother was beginning to work to bring him home.

After nine long months of confinement, she realized that we would not find a "placement" adapted to the medical care that the renal and hepatic condition of her son required. The social services team that I was part of pleaded with the psychiatrist who ran the institution, the whimsical Dr. Z, so that J. could obtain the legal right to return home.

J.'s mother was heard and I had the privilege of watching him leave the hospital the day she came to pick him up. It was a moment of great emotion: the social worker, who spoke to him like a three-year-old child and J.'s mother both began to cry. As they wept, I emitted a deep exhalation and sigh, feeling that it was the end of one chapter and the beginning of another one...

*

Unaware at the time of the existence of the concept of de-coincidence, *I could not characterize my work with J. using this term. In retrospect, however, it seems to me that this* je ne sais quoi *which was taking place in that little asylum nestled at the top of a hill illustrates the ethical, political, and therapeutic meaning of the concept. On the one hand, on the political level, we were discretely* resisting *the ideological language of the status quo: "sanity," "mental health," and "mindfulness." In a barely perceptible way, we were* cracking open from *within the very frameworks and terms that were imposed explicitly and implicitly to caregivers and patients. On the other hand, on the ethical and therapeutic level, we were* (re)opening *possibilities both in the life of this man who was dangerously close to physical, psychic, and social death, and in my own life. These privileged instances of aperture led me to work in the psychiatric field in Los Angeles for another year and have since then constituted the experiential basis of my doctoral research. Although I felt that this therapeutic practice in the making was intimately linked to a deep sense of ethics, politics, and narrative that I had inherited from my "classical" literary and philosophical training, it is only when I met Parisian psychoanalysts upon my return to France, and* encountered *François Jullien's thought, that I was able to conceptualize this singular approach to the clinic of psychosis in terms of* de-coincidence(s).

*

Since then, the concept of de-coincidence(s) *has given me the* capacity *to make sense of several other challenging (and arguably senseless) experiences. It has been a useful tool that continues to help me when I seek to re-open possibilities in situations, both personal and professional, which have imperceptibly blocked themselves.*

When I submitted paperwork in 2020 to receive accreditations for my clinical social work studies and my 2000+ hours of field experience in Los Angeles, in order to obtain the license necessary to seek out a job as a psychotherapist in France, the Ministry of Higher Education did not recognize my education nor my experience as being "equivalent" with the academic curriculum in psychology dispensed at French universities. I (literally) did not "coincide" with the French (academic) system; from the government's perspective, my training and work experience were in-adequate.

*

Three years down the line, I found myself in another (tragi-comic) position of de-coincidence as I began to take the necessary steps to unblock *the administrative deadlock that the government had cornered me into. At that point, I realized that I would have to de-coincide from my installed status as an "adjunct faculty member" to become both a student and a teacher at the University where I had been a doctoral fellow and a lecturer for the past two years. In addition to my doctorate, I had to complete another three years of coursework and (unpaid) internships at the Bachelors and Masters level in order to obtain the governmental license needed to seek out employment in psychiatry in France.*

While this typically French and truly Kafkaesque bureaucratic nightmare may seem to be nothing more than a regrettable series of unfortunate events that highlights the asphyxiating power of (ideological) coincidence, it is in fact a perfect illustration of de-coincidence's capacity to re-open possibilities *inside a* blocked *governmental system.*

Paradoxically, my position as an "insider/outsider" within French academia -I had first studied Ancient and Classical literature in public High School in France, but had done all my undergraduate and graduate studies in the US until my doctorate- allowed me to find a wider margin of operation *to de-coincide in my role as a lecturer and adjunct faculty member within the French public university system.*

When I detected *that the bureaucratic inertia of the university in fact gave me a great deal of latitude when it came to choosing teaching materials, I leveraged the* situation's potential *and began incorporating some of the Ancient Greek and Classical Chinese texts discussed in this book in the curriculum of the university's Bachelor's Degree in psychology.*

The disorderliness, decay, and general "stuckness" of the French public university system in fact allowed me to re-open a space for the Humanities in what is typically considered a "practical" and increasingly "scientific" field of the academy- psychology.Psychology is indeed an academic field where "theoretical" discussions most often take the form of elaborate (and sterile) rhetorical jousts between various representatives of the doctrines of coincidence *that populate its nebulous landscape across the globe: cognitive psychology, trans-cultural psychology, integrative psychology, clinical psychology, behavioral psychology, social psychology, neuro-psychology, evolutionary psychology, psycho-physiology, (neo)Lacanian psychoanalysis, (post)Freudian psychoanalysis, Jungian (psycho) analysis, Buddhist (ego)analysis, existential (dasein)analysis, relational analysis, to name but a few...*

*

As I write down these lines, I cannot help but be reminded of the "100 Schools of Thought" which flourished between the 8th and 2nd century BCE in Early China. When I think of Zhuang Zhou, the dreamer, ironist, and de-coincider *who lived in those troubled times and to whom the* Book of Master Zhuang *or the* Zhuangzi *is attributed, I imagine what would he could have written about the "100 Schools of Psychology" of the late 20th and early 21st century and find myself smiling. In the midst of a fanciful daydream, I suppose that he would have found the proliferation of these Schools and doctrines reminiscent of his own experience in Early China over 2300 years ago, and I envision him depicting the ideologies of the Scientists and Politicians of the Modern World with the same biting irony that he used to portray the ideologies of the mythical and historical Sages and Emperors of the Ancient World...*

*

If anything, this auto-biographical conclusion can provide a concrete inkling *of how the intercultural and philosophical concept of* de-coincidence *can indeed* re-open possibilities, *not just in the Humanities, but also across (non)academic fields. Even though the philosophical, sinological, and to a lesser extent, historical, and psychological contents of this book fall squarely within fields that are typically associated with academics and academia, it is my hope that the wide range of concepts and texts that it has covered in its effort to* transmit *a synthesis of François Jullien's philosophy has inspired You, the reader, whoever You may be, to* de-coincide, *even if just a little, from your habitual ways of thinking, and, above all,* living.

ANNEX I
The Universal, the Uniform, the Common and the Problem(s) of Human Rights.

1/ The universal, the uniform and the common: a genealogic and pedagogical approach.

a. Tracing the history of the strong universal, distinguishing it from the uniform and the common.

The intercultural understanding of universality is first and foremost pedagogical. The term "universal" remains equivocal, which is why it is important to insist on distinguishing a weak significance of this term from a strong one. The weak significance of the universal refers to generality, whereas the strong one refers to necessity. If we are to say that music is a universal feature of human culture, then we are using the term in its weak sense, we are stating that, based on empirical observation, it is possible to suggest that what we call "music" is generally found across human cultures. If we state that the universal equation used to calculate speed is distance divided by time ($s=d/t$), we are then referring to the strong significance of the term. The strong significance of the universal alludes to a Kantian *a priori,* transcendental, and pre-empirical dimension derived from logic and mathematics that can then be translated into the empirical realm.

It is the trail of this strong, Kantian significance of the universal that one must follow in order to determine the relevance of this concept in the globalized world and dispel the equivocations that dilute its potency.

As one follows the trail of the strong universal, it becomes impossible to elude the question of Western culture's geo-historical dominance in the Modern Era. As such, the globalized world of the 21st century has confronted us with the *singularity* of the Western world's conception of universality: it has made apparent the geo-historic conditions that enabled the development of a Modern science and technology rooted in the *logos* of the Greeks. In other words, if we are to take seriously the Kierkegaardian and later Sartrean critique of the universal as necessarily singular,[273] then we must relentlessly pursue that pre-empirical dimension of the universal aligned with necessity; *in spite of* the singularly Western heritage of the concept itself.

This question is of critical importance if we are to assess the possibility of a universalizing understanding of ethics. In order to attain one that isn't conditioned by cultural preconceptions, it becomes necessary to chart a geo-historical understanding of the universal. On the basis of this geo-historical understanding, we can *reflect upon* the necessarily singular history of the concept of "universal ethics."

The genealogical and geo-historic tracing of the universal is composite and chaotic, filled with problematic junctions that blur the boundaries separating the inner and the outer, the relevant and the irrelevant. In this effort to pedagogically restitute a strong notion of the universal, it seems useful to distinguish it from two other equivocal terms: the *uniform* and the *common*.

*

The ubiquity of the uniform in the globalized world might lead us to mistake it for the universal when, in effect, it represents a perversion of the universal. The uniform is derived from market forces, not logical abstraction. It represents the proliferation of standardized procedures and practices, the flattening of cultural differences, and the diffusion of a uniformized mode of existence determined by the technological structures of market economies. In an effort to revive

314

the universal and delineate the common, it is critical to resist the uniform and to denounce patterns of uniformization and standardization. It should therefore be clear that little attention will be devoted to the uniform in our attempt to retrieve the potency of the universal and articulate an effective understanding of the common.

*

Contrarily to the uniform, it seems as though the notion of the common still holds relevance. The common implies the idea of *sharing*, for example the *natural common* which refers to what a given species shares i.e, what they possess *in common*. The *political common* refers to a *chosen common,* to what we have *chosen together.* The common is not a prescriptible notion, it is noticed or built. The *choice of the common* reflects a political process in which the near and the far, the neighbor and the stranger, become potentially equivocal, it refers to an irreducible plurality of phenomena. On the one hand, choosing the common can reflect a process of (de)limitation where the shareable horizon of commonality is perpetually stretched in an effort to coalesce singular communities. On the other hand, the search for commonality can devolve into communitarian enclosures and entrapments. It is therefore crucial to maintain the universal as a *regulatory* point of reference for the common to prevent the advent of exclusionary communitarian logics within the political common. In order to do so, it is necessary to trace its chaotic and nearly impossible history composed of three distinct strata: a logical and philosophical stratum indebted to Aristotelian *logos,* a political stratum rooted not only in Greek, but also in Roman history, as well as a third theological stratum found in the Christian faith and in scholastic doctrine.[274]

b. The philosophical origins of the universal or Aristotle's "holism."

The original philosophical stratum of the universal can be found first and foremost in Aristotle's logic and metaphysics where the philosopher attempts to think from the perspective of the *all*: *to holon* in Greek.[275] For Aristotle the perspective of the universal constitutes a founding and commanding principle *(archè)* of philosophy. Aristotle thus establishes philosophy as a discourse that thinks in and on the *mode of the universal* by achieving a formalized, abstract logic that departs from the immediacy of sensory perception and from the singularity of empirical existence. Aristotelian metaphysics posit the universal as necessary for scientific clairvoyance: the concept of the universal is designed to guarantee science's *effectivity*, regardless of abstract and material determinations. Following Socrates' and Plato's footsteps, Aristotle's concept of the universal aims to separate the contingent from the necessary, opinion *(doxa)* from knowledge *(episteme)*. While *doxa* can hold some degree of equivocal truth, Aristotle' notion of a universal *logos* demands an unequivocal and *univocal* truth always identical to itself, regardless of individual determinations.

In this regard, Aristotle separates the individual from *logos*, setting the stage for scholasticism's position regarding the singularity of existence absorbed by the universal eternity of God. In this scholastic view of the world, God serves as the universal *end,* or *telos* in Greek, in which the individual is resorbed as his existence reaches a close. The scholastic and teleological understanding of the Aristotelian universal also prefigures Modern Science's understanding of the universal as an epistemic horizon ceaselessly pushed forward by the process of scientific discovery.

The teleological understanding of the universal developed by Aristotle and reprised by scholasticism and Modern Science constitutes both a decisive turning point in Western thought and also a traumatic instance. Traumatic in the sense that such a concept of the universal supposes a radical division, or *dissociation,* that squarely separates the vocal and embodied utterance of an individual truth from the silent scientific truth of the universal. The universal thus dissociates the existential from the scientific, as exemplified by the scholastic formulation *existentia est singularium, scientia est de universalibus*: "Existence is of the singular, science is towards the universal."[276] In this paradigm, existence is thus *composed* of singularities, as exemplified by the genitive *singularium*, whereas science is *directed towards* the universal, as exemplified by the dative formula-

316

tion *de universalibus*. In other words, the teleological and scientific universal derived from Aristotle's logic precludes the existential insofar as only it exists as an end, as a *telos*, and not as such. The logical tension that opposes the universal and the singular, the necessary and the contingent, the scientific and the existential, exemplifies a rift in Western thought where literary and philosophical discourse begin to compete with each other. Literature thus becomes the place of the singular and the subjective in the Western world, in near opposition to rational and technical scientific discourse, which aims to be as universal and objective as possible.[277]

c. The birth of the universal as a legal concept in Ancient Rome.

In order to detach ourselves from the logical and epistemological tension that arises in the teleological understanding of the universal derived from Aristotelian logic and metaphysics, it is necessary to investigate the political fate of the concept of the universal in the Roman Empire. We are in the habit of considering the influence of the Roman civilization as secondary to the Greek one in the development of Western thought, and yet when it comes to the universal the Roman Empire represents a striking moment of conceptual innovation. Indeed, in Ancient Rome the concept of universal finds a newfound usage as it becomes linked to the notion of the law, *juris*, which creates a *legal common* across the territory of the Empire. The progressive extension of Roman citizenship beyond the commonality of the *municipio,* the actual city of Rome, thus transformed Rome into not just a place but also into a universal.

The historical originality of Rome consists in this fusion of the universal and of the common made manifest by the universal citizenship, the *universa civitas,* extended to all the denizens of the Roman Empire by the Caracalla edict of 212. This extension of citizenship across the territory of the Empire institutes a linkage between the singular *urbs*, represented by the city of Rome, and the world, the *orbis*. Roman administrators viewed the universal city and its law not as moral compasses but as effective tools of political *governance*. Roman law became the effective universal link that binds together individuals living across a variety of territories into a *common* legal and political framework. As such, the *universal community* that the legal framework of Roman citizenship delineates attaches the citizens to a common political and legal body that extends beyond the singular territorial and cultural borders that compose the Empire. In the Roman world, the universal leaves its purely philosophical abode to form the basis of a series of legal statutes that are universally applicable throughout the Empire.

d. St. Paul and the advent of the theological universal.

The legal understanding of the universal forged by the Romans was then augmented by a third stratum of the universal: the theological one devised by St. Paul. In this regard, intercultural philosophy follows Alain Badiou's interpretation of Paul's tale as a story of the universal.[278] St. Paul's diffusion of the Gospels thus professes a doctrine in which the subject empties his plenitude of singularities into the universal void of God's Grace. The emergence of Christianity within the Roman context initiates a reversal where the universality of divine Love supplants the universality of temporal Law. Yet this universal Love, unlike Roman law, does not exist in full, as such; it is a void or rather a voiding zone in which the action of God's Grace empties the singular subject of his particularities. Once God's Grace has emptied the subject of his particularities, he then becomes a universal child of God in addition to being a singular individual, equal to *all* his brethren.

The motion of emptying that characterizes the Christian understanding of universal Grace reflects a tension inherent within the very story of Christ, the story of a man supposedly born of God, who died like a slave; a man whose death was rendered *impossible* because of the universal Love set forth by his Father's Grace.

In a sense, it is the *madness* of the Christian story which is most universal because it requires no justification beyond Faith. The story of Christ and its lack of abstraction are impervious to ideological particularities and to philosophical logic, the universality of the tale of suffering and of redemption that Paul tells does not require the existence of Christ as an individual. Rather it makes possible the construction of Christ as a universal figure of Love, as a True character of *fiction*. Although Paul was a contemporary of Christ, he never met him and did not speak his language; Paul initiated the "deterritorialization" of the Christian faith out of the semitic world and into the Greek and Roman world.

By folding Christ's message into the language of the universal, Greek *logos*, Paul turns the believers of Christian faith into a *universal body* where territorialities, singularities, and differences dissolve into Christ as in Galateans 3:28: "There is neither Jew nor Greek, slave nor free, male nor female, for you are all one in Christ Jesus." Paul folded the semitic tale of Christ into the language of the universal: he accentuated the universalizing propensity contained within the Christian narrative of Resurrection and transformed it into a message that obliterates cultural, social, and biological differences. Through Paul's Word, Christ becomes a figure of historic *self-realization*; the universal representation of a God that transcends borders. Unlike the Jewish God, the Christian God invented by Paul is not assigned to a people: His Love embraces the totality of humanity. Paul became the promoter of a newfound universal; the universal community of *humankind*. While Christ's existence and the narrative surrounding it tell the tale of a singular individual born in a moment in time, the Resurrection diffuses a message of transcendence woven into a universal *credo*. The *credo* or testimonial of Faith that the Resurrection requires relays a fundamental Christian belief: human singularities, however uncanny they may be, are *necessarily* reabsorbed into the universal and eternal Grace of God's Oneness.

Paul's Christian understanding of a universal community of humankind prefigures later conceptual elaborations on the universal, namely those born out of the Enlightenment. Hegel and Marx in particular bear a great debt to Paul's understanding of the universal: for both thinkers, the singularity of humanity is reabsorbed into a universal totality- the "End of History." Hegel's "Great Man" and Marx's "Proletariat" offer a variation on the Christian theme of an earthly body destined to transcend material determinations in a dialectic where transcendent, universal, and eternal Liberty *incarnate* the immanent self-realization of the Spirit of History.[279]

e. Leveraging Ancient China's exteriority to detach the universal from ethnocentric universalism.

The universal acts as a root concept in Western thought and yet we cannot take its universality for granted. As we trace the history of the universal beginning with Aristotle, moving through Descartes, Kant, Hegel, all the way to Marx, it becomes impossible to silence the dissenting voices of philosophers like Hume, Kierkegaard or Nietzsche who emphasized the concreteness of the singular and the empirical over the emptiness and abstraction of the universal. Hume's suspicious voice made even Kant question the very substance or substrate, *hupokaimenon* in Greek, that our categories of thought rely on, forcing him to devise newfound strategies to promote the universal in all of its logical and philosophical glory.[280] The recourse to the exteriority of Ancient China awakens philosophy from its dogmatic slumber just like Kant was awoken by Hume: it compels philosophers to devise newfound approaches to promote a strong universal in an era where the legitimacy of the very notions of universality and necessity are being pulled into question. When (Western) philosophy takes into account the singularity of Ancient Chinese thought, it is compelled to seek out the universal *outside* of the habitual Aristotelian "universal categories" of substance, essence, and necessity. The recourse to Ancient China makes philosophy understand that the concept of the universal was in no way necessary for the development of civilization; tracing its chaotic history reveals the very singularity of its development as a concept across the Greek, Roman, and Christian world.

Ancient Chinese thought forces philosophical discourse to accept that the universal does not exist *as such*; it demonstrates that the concept itself is the product of a singularity and not a transcendent(al) category of thought that (potentially) exists beyond Space and Time. We must indeed cease to understand the universal as a *given* that exists as such when we trace its history and instead learn to draw our attention to the very *constructed* nature of this concept. Doing so will allow us to better appreciate the resources it holds and thus determine its appropriate regulatory usage in today's globalized context.

Determining how to potently leverage the strength of the universal requires us to go beyond the recourse to Ancient China's exteriority, it demands the critical appraisal of a universalist ideology that was too often used as a pretext to justify ethnocentrism, colonialism, and exploitation. Universalism is indeed but a thinly disguised imperialism and it is therefore imperative that we separate the concept of the universal from this universalist and imperialistic legacy if we are to preserve its credibility in the globalized world. Whereas universalism represents an effusive ideological saturation that overflows toxic waste, the concept of the universal represents an empty vessel that induces a *lack* capable of destabilizing ideological, political, and economic forces.

When the universal serves as a basis for rebellion, not conformity, it acts as a horizon destined to be pushed, as a negative force of *resistance* that counters the totalization of universalism. In this regard, the intercultural understanding of the universal remains faithful to the genius of Kant who was able to not just posit the universal as a constitutive category of thought, but also to construct it as an empty, *regulatory principle*.

2/ The problem(s) of the (in)human(e): intercultural perspectives in ethics and international law.

a. The People's Republic of China and the supposed "Western-ness" of Human Rights.

If the pedagogical approach to the universal has demonstrated anything, it is the embeddedness of this concept in the geo-historic context of Western thought and civilization. Could the necessity of this concept therefore be solely relative to the geo-historical determinations of the West? How can it be separated from the problematic imperialism of Western universalism? In other words, how does the universal remain relevant in a world where the West's supremacist history is being pulled more and more into question?

The People's Republic of China certainly seems to be aware of this tension: it fortuitously exploits the erosion of Western universalism to elude justifications regarding its documented (and atrocious) exactions in Xinjiang province and in Tibet. The leaders of the

Chinese communist party have even gone as far as to condemn the universalism of the legal and normative framework of human rights in the name of a self-professed ideal of Harmony that is supposedly more reflective of China's "5000 year old cultural identity."[281] The People's Republic of China's actions in Xinjiang province and in Tibet are of course contrary to the universalizing principles of human rights set forth by international institutions like the UN ; and yet, through their very discourse and actions, the perpetrators of atrocity at the head of the Chinese regime brazenly expose the powerlessness of these international institutions that they claim to be beholden to the ideological and imperialistic agenda of the West.

How can we therefore preserve and defend the universal principles that these institutions uphold, while also departing from the Western universalist and imperialistic ideology that these perpetrators forcefully challenge with their violence? In other words, how do we maintain the relevance of the *concept* of "human rights" in a world where they are so brazenly violated in the name of cultural exceptionalism?

*

The singular history of the notion of human rights is indeed tied to the Western history of the universal, emerging first with Hobbes and Rousseau's theorization of the social contract.[282] While it was critical to investigate the history of the universal to clean it up from a thinly veiled ethnocentric and imperialistic form of universalism, it is now of the utmost importance to preserve the *universalizing* emancipatory reach of the *concept* of universal human rights.

The very notion of human rights confronts us to a translation challenge. Derived in part from the French *Déclaration Universelle des Droits de l'Homme*, the legal framework of human rights and international law does not capture the abstraction contained in the French genitive formation *"droits de l'homme."* What is important in the original French formulation is that the construction of the legal apparatus of "rights" (*"droits"*) *precedes* the definition of what constitutes "Man" (l'*Homme*), or in more modern terms, a human.

The apparatus put forth by these legal rights is not dependent on some positive understanding of humans and of their basic needs. Instead, it depends on an *abstracted,* legal understanding of a *universal community* of *humankind.* In other words, the intercultural, and thus legal, approach to human rights does not represent an adhesion to a set of pre-existing values like dignity or respect that define the "human" in some positive capacity; it functions instead like an abstracting and universalizing *regulatory tool* intended to be shared across cultures to *resist* the *inhumane.*

*

In an era where ideals of harmony and integration begin to shape the global discourse, not only due to the influence of the People's Republic of China, but also in response to the global ecological crisis, the concept of a universal community of humankind can remain relevant if it is understood as a *tool for resistance.* It is this absolute dimension of this universal community, the one that cannot be dissolved by cultural relativism, which needs to be preserved and *utilized* to resist atrocity. In order to dissociate human rights from their universalist ideological provenance, it is necessary to preserve the force of *abstraction* contained in the universal. To become operative and useful, human rights must reach beyond "feel-good" PR strategies, they need to be leveraged and effectively *put to use.*

One could argue that the abstraction inherent to the negative, conceptual, and intercultural approach to rights of the universal community of humankind is less tangible than the values-based understanding of individual human rights. Yet it is the very unconditionality, neutrality, and *indeterminacy* of abstraction that upholds the universalizing force of the *concept* of human rights and which strengthens their *legal capacity* to act as a *regulatory ground* for human living.

*

b. Master Meng's encounter with the Emperor or the negative universality of the inhuman(e).

We must therefore cease to understand human rights as given and transcendent principles but rather understand how we can make them *operative*. It seems as though the operativity of human rights is not to be found in a positive approach where one must adhere to them as values but rather in a *negative* approach that crafts tools designed to protest, reject, and denounce atrocity. A negative and conceptual understanding of the "human" does not constitute a *credo*. Rather, it is a tool born out of *necessity* that can be operationalized to challenge *inhumaneness*.

The negative universality of human rights demonstrates not a surplus of humanity or of humaneness, but rather a *lack* thereof. The rebellious understanding of universal human rights gives us a tool to open a breach in the ideological saturations that diffuse inhumaneness across the world. Human rights do not give us the means to adhere to a set of preconstructed values. Instead they give us the strength to *refuse inhumaneness* on a legal and existential basis. This refusal and this resistance are not done in the name of culturally-determined moral values, they constitute a reaction to *abjection*, a relinquishing of the inhumane.[283] The intercultural understanding of human rights therefore forms the basis for an ethical refusal of the *abject*, it represents a recusal of the inhumane on the simple basis of *non-recognition*. In other words, universal human rights are tied to a sensible, elementary, and, above all, *necessary* reaction to the *inhumane*.

*

To demonstrate the intercultural operativity of this negative understanding of human rights, it might prove useful to allude to the closing story of the opening chapter of the Classical Chinese text *Mengzi* or *Mencius*.

In this short narrative, the Emperor questions the Master's teachings regarding the moral propensity of the human being.[284] In an effort to address the Emperor's questioning, the Master tells the sovereign that he once heard a story where the Emperor refused to slay an ox for a sacrifice, and offered instead a sheep. Master Meng then goes on to state that the Emperor refused to slay the ox because he sensed the animal's distress after gazing into its eyes, thus demonstrating a human propensity towards sympathy that even reaches beyond the human realm and extends towards the non-human.

In another passage, Master Meng evokes the example of someone reacting when he sees a child falling in a well and argues that any true human wi ll reach out in an effort to save the child, regardless of personal interest. The *Mengzi* thus offers us a *reactive* understanding of the humane where moral action is not the product of an action referred to a universally valid judgment of what is right and what is wrong (Kant). Instead, morality and ethics become a simple reaction, a manifestation of "humaneness" or *ren* (仁). Master Meng's disqualification of those who would not reach out to help the child is both lapidary and beautiful: they "betray themselves" (自賊) and thus become *inhuman(e)*.[285] This episode of the *Mengzi* highlights the strength of the negative understanding of humaneness and inhumanness because it shows that it is much simpler to negatively demonstrate the nature of what is inhumane, as opposed to positively define or identify the nature of what is human(e). In other words, the kind of morality that Master Meng delineates does not offer a positive assessment of what constitutes humanity and humaneness. Rather, it offers a simple basis for justifying our reactions to the inhumane.

*

Master Meng's stories show us that a *neg-active* ethics grounded in a rejection of the inhumane can provide a strong foundation for the construction of a universal community inclusive, not only of humans, but also of non-humans. On the basis of such an understanding of ethics, it is possible to refuse the inhumaneness of factory farms and mass deforestations, to deplore the senselessness of the obliteration of cultural artifacts, and to react to the sheer horrors of war and colonization without invoking a positive and ideologically conditioned ideal of dignity, morality, or even "nature." The simple refusal of the abject and of the inhumane demonstrates a moral propensity that lies beneath any adherence to a set of values, it represents the simple recognition of an inhumane activity and the *non-recognition* of the humane within the human. As such, a negative and universalizing understanding of the inhumane can indeed provide a solid ground for an intercultural ethics predicated not upon a definition of "the human," but rather upon a simple recognition of the inhumane.

It should therefore be clear to the reader that the negativistic and intercultural approach to the universal resists any kind of assimilationism and any kind of cultural appropriation. It does not seek to fold cultures into each other in the name of a positive and prefabricated universalist ideology. Instead, it simply stresses the *effectiveness* of universalizing concepts like *human(e) rights,* as well as their capacity to offer means of resistance. From an intercultural perspective, the rights of humankind thus constitute a set of legal and conceptual tools born out of necessity, tools designed to construct an ever-expanding *common horizon* that can never be enclosed. The *common horizon* traced by universalizing concepts breaches patterns of similarity and dissemblance: it demonstrates a *lack* within each totality, a *resistance* to the enclosing of commonality and assimilation.

*

Against all forms of communitarianism and cultural exceptionalism, the intercultural understanding of the universal aims to form the basis of a genuine dialog where one does not differentiate nor assimilate an "Other" and where one instead begins to *weave together* the threads that lie *in between* cultures to patch together a strong *constructible common.* This ever- inclusive, and yet ever- demanding, constructible common is born out of the necessary *labor* of dialog which unfolds at its own rhythm and pace, surely far slower than the rapid march of ideology and discourse.

ANNEX II
Landscape(s) as the unthought of Reason.

1/ Neither objective nor subjective: the specular biases of landscape(s).

Our global, and in appearance rational, conception of the "subject" and of the "object" seems intrinsically tied to the European conception of the landscape that emerged in the Early Modern era. The emergence of "landscape" (*landschapt* in German, *paysage* in French) as a common term in 17th century Europe coincides with the advent of Early Modern thought, that is to say with the arising of what can loosely and imperfectly be characterized as "rationalism." The European definition of the landscape emphasizes the idea of vantage point from which the subject can "scope out" an objective visual field that extends before his eyes. In other words, the European view of the landscape supposes a primarily *visual* understanding of *perception* grounded in a dual subject/object distinction that emphasizes the primacy of *spectatorship*.

*

As hinted at in the 5th chapter, the notion of "*Shan-Shui*" (山水) or *mountain(s)-water(s)* articulated in the texts of the scholars, poets, and painters of Imperial China, commonly translated as "landscape" in English, wanders *on the wayside* of such distinctions. To invigorate and lay bare the binding material which ties the Early Modern view of the landscape to the subjective schemata of perception, it will prove useful to leverage once more the conceptual devices of intercultural philosophy. Once again, the point is not to "compare and contrast" but instead to construct a *reflexive vis-à-vis*, a mirroring device capable of *reflecting* an *intercultural common(s)* which remains *unthought*. Putting "landscape" face to face with 山水 or "mountain(s)-water(s)" *alters* the contemporary globalized notions of landscape, subject, and object: it facilitates the emergences of an intercultural *in between* that can renew thought in both the Arts *and* Sciences, be they "Eastern" or "Western." The mirroring devices of intercultural reflection induce a diffuse effect of *refraction* which manifests itself in the "here and now" of a paradoxical moment of *unhomeliness,* that (un)fathomable and (un)certain feeling-apparition captured in Sigmund Freud's 1919 essay *The Uncanny* or *Das Unheimlich*.[286] The cultural biases of landscape(s) allow us to appreciate the distance which separates the mirroring from the mirrored; they also highlight the *liminal space* that that lies *in between* the two, however *altered* and *unhomely* it may be.

2/ From visual perception to perceptual-affective backgrounds: correlations, polarities, and shifts.

Confining ourselves to the pictorial field (discussing only pictorial representations of landscapes across cultures for example) would betray the amplitude of the distance which separates a "landscape paradigm" from a "*Shan-Shui* paradigm."[287] Indeed, the "mountain(s)-water(s)" of Classical Chinese literature introduce *the sonic within the visual* as well as *processuality within representativity*. The distance separating these two "esthetic paradigms" brings into play the *tension* that pulls them apart; the vis-à-vis of "landscape" and of *Shan-Shui* reflects a *figurable field* which allows us to *step outside* the language-thought of Being. In the *Shan-Shui* context, the visual transforms itself into the sonorous. The notion of "mountain(s)-water(s)" evokes just as much the soft sound of the babbling brook as it does the stark visual of the mineral mountain piercing through clouds. The juxtaposition of "landscape" and *Shan-Shui* allows us to gain an enhanced perspective of the *dualist impulse(s)* that would want us to neatly separate a *visual-intellective* field (fine arts, calligraphy, and literature) from a *sonic-affective* field (performative arts, music and dramaturgy).

As we shall see, *both* these fields of sensory experience can be *accessed* through the *Shan Shui* repertoire of *sound-images* as played on the Classical Chinese *Guqin* zither first mentioned in chapter V. The shift from the visual to the sonic makes possible the emergence of an intercultural *common ground(s)*- the *perceptual-affective,* which is neither purely visual nor purely sonic; neither purely intellective nor purely affective; neither purely cultural nor purely individual. Thus, the *Shan-Shui* or "mountain(s)-water(s)" sounds that emanate from the *Guqin* do not reflect a sound *or* an image, but rather *a sound-image*. In other words, the *sonic reflections* that emanate from the *Guqin* not only produce a *mise-en-abyme* that sonically *re-presents* the visual elements of a "landscape," they also tear through *the fabric of silence*, thus generating *sound-images* that mirror the *abyssal marking(s)* of *(ab)sensitivity.*

3/ Soundscape(s) and floating listening.

a. The strangeness of the between-two-notes and the common constancy of (dys)harmonic distance.

If one were to describe Guqin music in purely perceptual and objective terms, one could allude to the sliding, pinching, and friction that characterizes it. Its *(a)tonal ressources* come from the co-implication of sound and silence that the playing of the instrument requires. The sonorities of a famous Guqin piece like "Flowing-Water(s)" or Liu Shui (流水)[288] evoke both the visual and sonic elements of landscape(s): the pulsating vibrations and the resonant activity of the tones bring into play the dynamic polarities and the harmonic correlations that animate a sonic landscape or *soundscape* where we are no longer referred to a subjective position of objective spectatorship. Instead, the resonant tones of the soundscape open us up to a *(en)livened field of (un)awareness,* a flotational and transitional *living zone* that is as much inhabited as it is observed. The "mountain(s)-water(s)" and landscape(s) of *Shan-Shui*, which are both sonic and visual, affective, and perceptive, emerge *out of the Guqin* tones; they emphasize the *living (de) tension* of the *oscillations* and *reverberations* of a soundscape that revolves around polarities and correlations. The towering ascent of the rocky mountain vs. the lush descent of the flowing water, the hard silence of shapely stone vs. the soft sound of the formless wind, the grave density of the calligraphic gesture vs. the alert levity of the painted mark… Such are the kind of correlative and bipolar parallelisms that structure the poetic and allusive sound-images of Shan Shui.

b. Beneath Being and universal harmony: evanescent reverberation(s) and floating listening.

The sound-images of the *Guqin* reflect a paradoxical (a)temporality that appeals to both the ephemeral and the eternal. They transpose the landscape from a visual field into a sonic field and thus produce a *soundscape* that is structured by the *mathematical harmonies* common to all cultures *and* by the singular *microtonal distances* that reflect their incommensurability. The sounds of *Guqin* therefore seem to open up a *reflective space-time* imbued with textural and sonic colorations that diffuse seemingly infinite *waves of resonance.*

If one were to hear an *intelligible common* in the sounds of the *Guqin,* one would have to listen not to the tones or even to their harmonic resonance but instead to their *reverberations.* Asserting the transcendental universality of mathematically identifiable forms of harmonic resonance reflects a metaphysical idea of difference that separates, and thus transcends, the always singular and contingent discrepancies of various musical languages. Such a metaphysical understanding of harmony as a transcendent or transcendental metaphysical differentiator aligns both with the ideological discourse of "the music of the spheres" or *harmonia mundi* of the West, and with the Chinese imperial ideology of Harmony *(Hé* 和).[289] Analyzing *Guqin* music solely from the perspective of harmony or harmonics would make us miss the fertile resources contained in the familiar and yet foreign *reflexivity* of *floating listening.*

Floating listening is of course a concept which pertains to *Guqin* music and which alludes to psychotherapeutic technique insofar as it offhandedly references the famous Freudian notion of "evenly suspended attention" or *Gleichschwebende Aufmersamkeit.*[290] Floating listening dissolves the limits separating the perceptual from the affective, the subjective from the objective, the universal from the singular, the sonorous from the silent. The reverberations of musical tones and of discourse *un-anchor* the listening experience: listening ceases to be a *spectatorial* experience and becomes instead a *floating* one. The tones and the discourse do not appeal to an ontological "quiddity" or "thingness" of the notes or of the words; they do not stand in as *representatives* of a metaphysical "thing in-itself," nor do they point towards some kind of definitive signification. Instead, their continuous and processual *waxing-waning* brings into focus the emergence of a *floating field of (un)awareness* (another possible translation of *Gleichschwebende Aufmersamkeit*), thus pointing in the direction of a *reflective transparency.* These transparent reflections unfold in the wake of the *perceptive-affective reverberations* of music and discourse, which are understood here not as representative or significant objects of (psychoanalytic) art or science, but instead as *living landscapes.* Reverberations and echoes hint towards a *crystalline imperceptible* which renders impossible any form of subjective synthesis that would want to neatly separate the subject from the object, the self from the other, the end from the beginning, or the sonorous from the silent.

Floating (un)awareness, as it *attunes* to the reverberations of soundscapes where the visual switches into the sonic and vice-versa, makes possible the emergence of a *specularity,* of a *mirroring space.* In the specular space of the soundscape, hearing becomes the witness of the ephemeral passages of a sound whose *unheard* "becoming-imperceptible"[291] both repels and *opacifies* the *a priori* limits of understanding. The soundscape's reverberations *cannot be* sound in loss of Being; on the contrary, they *become* the *living manifestations* of the seemingly infinite transformations of sound into silence and of silence into sound. The crystalline specularity of the soundscape and of its compact webs of infinite sonic matrixes of reverberations thus *transform* the listener, not into an ego-centered Subject or into an object-centric Thing, but rather into a *transitional vehicle* that stresses the core *inter-activity* of a renewed intercultural appreciation of *living landscape(s)*.

c. On the absence of the body as a transformation of living.

How can this specular hearing in which the transformation of living unfolds be characterized? If we admit that the soundscape brings out a life that escapes the onto-logic of Being, then can we consider how the sounds of *Guqin* make possible the reflection of an *emotionality* or tonality that spreads and responds *beneath all emotion*? Listening to the *Guqin* piece "Missing an Old Friend" or "*Yi Guren*" (憶故人)[292] allows us to hear both the induction and the tensioning of a perceptual-affective process which diffuses seemingly inexhaustible reverberations. This effect of consciousness put in tension by the soundscape emphasizes both the bodily absence of the "old friend (故人)" and the sensitive presence of the tonal reverberations that make the invisible spirit(s) or *shen* (神) of the landscape come alive. It is as if the silent distance *in between* the tones evoked a flowing *continuum of spirit(s)*. Amidst this perceptive, affective, and spiritual continuum, death and absence are no longer the painful expressions of a lustful lack engrossed in an illusory search for a forever lost *being*. Instead, they become a fertilizing *memorial tension* which results from the *transformation(s) of living*.

The *sonic-affective backgrounds* that emerge from the piece "*Yi Guren*" bring into tension both the melancholy of disappearance and the quiet serenity of contemplation. The piece indeed *transmits the specular reverberations* of a *living breath* that lies *in between* notes. The specular reverberations that emanate from a piece like "*Yi Guren*" promote the fundamental resources of an intercultural *intelligible common* that is neither objective nor subjective, neither ancient nor modern, neither Eastern nor Western.

BIBLIOGRAPHY

BOOKS ABOUT JULLIEN'S WORK:

François Jullien's unexceptional thought, A Critical Introduction, Arne de Boever, Rowman/Littlefield, London/New-York, 149 p., 2020

Against Ontology: Chinese Thought and François Jullien', Shiqiao Li et Scott Lash, TCS Special Issue, Sage, 2023.

ARTICLES AND CONVERSATIONS :

Critical Inquiry, "Did Philosophers Have to Become Fixated on Truth?", Sommer 2002, Volume 28, Number 4

"The Shadow on the Picture: Of Evil or the Negative", Autumn 2005, Volume 32, Number 1

Thesis Eleven, Notes and Discussion, "A Philosophical Use of China: An Interview with François Jullien", Number 57, May 1999, 113-130

Diogenes, "China as Philosophical Tool: François Jullien in convervation with Thierry Zarcone", 2003

Modern Langage Quarterly, "Rethinking Comparison", Volume 73, Number 4, December 2012

Qui parle, "Thinking between China and Greece: Breaking New Ground", an Interview with Marcel Gauchet, Volume 18, Number 1, Fall/Winter 2009

Comparative strategy, an International Journal, Paul Dragos Aligica, "Efficacy, East and West: François Jullien's explorations in Strategy », Online publication 01 July 2007

Revue Harvard Design Magazine, François Jullien and Sarah M. Whiting "A mondialisation to strive for, rather than a globalization to succumb to", SS 22, p.78-85, 2022

Li, S., & Lash, S. (2023). Against Ontology: Chinese Thought and François Jullien: An Introduction. Theory, Culture & Society, 40(4–5), 3–23.

Heubel, Fabian (2023). "The Other Between. Critical Reflections on François Jullien's Approach to "Chinese Thought"" Yearbook for Eastern and Western Philosophy, vol. 6, no. 1, pp. 3-34

FROM FRANCOIS JULLIEN

The Propensity of Things (Toward a history of Efficacy in China), "La Propension des choses : Pour une histoire de l'efficacité en Chine", Seuil. Translated by Janet Lloyd, Zone Books, 1995

Detour and Access: Strategies of Meaning in China and Greece, "Le detour et l'Accès : Stratégie du sens en Chine, en Grèce", Grasset, translated by Sophie Hawkes, Zone Book, 2000

In praise of Blandness: Proceeding from Chinese thought and Aesthetics, "Eloge de la fadeur", Picquier, translated by Paula M. Varsano, Zone Books, 2004

A Treatise on Efficacy, Between Western and Chinese thinking, "Traité de l'efficacité", Grasset, translated by Janet Lloyd, University of Hawai's Press, 2004

Vital Nourishment, Departing from Happiness, "Nourrir sa vie : A l'écart du Bonheur", Seuil, translated by Arthur Goldhammer, 2007

The Impossible Nude: Chinese Art and Western Aesthetics, "De l'Essence ou du Nu", Seuil, translated by Maev de la Guardia, The University of Chicago Press, 2007

The great image has no form, or on the nonobject through painting, "La grande image n'a pas de forme ou du non-objet par la peinture", Seuil, translated by Jane Marie Todd, The University of Chicago Press, 2009

The Silent Transformations, "Les transformations silencieuses", Grasset & Fasquelle, translated by Krzysztof Fijalkowski and Michael Richardson, Seagull Books, 2011

On the Universal: the uniform, the common and dialogue between cultures, "De l'universel, de l'uniforme, du commun et du dialogue entre les cultures", Librairie Arthème Fayard, translated by Krzysztof Fijalkowski and Michael Richardson, Polity Press, Cambridge, 2014

The Book of Beginnings, "Entrer dans une pensée, ou Des possibles de l'esprit", Gallimard, translated by Jody Gladding, Yale University, 2015

The Strange Idea of the beautiful, "Cette étrange idée du Beau", Grasset & Fasquelle, translated by Krzysztof Fijalkowski and Michael Richardson, Seagull Books, 2016

The Philosophy of Living, "Philosophie du Vivre", Gallimard, translated by Krzysztof Fijalkowski and Michael Richardson, Seagull Books, 2016

Our Worlds in Tongues, "Nos mondes en langues", Huang Yong Ping et François Jullien, Donatien Grau. In French, English and Chinese, English translation by Pedro Rodriguez, Klincksieck, 2016

De-coincidence: Where Art and Existence Come From (Billingual edition), "Dé-coïncidence, d'où viennent l'art et l'existence", Grasset & Fasquelle, English translation by Pedro Rodriguez, National Taiwan University of Art, 2018

Living off Landscape: or the unthought-of in Reason, "Vivre de paysage ou L'impensé de la raison", Gallimard, English translation by Pedro Rodriguez, Rowman & Littlefield, 2018

From Being to Living: a Euro-Chinese lexicon of thought, "De l'Être au Vivre" Gallimard, translated by Krzysztof Fijalkowski and Michael Richardson, Sage, 2020

There Is No Cultural Identity (A Defense of Cultural Resources), "Il n'y a pas d'identité Culturelle", Ed. L'Herne, translated by Pedro Rodrigues, Polity Press, Cambridge, 2021

Resources of Christianity, "Ressources du christianisme", Ed. L'Herne, translated by Pedro Rodrigues, Polity Press, Cambridge, 2021

Acknowledgements:

I would like to thank McNeil Taylor for his thoughtful and insightful editing, Henri Moreau de Balasy for his thorough proofreading, and Linda Branco for her invaluable help with the formatting and design of this book, which was generously funded by the Association De-coincidence, the non-profit organization started by François Jullien at the onset of the COVID-19 pandemic. I would also like to thank Aiko for her unconditional support throughout the process of writing this book and for her help locating the origin of the Japanese poem in Chapter IX. A special thought goes out to my doctoral advisor Derek Humphreys without whom I may have never had the opportunity to encounter FJ's writing, and to my uncles Will and Dave who always nurtured and nourished my lifelong passion for Ancient China and who so generously gave me the opportunity to go see Qin Shi Huangdi's terra cotta army in Xi'an over 15 years ago. It also goes without saying that I would also like to thank FJ for giving me the opportunity to realize this project, for his philosophical inspiration, and for having granted me access to his sinological erudition.

Endnotes

Foreword

1   Psychoanalysis remains very prevalent in the French university and to a lesser extent in clinical institutions. Moreover, the writings and teachings of the psychiatrist and psychoanalyst Jacques Lacan (1901-1980) hold far greater clinical influence in France and in the Latin world than they do in the anglophone world.

2   I have since then become highly critical of the blanket-category of "Eastern Spirituality" as it tends to subsume an incredible diversity of a wide range of texts, practices, traditions and languages under a single auspice. In many ways, this book deconstructs the imaginary colonial construction of a mystical, detached and passive "Oriental Other" that serves as convenient foil to an equally imaginary active and industrious Western "doer." cf. *infra* Ch. III. Readers interested in the legacy of Edward Said's critical approach to Orientalism can refer themselves to Lidan Lin's excellent article *The Legacy and Future of Orientalism in Paradoxical Citizenship: Edward Said*, ed. Silvia Nagy-Zekmi, Lexington Books, Washington, D.C, p. 129-141

3   French academics in the social as well as medical sciences remain highly dubitative when it comes to the slew of English-language "integrative research" that has sprung up in recent years; this kind of research affiliated with "happiness studies" and "positive psychology" associates contemporary quantitative clinical research methodologies like Randomized Clinical Trials with qualitative objects of study traditionally reserved to the Humanities or the Social Sciences, "spirituality" chiefly among them. Despite having once been an "integrative researcher" myself, I have come to understand my European colleague's skepticism. My personal observation is that the fashionable, "West-Coast-gone-global" discourse of "integrative medicine" which wants us to bridge interdisciplinary and intercultural divides in an effort to develop innovative practices, re-iterates, despite all its good intentions, a standardized biomedical mode of reasoning founded upon a worldview where even the unquantifiable, the incommensurable, and the subjective- i.e. the *spiritual* (cf. *infra* Ch. II, VI, VII, VIII) - can somehow be "integrated" into the quantitative "meta-discourse" of Evidence-Based Medicine. Perhaps I am myself too French, but this kind of intellectual shortchanging that glosses over the fecundity of *contradiction* and that does not engage with the traditional research methodologies of the Humanities like philology, hermeneutics, and exegesis falls short of standards of scientific

rigor in both the "hard" sciences and the "soft" sciences: it contributes to a form of *pseudo-thinking* (cf. Ch. IX, X) that proliferates in traditional and digital media where broad overgeneralizations and blanket statements are too often accompanied by the sempiternally misleading sentence: "studies have show that xyz may contribute to *zxy*..."

4   Lacan nurtured a strong interest in Ancient China, he studied Classical Chinese with the eminent scholars and sinologists Paul Demiéville and François Cheng. Lacan's interest in Chinese writing is becoming the object of more intense scholarship not only in France but also in China cf. Lin, Lidan *art.cit.* p. 136-140.

5   The medical historian Paul Unschuld has offered the most scholarly approach to Ancient Chinese medical treatises to date with his monumental philological translation of the Han-dynasty era text *Huangdi Nei Jing* or "Yellow Emperor's Canon" cf. P. Unschuld and H. Tessenow (2011) *Huangdi Nei Jing Su Wen, an annotated translation*, University of California Press, Berkeley CA as well as P. Unschuld (2003) *Huangdi Nei Jing Su Wen: Nature, Knowledge and Imagery in an Ancient Chinese Medical Text*, University of California Press, Berkeley, CA.

6   F. Jullien (2005) *Conférence sur l'efficacité*, Presses Universitaires de France, Paris FR. This text has been translated in English but has yet to be published, it is one of Jullien's most widely diffused texts in France.

7   This is an allusion to the (in)famous cultural "divide" that has been the source of much quarreling in (academic) philosophy throughout the second half of the 20th century: Anglo-Saxon "analytic" philosophy is opposed to German and French "continental" philosophy; François Jullien's work falls squarely in the "continental" camp. For a broader and nuanced overview of the opposition between the two approaches to philosophy cf. CHASE, J., & REYNOLDS, J. (2010). *Analytic versus Continental: Arguments on the Methods and Value of Philosophy.* McGill-Queen's University Press.

8   Cf. *5 concepts proposés à la psychanalyse*, Grasset, Paris, 2012 (untranslated). F. Jullien's work is widely diffused and discussed in the fields of clinical psychology, psychiatry, and psychoanalysis in France; he is frequently invited by a range of practitioners working across a wide range of settings and populations and works closely with clinicians working with addiction as well as clinicians transmitting psychoanalysis in China. Cf. *Dé-coïncider de l'addiction*, eds. Couteron, JP and Vitry, G., Descartes et Cie, Paris, 2023 (untranslated).

9   Scholars who wish to approach Jullien's work from a critical perspective should refer to De Boever, Arne (2020). *Francois Jullien's Unexceptional Thought: A Critical Introduction.* Rowman & Littlefield International, Washington DC or to Heubel, Fabian (2023) "The Other Between. Critical Reflections

on François Jullien's Approach to "Chinese Thought"" *Yearbook for Eastern and Western Philosophy*, vol. 6, no. 1, pp. 3-34

10   *De l'intime, loin du bruyant Amour,* Grasset, Paris, 2013; *Décoïncidence, d'où viennent l'art et l'existence,* Grasset, Paris, 2017; *L'inouï ou l'autre nom de ce si lassant Réel,* Grasset, Paris, 2019; *De la vraie vie,* Ed. de l'Observatoire, Paris, 2020; *Ce point obscur d'où tout a basculé,* Ed. de l'Observatoire, Paris, 2021; *L'incommensurable,* Editions de l'Observatoire, Paris, 2022.

11   François Jullien recuses the "comparatist" etiquette that is so often attached to his world in the anglophone world. Ch. I develops the point which separate his intercultural approach to philosophy from comparatism.

12   From the Wayside to the Unheard, editions de l'Herne, Paris, 2018 (untranslated) p.57; cf. ch. I for further elaboration how the intercultural philosophy of the wayside demarcates itself from the Deleuzian and Derridean "philosophies of difference" that François Jullien both inherits and departs from.

13   Cf. *There is no cultural identity,* Polity Press, London, 2021

14   A. Badiou (2007), "Jullien l'Apostat" in *Cahiers de l'Herne no. 121: François Jullien* eds. Daniel Bougnoux and François L'Yvonnet, Editions de l'Herne, Paris, 2018, p.98

15   The transliteration of Classical Chinese is a complex affair; for the sake of consistency, I have followed François Jullien's approach and provided an un-accented pinyin transliteration of all Chinese characters. This provides a rudimentary understanding of the monosyllabic structure of the language and rough indications for approximate readings when consulting original sources. From a scholarly perspective, this choice is debatable: pinyin is a transliteration system for a spoken language (Mandarin Chinese); all the works cited in this book are in Classical Chinese, an essentially written language. Aside from a few scholars of Old and Middle Chinese, there is virtually no one today in China, let alone in the rest of the world, that knows how to read these texts in their (most often conjectural) "original" pronunciation; that is why it did not make sense in my opinion to provide tonal accents to pronounce the text in "correct" contemporary Mandarin Chinese. For readers that are unfamiliar with the basic sounds of pinyin transliteration the following indications can be helpful: "zh-" reads as "Dj-" as in James, "-ou" reads like like the verb "to owe," "-i" reads like the guttural sound "Uhh," "z-" reads like "dz-," "q-" reads as "tch-" as in "chip," the vowel "u" reads like two o's as in the verb "to woo."

Chapter I

16   One can refer to the seminal works of the classicist Charles H. Kahn

for further details concerning the importance of Being (the verb to *einai*) and its relationship to *truth* when it comes to not only the syntactic structure of the Ancient Greek language but also the history of Ancient Greek philosophy cf. *Essays on Being*, Oxford University Press, 2009. A thorough and scholarly summary of the contents of each chapter can be freely accessed at https://bmcr. brynmawr.edu/2009/2009.11.21/

17   Fragment II, original translation.

18   Barbara Cassin's work *Sophistic Practice: towards a consistent relativism*, Fordham, 2014 remains the definitive work on this often misunderstood and yet crucial school of Ancient Greek thought.

19   240c

20   Cf J. Derrida, *Plato's Pharmacy Dissemination*, Chicago: University of Chicago Press, 1981

21   Cf. L. Lin (2006) *The Legacy and Future of Orientalism*, op.cit.

22   The Ancient Greek term "aporia" designates a point of impasse in reasoning, it arguably constitutes the bedrock of philosophical reflection cf. Palmer, J. (2017). Contradiction and Aporia in Early Greek Philosophy. In G. Karamanolis & V. Politis (Eds.), *The Aporetic Tradition in Ancient Philosophy* (pp. 9-28). Cambridge: Cambridge University Press. doi:10.1017/9781316274293.002

23   The (unfortunately untranslated) works of the French sinologist Léon Vandermeersch (1928-2021) convincingly argue that the ideographic tradition derived from the oracle bone shard divination practices of Bronze-Age China constitutes a cogent and autonomous form of rationality that bears no common measure with the rationality of *logos* cf. *Les deux raisons de la pensée chinoise: divination et idéographie*, Paris, Gallimard, 2013.

24   For further developments on the critical structure of predication in the Ancient Greek language and in Ancient Greek philosophy refer to C.H. Kahn "The Greek Verb "To Be" and the Concept of Being," in Essays on Being, op.cit.

25   Although Classical Chinese does not reason on an ontological mode, it of course possesses its own cogent form of operational logic: the one derived from the "divinatory equations" of the seers of Bronze Age China cf. L .Vandermeersch, *Les deux raisons de la pensée chinoise*, op.cit, p. 17-18

26   For a more technical and precise appraisal of Early Chinese "transphenomenal meta-cosmology" vs. Greek "metaphysical onto-theology' cf. L. Vandermeersch, *ibid.* p.108-109

27   G. Dumézil (1898-1986) and E. Benveniste (1902-1976) were highly influential philologists and linguists who bore a decisive influence on post-war French intellectual life; major works of theirs like Benveniste's *Dictionary of*

Indo-European Concepts and Society (University of Chicago Press, 2016) and Dumézil's *Mitra-Varuna: An Essay on Two Indo-European Representations of Sovereignty* (Zone Books, 1990) continue to exert a lasting influence in the Humanities.

28   Cf. *infra* Ch. II and VII for more extensive analyses of Early Chinese cosmological and ideographic thinking.

29   The kantian critical concept of "conditions of possibility" refers to the understanding of Time and Space as the transcendental a priori categories of intuition that make experience possible as elaborated in the *Critique of Pure Reason*; it also refers to the historical understanding of knowledge as an epistemological field shaped by and within the mechanisms, structures, and techniques of discourse understood as an episteme, a point forcefully developed by Michel Foucault in *The Order of Things*. For further reading cf. Piché, C. (2016). Kant on the "Conditions of the Possibility" of Experience. In: Kim, H., Hoeltzel, S. (eds) *Transcendental Inquiry*. Palgrave Macmillan and Koopman, C. (2010). Historical Critique or Transcendental Critique in Foucault: Two Kantian Lineages. *Foucault Studies* 8:100-121.

30   For an extensive comparative analysis of the status of difference in the philosophies of Derrida and Deleuze cf. V. Cisney (2018) *Deleuze and Derrida: Difference and the Power of the Negative*, Edinburgh University Press.

31   Deleuze's *Nietzsche and Philosophy*, New York: Columbia University Press, 1983, offers perhaps the most brazen endorsement of such a radical "reversal of Platonism."

32   The Lewis Elementary dictionary that can be consulted freely using the following link http://www.perseus.tufts.edu/hopper/morph?la=la offers the following definitions: "to step out, come forth, emerge, appear."

Chapter II

33   The usage of *Yang Sheng* literature in care work is an emerging field of study and is the object of my upcoming dissertation. For a pedagogical and concise introduction discussing the significance of Yang Sheng literature in the medical context cf. Wilcox, Lorraine. "Nourishing life (Yang Sheng): an ancient love of lists." *The Journal of Chinese Medicine*, no. 113, Feb. 2017, pp. 28-31.

34   Itzkowitz, Sheldon. "THE DISSOCIATIVE TURN IN PSYCHO-ANALYSIS." *American journal of psychoanalysis* vol. 75,2 (2015): 145-53. doi:10.1057/ajp.2015.15

35   *Phaedo* (64c-d), trans. B. Jowett

36   *Process and reality*, New York: Free Press., p. 39

37   It is worth noting that the object of this chapter is not to argue "for" or "against" dualism, holism, or any other "ism"- unlike Edward Slingerland's book *Mind and Body in Early China: Beyond Orientalism and the Myth of Holism* (Oxford University Press, 2018) which expounds the virtues of a universal "weak" mind-body dualism, the argument developed here aims to illustrate how Ancient Chinese thought gives us the means to think outside the categories of "mind" and "body" born in the Western intellectual scenery.

38   The significance of pneuma in Aristotle's philosophy and the relationship it bears to psychè is a complex and largely unsettled matter which continues to generate considerable scholarly interest and debate; for further reading *The Concept of Pneuma after Aristotle* (2021), eds S. Coughlin, D. Leith & O. Lewis, Topoi Editions, Berlin., DE: Topoi Editions

39   For the roots of Aristotle's "hylomorphic" doctrine of the soul where bodies (*somaton*) are said to be "organs" or "instruments" (*organa*) of the soul cf *De anima* 415b

40   The excerpts cited are available (in French) for free below. http://dx. doi.org/doi:10.1522/cla.der.tra. For recent scholarship on the text the following review can be consulted Fabrizio Baldassarri (2018) Descartes' treatise on man and its reception, British Journal for the History of Philosophy, 26:6, 1234-1236

41   Cf Damrosch, David (2003) *What is World Literature,* Princeton University Press. p. 15 for the useful "masterpiece vs. classic" distinction: "The "classic" is a work of transcendent, even foundational, value [...] and often closely associated with imperial values [...] The masterpiece, on the other hand [...] need not have any foundational cultural force." Indeed, the *Zhuangzi* never received the kind of institutional prestige granted to the Classic texts (經 or *jing*); its diffusion and transmission across the world has always followed a more "rhizomatic " as opposed to "arborescent" dynamic even though it is obviously a "foundational" work and thus possesses some of the aura associated with the "classic."

42   The seemingly ever-increasing amounts of scholarship surrounding the *Zhuangzi* and the many translations of the text across languages is a testimonial of the enduring fascination and influence of this seminal work of world literature. Given its highly idiosyncratic form, the *Zhuangzi* is a notoriously difficult text to translate. Whenever possible, I will refer to A.C. Graham's (1981) translation as it both stays close to the text's singular style and syntax while also being elegant and intelligible: *Chuang-tzu: The Seven Inner Chapters and Other Writings from the Book Chuang-tzu,* Boston: Allen and Unwin. Graham's translation is nonetheless incomplete and certain passages are omitted; I will therefore also always refer readers back to James Legge's dated yet complete translation and to the original text which can be found at online at ctext.org/ zhuangzi

43   For an excellent overview of the crucial role of fiction in the *Zhuangzi* cf. Romain Graziani's (2021) *Fiction and Philosophy in the Zhuangzi: An Introduction to Early Chinese Taoist Thought*, London: Bloomsbury Academic.

44   The *Zhuangzi* is of course considered a foundational text of what Western scholars call "Daoism" and of what Chinese scholars refer to as Dao Jiao 道教 (literally *Dao* tradition). While it is interesting and worthwhile to deconstruct (in a Derridean sense) such an *a posteriori* act of scholarly classification, such a strategic enterprise does not constitute the primary aim of this chapter which is instead to offer anglophone readers an alternate *point of entry* into the philosophical, intercultural, and existential dimensions of "nourishment" as it relates to "our" common, human experience of *living*.

45   trans. A.C Graham with modifications in bold, p.82-85; Legge 11.3 at ctext.org

46   It should be noted that the character jing (精) which connotates "semen," "essence" and "spirit" denotes the hulled and uncooked grain of rice (米), giving us yet another indication that the process of nourishment in the *Zhuangzi* is indissociable from a nutritive process of spiritual *transformation*.

47   Attentive readers will notice that knowledge or *zhi* (知) in the *Zhuangzi* bears none of the positive connotations associated with *episteme* in Greek. Whereas the Western body/soul distinction is predicated upon an epistemological dissociation that attempts to determine the knowable and separate it from the unknowable, the cultivation of the jing seminal-quintessence which

48   The subtle *shen* invisible spirit discussed here should not be confused with an immaterial spirit that transcends physicality. The *shen* spirit is akin to the spirit of a wine or a perfume, a subtle and evasive diffusion, an emanation which oscillates *in between* the sensible and the non-sensible, the perceptible and the imperceptible, the visible and the invisible. *Shen* also refers to the spirits of the dead that continue to inhabit the world of the living, hence the reference to the Greek *daemon*.

49   The translation of *xin* (心) remains an area of intense scholarly debate amongst sinologist as Edward Slingerland's recent book (*op.cit.*) can attest; the term indeed connotates both the mind in its spiritual dimension as well as the physical organ of the heart. Although translating xin as "heart-mind" bears the inconvenience of substituting one word with two, it nonetheless faithfully captures the equally spiritual and physical dimensions that this term carries along with it.

50   The full anecdote, which is omitted from A.C. Graham's translation, can be found at Chapter 19 "The Full Understanding of Life" section five on ctext.org

51   Freud in particular comes to mind, the term "way" or "weg" in German is indeed a crucial term in the Viennese neurologist's vocabulary, particularly when it comes to his metapsychological theory of the drives or Trieben. Unlike the Way of *Dao* in the *Zhuangzi*, Freud's Weg in fact always supposes a destination and a predetermined destination as it is the topological and representative psychic ground which leads the drive to its object (satisfaction or destruction) cf. *infra* ch.8.3 for a more detailed discussion of Freud's drive theory.

52   The attentive reader will have noticed that in the anecdote of the Yellow Emperor and Guang-Chenzi there were already two designations that can be translated as "body:" *shen* (身), which refers to one's own body and and *xing* (形), the bodily form..

53   The importance of *shen* (神) in Early Chinese medicine is well known and it bears a tight relationship to the medical understanding of *Yang Sheng* as can be seen in the great treatise of Classical Chinese medicine known as "The Yellow Emperor's Cannon" cf. P. Unschuld & H. Tessenow (2011) *Huangdi Nei Jing Su Wen: An Annotated Translation, op.cit.* p.47-49 ch. 2 section 10.1

54   Cf. Unschuld (1985) *Huangdi Nei Jing Su Wen: Nature, Knowledge, Imagery in an Ancient Chinese Medical Text, op.cit.*, ch. V section 7.2 "Wind Etiology and Pathology" p.183-189

55   Cf. M. Granet (1934/1999) *La Pensée Chinoise*, ch. II, "Le Yin et le Yang", p. 102-103, Paris, Albin Michel.

56   P. Unschuld & H. Tessenow, *Huangdi Nei Jing Su Wen, op.cit.*, p.16-18

57   J. Lacan, *Le séminaire XXIII: Le sinthome*, Paris, Le Seuil, Coll. "Le champ freudien", 2005, p.31

58   Section 28, translation Hsieh, L., & Shih, V. Y. (2015). *The Literary Mind and the Carving of Dragons*. The Chinese University of Hong Kong Press. https://doi.org/10.2307/j.ctt1p6qr6g; Chinese text available at ctext.org https://ctext.org/wenxin-diaolong/feng-gu

59   For further discussions of *Ch'an* or Zen Buddhism cf. infra ch. IX

60   The *Zhuangzi* indeed played a central role in the translation of Sanskrit and Pali Buddhist texts in Chinese at the beginning of the 2nd century CE as shown in Haun Saussy's (2018) recent book *Translation as Citation: Zhuangzi Inside Out*, Oxford University Press.

61   I am unfortunately unable to locate the precise source of this irreverent anecdote at this moment time; it was transmitted to me by Janest Gyatso, Hershey Professor of Buddhist Studies at Harvard Divinity School, during my undergraduate studies.

62   Cf. *infra* ch. IX for further elaboration on the Zen understanding of enlightening.

63   Chinese text and J. Legge translation available at https://ctext.org/mengzi/gaozi-i in *Mengzi, Gaozi* I section 8.

64   "故苟得其養，無物不長；苟失其養，無物不消"

65   A.C. Graham translation with slight modifications (1981), *op.cit.*, p. 23-24, also available on https://ctext.org/zhuangzi/nourishing-the-lord-of-life section 2.

66   265e-266b

67   Cf. *infra*-Ch.VIII for a detailed discussion of the eros and thanatos distinction in Freud.

68   The word that is commonly translated as "unconscious" in English is in fact *Unbewusst* in German which is more accurately translated as unbeknownst.

69   Lacan's infamous adage "*L'impossible, c'est le réel*" i.e "The impossible is the real" is in fact borrowed from Alexander Koyré's epistemology and from his assessment of modern physics. Readers who can read French and who wish to learn more about this fascinating confluence of physics, psychoanalysis, philosophy can find more information in this excellent article by the physicist Etienne Klein (2011). "Comment dire ce dont parle la physique ?". *Champ lacanien*, 10, 181-194. https://doi.org/10.3917/chla.010.0181

70   Heraclitus, fr. 119, *Die Fragmente der Vorsokatiker,* Diels-Kranz, I, p.177; Democritus, fr. 170-171, *ibid.*, II, p.178-179

71   Cf. ZZ Chapter 4 "Good luck (福) is lighter than a feather, none knows how to bear its weight." in A.C Graham, *op.cit.*, p.36 and https://ctext.org/zhuangzi/man-in-the-world-associated-with section 8

72   The 10th century AD Japanese text *Ishimpô* compiled by Yasuyori Tamba offers precise descriptions of such techniques in chapters 26 "obtaining longevity" and chapters 27 "nourishing life" cf. *The Essentials of Medicine in Ancient China and Japan:* Yasuyori Tamba's Ishimpô" translation, introduction and notes by E. Hsia, I. Veith, & R. Geerstma (1986), Vol. 2, E.J. Brill, Leyde.

73   Cf. R. G. Henricks (1985) *Philosophy and Argumentation in Third-Century China, The Essays of Hsi K'ang*, Princeton University Press.

Chapter III

74   The definitive analysis of "metis" can be found in Vernant, J.P. & Detienne, M. *Cunning Intelligence in Ancient Greece*, Chicago: University Press, 1981. JP Vernant was François Jullien's mentor and teacher when he studied Classics at École Normale Supérieure; it was under his influence that he opted to make the journey to then Maoist China.

75   Hesiod, *Theogony*, 890

76   *On War, Book I*, ch. 2. Freely available in German and in the English translation at Clausewitz.com

77   Joseph Needham's (1900-1985) magnum opus *Science and Civilization in China*, a massive study divided into 7 volumes, remains the definitive enquiry on the topic to this day, depiste a few scholarly controversies that cannot be delved into within the context of this book.

78   Original of Galileo's 1623 text *Il Saggiatore*, ch. 6:

"La filosofia è scritta in questo grandissimo libro che continuamente ci sta aperto innanzi agli occhi (io dico l'universo), ma non si può intendere se prima non s'impara a intendere la lingua, e a conoscere i caratteri nei quali è scritto. Egli è scritto in lingua matematica, e i caratteri son triangoli, cerchi e altre figure geometriche, senza i quali mezi è impossibile a intenderne umanamente parola; senza questi è un aggirarsi vanamente per un oscuro laberinto."

79   In R. Descartes' 1637 *Discourse on Method*, ch. 6 par. 2

80   Cf. Klein, É. (2011). *Comment dire ce dont parle la physique ?* art.cit.

81   "Sun Tzu" (孫子) or "Master Sun" is thought to be the author of the most famous *Bin Fa* (兵法) treatise which is commonly translated as "Art of War." While the character *Bin* (兵) indeed refers to "war," the character Fa (法) relates more to the notion of "law" or "rule" than to the notion of "art." Further references to *Sunzi Binfa* will be abridged to *SZBF* and point directly towards the source text and translation available at https://ctext.org/art-of-war

82   *SZBF*, ch. 1, "計", par. 3

83   *SZBF*, ch. 4

84   *SZBF*, ch. 5

85   *SZBF*, ch. 4, par. 4 and ch. 6, par. 7

86   *Huangdi Nei Jing Su Wen*, ch. 70, 70-445-6, p. 328, Vol. II, in P. Unschuld & H. Tessenow, *op.cit.*

87   *Metaphysics*, book 2, 994a

88   The character *Li* (利) is the third caracter of the opening stanza (乾 or

Qian) of the *Yi Jing* Cf. *infra* Ch. VII section 5.a for an in-depth translation and commentary which details the crucial significance of this stanza in Early Chinese thought.

89   *SZBF*, ch. 4, par.3

90   Although he takes issues with François Jullien's work because he misunderstands it when he assumes it to be culturalist, Edward Slingerland has nonetheless authored two books that are useful references on the notion of wu wei: the scholarly Effortless Action: Wu-wei as Conceptual Metaphor and Spiritual Idea in Early China, Oxford: Oxford University Press, 2003 and the trade book Trying to Not Try: Ancient China, Modern Science, and the Power of Spontaneity.

91   Cf. Sells, M., *Mystical Languages of Unsaying*, Chicago: University of Chicago Press, 1994 for a detailed analysis of the Greek notion of "apophasis" or "unsaying" in Mediterranean and European mystical traditions.

92   *Hanfei Zi*, ch. 20, concluding citation in par. 2: "上德無為而無不為也"

93   Cf. *infra* ch. IV section 5.b for a more detailed discussion of the significance of hua in Classical Chinese thought.

94   *Gong Sun Chou*, I.2, par. 15

95   *The Silent Transformations* is also the title of one of François Jullien's later works cf. Bibliography. Esther Lin, who translates François Jullien's works into Chinese, comments on the significance of his usage of Wang Fuzhi's four letter idiom (潛移默化) or *chengyu* in the following conference: https://francoisjullien.hypotheses.org/1025

96   Deng indeed explicitly referred to the ancient Confucian governmental doctrine of "small prosperity" (小康, *xiaokang*) first described in the *Book of Rites* (Ch. 9. Par. 2) when he outlined out his project to transform China Cf. E. Vogel, *Deng Xiaoping and the Transformation of China*, Harvard University Press: Cambridge, MA, 2011, p.52-57 and L. Vandermeersch, *Les deux raisons de la pensée chinoise, op.cit.* p. 177, p.185-186, and p.193

97   Most famously, the First Emperor burned the Confucian books of Poetry (詩) and Historical Records (書) as referenced in Sima Qian's historical chronicle *Shiji*, Ch. 6, section 38. 臣請史官非秦記皆燒之。非博士官所職，天下敢有藏詩、書、百家語者，悉詣守、尉雜燒之。有敢偶語詩書者棄市

98   *Han Fei Zi*, ch. 5 "明君無為於上，群臣竦懼乎下"

99   Leon Vandermeersch convincingly argues that the "One Party" system of the PRC mirrors the "Department of Heaven" from the imperial era; to avoid

any easy (and arguable racist) characterization of China's political history, Vandermeersch makes a crucial point when he states that "anti-totalitarianism" has also always been at the heart of "Chinese political consciousness" cf *Les deux raisons de la pensée chinoise, op.cit.*, p.194-195

100	*SZBF*, ch. 11, par. 5

101	Cassin, B. *Sophistical Practice, op.cit.*

102	*Physics*, II. ch.4-6.

103	Aristotle's habitual insistence on his contradictors and his logical style of refutation bear witness to the effective difficulty associated with the implementation of "theory" into "practice, let alone "science."

104	Cf. Paul, J. (2014). The Use of Kairos in Renaissance Political Philosophy*. *Renaissance Quarterly*, 67(1), 43-78. doi:10.1086/676152

Chapter IV

105	*Critique of Pure Reason*, "Transcendental Aesthetics," par. 6

106	*Georgics*, III, v. 284

107	*Confessions*, XI, 23.

108	*Physics*, IV, 10.

109	J. Needham, *Science and Civilization in China*, vol.4, 1, "Physics."

110	*Les Fleurs du Mal*, "L'Ennemi"

111	As quoted in Diogenes Laertius, *The Lives and Opinions of Eminent Philosophers*, I. 35. *Ζὰς μὲν καὶ Χρόνος ἦσαν ἀεὶ καὶ Χθονίη*

112	*Ibid.*, I. 49

113	*Ibid*, I. 119

114	*Olympian*, II.17

115	As quoted in Plato, *Cratylus*, 402a

116	v. 609

117	221a

118	*La Pensée Chinoise*, 1934 [1999], Paris, Albin Michel, book II "Les Idées Directirces," ch. 1 "Le Temps et l'Espace"

119	*On the "Logic" of Togetherness, A Cultural Hermeneutic*, Leiden,

Brill, 1998, 5, 5 "Time in China", p.342s

120   Granet famously dedicated his magnum opus *Dances and Legends of Ancient China* to his dear friend and mentor Marcel Mauss.

121   The final paragraph of Granet's fascinating and nearly forgotten article on funerary rites in Ancient China Le Langage de la Douleur original published in the Journal de Psychologie in 1922 is striking in this regard: *"C'est pourquoi les gestes de la douleur se sont ordonnés en une suite de rites qui sont aussi un système de signes. Ils constituent une technique et une symbolique ; ils forment un langage pratique qui a ses besoins d'ordre, de correction, de clarté, qui a sa grammaire, sa syntaxe, sa philosophie, et, je dirais aussi, sa morale."* French text available online at https://www.chineancienne.fr/d%C3%A9but-20e-s/granet-le-langage-de-la-douleur/

122   *La Pensée Chinoise*, original translation, op.cit., p.78

123   Cf. *Infra*. Ch.VII.4 for further analysis of the significance of 禮 in Early China and for further commentary of Xunzi's *Lilun* or "discourse on li."

124   A.C. Graham, *Later Mohist Logic, Ethics and Science*, CUP/SOAS, 1978, p. 298 and p. 288

125   Ch. 17 par. 3 夫物，量無窮，時無止，分無常，終始無故

126   Cf. Graham, *op.cit.*, p. 364s

127   *Huainanzi*, ch. 11 "Qi Su Xun," par. 18 available at https://ctext.org/huainanzi/qi-su-xun#n3206

128   *Time and Place in Ancient China*, p.56, eds Huang & Leider, Brill, Leiden, 1995.

129   In *Mozi*, Book 10, Canon I, par. 40 and 41. Available online at https://ctext.org/mozi/canon-i

130   J. Needham, Science and Civilization in China: Volume 4, Physics and Physical Technology, Part 2, Mechanical Engineering. Cambridge University Press, p.479

131   *Confessions*, XI.29

132   Readers interested in further detail regarding the capital significance of *Bian Hua* in the Classical Chinese tradition -in particular its importance when considering translation of Sanskrit and Pali Buddhist texts in China and East Asia - can refer to the admirably scholarly Wikipedia article on the topic https://en.wikipedia.org/wiki/Bianhua.For example-usages cf. *Zhuangzi* chap. 33 par. 6 以天為宗，以德為本，以道為門，兆於變化，謂之聖人 or *Huangdi Nei Jing Su Wen* ch.5 par. 1 黃帝曰：陰陽者，天地之道也，萬物之綱紀，變化

之父母，生殺之本始，神明之府也，治病必求於本.

133   The great sinologist Roger Ames offers a clear, concise, and incisive take on the utmost significance of the *Great Commentary* of the *Yijing* in Early Chinese cosmology Ames, R.T. The *Great Commentary* (Dazhuan 大傳) and Chinese natural cosmology. *Int. Commun.* Chin. Cult 2, 1–18 (2015). https://doi.org/10.1007/s40636-015-0013-2

134   *Xici*, I.6

135   *Ibid*, I.11.B

136   *Physics* 223a and *Nicomachean Ethics* 1174b

137   Cf. Emilsson, Eyjólfur Kjalar, 'On Happiness and Time', in Øyvind Rabbås and others (eds), *The Quest for the Good Life: Ancient Philosophers on Happiness*, Oxford University Press, 2015

138   Cf. *Phenomenology of Intimate Time Consciousness*, Indiana University Press, 1964

139   *Beyond Nature and Culture*, trans. Janet Lloyd, University of Chicago Press, 2013.

140   For an example of contemporary usages of Heidegger in "care studies" cf. Stevens, R. (2022), An Existential Foundation for an *Ethics* of Care in Heidegger's Being and Time. J Ethics 26, 415–431

141   *Essais*, III, 13 "De l'expérience", original translation.

142   *Zhuangzi*, ch.6 par. 1d

143   *Ibid*, par. 1c

Chapter V

144   In *Liji*, "Zhongyong" par. 33 君子之道：淡而不厭，簡而文，溫而理，知遠之近，知風之自，知微之顯，可與入德矣.Available at https://ctext.org/liji/zhong-yong

145   *Laozi* par. 35 道之出口，淡乎其無味，視之不足見，聽之不足聞，用之不足既 available at https://ctext.org/dao-de-jing

146   This formulation can be traced to a Chinese Buddhist text which is a supposed translation of an arguably imaginary "Sutra of Perfect Enlightenment" (大方廣圓覺修多羅了義經) which dates back to the 7th or 8th century CE. Par. 46 不即、不離，無縛、無脫. Available at https://ctext.org/wiki.pl?if=en&chapter=579285

147   Liu Shiao is evoked in 14th century classic Chinese novel, the *Romance of the Three Kingdoms* attributed to Luo Guanzhong. The novel lies at the heart of the most ubiquitous representations of Ancient China in contemporary pop culture: it has been adapted into countless films, manga, and video games like the famous slasher series Dynasty Warriors. Liu Shiao as an NPC in the game and appears in Ch. 103 of the classic novel which is available without translation at https://ctext.org/sanguo-yanyi/ch103

148   Ch. 1 par. 3. François Jullien translation of 凡人之質量，中和最貴矣。中和之質，必平淡無味；故能調成五材，變化應節。是故，觀人察質，必先察其平淡，而後求其聰明 available at https://ctext.org/renwuzhi/jiu-zheng

149   On more than one occasion during our work together, François Jullien energetically and emphatically stated that "Confucianism" and "Daoism" do not "exist." François Jullien is indeed critical of the traditional categorizations developed during and after the Han dynasty which tended to cement Chinese thought into three distinct "schools": The School of Letters (*Ru jia* cf. *infra* ch.VII) aka "the Confucians", the School of the Way (*Dao Jia*) aka the "Daoists," and the School of the Buddha (*Fu Jia*). What Jullien seeks to emphasize is that these categorizations ***cover up*** the texts with pre-conceived explanations and expectations: nothing can replace the patient and arduous study of their traditional commentaries to situate the ways in which overlapping layers of coherence were brought out by a slew of literati disciples, commentators, and translators throughout the ages; many of whom relied extensively on verbatim citation as a mode both of argumentation and translation as showcased in Haun Saussy's brilliant book *Translation as Citation: Zhuangzi Inside Out*, 2017, op.cit.

150   *Liji*, "Yue Ji" par. 6 "是 故 樂 之 隆，非 極 音 也. 食 饗 之 禮, 非 致 味 也"

151   Xi Kang, author of the "discourse on Yang Sheng" (養生論) and of a "discourse on sound without grief or joy" (聲無哀樂論) was indeed also associated with the *Xuanxue* movement. cf. *supra* II and III.

152   *Republic*, III, 401e-402b

153   *Politics* VIII.5. Adventuresome readers can refer back to Ford, Andrew, 'Catharsis: The Power of Music in Aristotle's *Politics*', in Penelope Murray, and Peter Wilson (eds), *Music and the Muses: The Culture of Mousike in the Classical Athenian City*, Oxford university Press, 2004 and to "Musique et Catharsis… Autour d'un texte d'Aristote" for detailed discussions on the significance of the concept of *katharsis* in Aristotle's philosophy as it relates to the theatric tradition of tragedy and to psychoanalysis. Available online at https://gil-conflit.over-blog.org/article-musique-et-catharsis-110420068.html

154   If the reader is unfamiliar with the sound of this instrument and wishes to hear it for himself, there is a wealth of videos on YouTube where the instrument is played. One video entitled *"The beacon tower of Han dynasty Great Wall are listening minstrel Jie playing Guqin"* is particularly evocative of the themes we explored in our commentary of *Laozi* par. 41 as it prominently features the sound of the wind and birds with a stunning backdrop of ruins and deserted landscapes. The second annex offers a detailed discussion of *Guqin* music as it relates to landscape.

155   Cf. *infra* VI.1 for further discussion on the relevance of *"Shan Shui"* as an esthetic category.

156   This rather obvious observation remains controversial: when François Jullien presented his work on the nude in Chicago in 2005, a distinguished sinologist violently reacted to his conference and stormed out, saying that Jullien's take was "completely false."

157   Cf. *supra* II.3

158   *Symposium*, 211a-211c

159   *Metaphysics*, 1072b.3

160   Cf. *Supra* II.3

161   We find an evocation of the "ming men" point in *Huangdi Nei Jing Su Wen* ch.6 par.2 when the counselor Qi Bo describes the "fronts" and "backs" of the Ancient Sage's perfected bodily forms (形).: "When the Sages stand facing the South, their frontside is called broad brilliance; their backside is called great thoroughfare; the earth-side of the great thoroughfare is called minor yin, above minor yin is called major yang. What is called major yang originates and rises from Utmost Yin (至陰), it ends at the gate of life (命門); it is called yang centering the yin (曰陰中之陽)" Trans. Unschuld and Tessenow with mods, *op.cit.*, p.129-130

162   Par. 15 曠兮其若谷；混兮其若濁

163   Par. 41 大象無形

164   Modified translation, another version can be found at T.W. Adorno *Aesthetic Theory* trans. Robert Hullot-Kentor, London, Continuum Books, 2002, p.51

165   First edition of the *Encyclopedia*, article "the Beautiful," p.169-181, original available in French on wikisource.

166   A simple search on the CTEXT dictionary shows that the usage of the character 美 in Early Chinese thought has much more to do with the notion of the "agreeable" or the "pleasant" than with the metaphysical and/or ontolog-

ical reflection on "the Beautiful" (*to kalos*) developed in Ancient Greek philosophy. Whereas the Beautiful is systematically associated with the Good in Greek philosophy (*kaloskagathos*), thinkers across schools in Early China seem to agree on the contrary: the beautiful is not necessarily good. One can find in the Mengzi (Jin Xin I par. 41) a plain and lucid assessment of the beautiful as an impossible: the wise Sage named Gong Sun Chou both flatters, mocks and warns the Emperor when he tells him: "Your lofty Regulatory Principles are really something, truly they're delightful (美), fit for heavenly ascent, as if they could never be reached." (道則高矣，美矣，宜若登天然，似不可及也).

167   *Phaedrus* 250b-d

168   *Enneads* V 9.36-42

169   Cf. *supra* II.2

170   The theory of *Chuan Shen* was first elaborated by Gu Kaizhi, a 3rd and 4th century CE painter and theorist; for an excellent overview cf. p.266 in Yu, H. C. (2021). The Influence of Confucianism and Daoism on the Changes of Chinese Painting Theories. From Figure Painting to Landscape (shanshui) Painting. *Synthesis philosophica*, 36(2), 257-276.

171   While it is beyond my sinological capacities to point towards specific textual instances of the expression "神彩" in Chinese sources, readers interested in doing further research this notion can consult this interview of the art historian Maurizio Paolillo as well as his interpretation of the expression as "ornamental expression of spirit" in the excellent online academic resource *Shan Shui Projects*: https://www.shanshuiprojects.net/interview-with-maurizio-paolillo/.

172   For a critical analysis of the reception of this term in Western aesthetic theory cf Xia Wang (2020) Reception and Dissemination of *Qiyun Shengdong* in the Western Art Criticism, Critical Arts, 34:2, 43-54, DOI: 10.1080/02560046.2019.1690536

173   Cf. *infra* VII.

174   自然 or *chizen* has become the common translation of the Western concept of "Nature" in Japanese: astute sinologists will know that the notion of *ziran* 自然 is of critical importance in Guo Xiang's canonical edition and commentary of the *Zhuangzi*. While it is tempting to brush this off as a coincidental instance, further research is needed to elucidate the complex rationales which led 19th century East Asian translators to adopt 自然, a two-character idiom of ancient origin, as their preferred translation for the European notion of "nature."

175   304c-e

176   *Aesthetic Theory*, op.cit., p.51

177   There is an ongoing development of fascinating studies in early 20th Century Japanese philosophy happening in European scholarship at this time. The culturalism of the esthetics of iki in Kuki Shuzo's philosophy has been well commented on by S. Ebersolt, *Contigence et Communauté: Kuki Shuzo, Philosophe Japonais*, Paris: Editions Vrin, 2021

Chapter VI

178   3.6.11

179   Readers interested in an English translation can consult the following edition: *Six Records on the Floating Life* trans. Leonard Pratt and Chiang Su-Hui, New York: Viking Press, 1983.

180   Cf. Ch. 3 par. 12 "the utmost man, both simple (*pu*) and sincere" (人極樸誠)

181   Du shu xing ling (獨抒性靈) or "lonely outpouring of natural brightness is a common 4- character idiom or chengyu in Chinese literary criticism.

182   Ch. 1 par. 6, original translation

183   It is critical to emphasize that the usage of the character 親 or *qin* in Classical Chinese, which I translate here as "intimate shared living," strongly connotes familial and filial, as opposed to "romantic," let alone sexual, intimate relationships cf *Analects* I.6 "The Master said: a youth inside the home should be obedient; outside the home he should be respectful of elders; prudent as well as truthful; dispensing fondness to all; and thus [showing] intimate humaneness. When an excess of capacity occurs, he should study literature" (子曰：弟子入則孝，出則弟，謹而信，汎愛眾，而親仁。行有餘力，則以學文.). Original translation.

184   Although the character 愛 or ai has become the ubiquitous translation for the term "love" in both Chinese and Japanese, I prefer to follow François Jullien's suggestion and render it here as "affection" to strip it from the universalist and metaphysical pretense so commonly associated with the concept of "Love" nowadays; it is worth reminding readers that *ai* bears far less metaphysical significance in the Classical Chinese tradition than in the Western philosophical and theological tradition. cf. *Analects* I.6 cited above or the more cryptic *Zhuangzi* 2.7 "And so, as with the ruin of the *Dao*, so does love reach its completion" 道之所以虧，愛之所以成"

185   The notion of "impermanence" or 無常, *Wuchang* in Chinese and *mujo* in Japanese, is the common sinographic translation of the Pali term *annica*; it is of course of one of the three key doctrines of Buddhism (the others being *dukka* or "suffering" and *annatta* "no self); its usage can be found as early as the 7th

century CE in the *Sangyo Gisho* (三経義疏), which is itself a Japanese adaptation of the Chinese *Fahuayiji* (法華義記) from the 5th century CE. While Shen Fu does not explicitly refer to 無常, it is obvious that his worldview bears the weight of the centuries of Buddhist influence on Classical Chinese literature.

186   *Notes on Floating Living* ch. 1 par. 8; the image of the "moonlight spirits" of the two spouses "transforming" themselves "absent-mindedly' into "smoke and mist" as they join hands. (握手未通片語，而兩人魂魄恍恍然化煙成霧).

187   For further details on the crucial political significance of the notion of the "Mandate of Heaven" or tian ming (天命) cf *infra* VII.3.b.

188   Readers who can read French and who want to do a "deep dive" into this well-trodden topic can refer to the following recent article: Jean-Philippe Watbled. "Si je me trompe, je suis" : saint Augustin précurseur de Descartes ?. Travaux& documents, 2019, Journée de l'antiquité et des temps anciens 2018-2019, 54, pp.207-220. hal-02992452

189   無我, *wumo* in Chinese and *muga* in Japanese, is the translation for the Pali term *annatta*, literally "no self," one of the three key doctrinal assertions of Buddhism; readers interested in further exploring the translation dynamics that have shaped Chan and Zen Buddhism can refer to John McCrae's magisterial *Seeing through Zen: Encounter, Transformation, and Geneaology in Chinese Chan Buddhism*, Berkeley: University of California Press, 2003

190   *Confessions* I, opening paragraphs, original translation

191   *Ibid.*, original translation

192   Cf. A. Soble *Eros, Agape, and Philia: Readings in the Philosophy of Love*, Saint Paul, MN: Paragon House, 1998

193   "RSI" 1975 seminar, unedited, p.139 of the edition available on valas. fr

194   Lacan first refers to "extimacy" (*extimité*) on February 10th 1960 in Seminar VII "The Ethics of Psychoanalysis" when discussing pre-historic cave paintings of Altamira and their relationship to the psychoanalytic notion of "sublimation": "At the end of the day, if we begin from what we describe as that *central place*, that *intimate exteriority*, that *extimacy* which is *the Thing*, maybe that will clarify for us what remains still a question, even perhaps a mystery for those who are interested *in this prehistoric art*" p. 285, original translation of the Staferla transcript available at Valas.fr

195   cf. Lidan, Lin. *The Legacy and Future of Orientalism, art. cit.*

Chapter VII

196   *Essays,*III, 13 "On Experience," original translation.

197   Brunschvicg edition, paragraph 593

198   It is surprising that Father Martino Martini's exceptional destiny has not yet been the subject of a fictional adaptation: in addition to being a swashbuckling traveler of the early 17th century, he played a central role in the "Chinese rites controversy" that shook the Catholic Church for over 150 years. Readers that want an extensive historical and critical overview of the controversy, particularly when it comes to its central role in the development of Orientalism, can consult the following article: Giovannetti-Singh, G. (2022). Rethinking the Rites Controversy: Kilian Stumpf's Acta Pekinensia and the Historical Dimensions of a Religious Quarrel. *Modern Intellectual History*, 19(1), 29-53

199   While the term 儒 is habitually translated by "Confucian scholar," I prefer to leave it untranslated following François Jullien's advice: the habitual classificatory categories which emphasizes the difference of "Confucianism" and "Daoism" tends to cover up the broad patterns which tie together "the school of scholars" or *Ru Jiao* (儒家)to the "School of the Way" or *Dao Jiao* (道家).

200   *Chandogya Upanishad* 6.8.7

201   *Mandukya Upanishad* 1.2

202   In Diels-Kranz, *Fragmenter der Vorsokratiker*, 80B4 "περὶ μὲν θεῶν οὐκ ἔχω εἰδέναι, οὔθ᾽ ὡς εἰσὶν οὔθ᾽ ὡς οὐκ εἰσιν οὔθ ὁποῖοί τινες ἰδέαν· πολλὰ γὰρ τὰ κωλύοντά με εἰδέναι, ἥ τε ἀδηλότης καὶ βραχὺς ὢν ὁ βίος ἀνθρώπου.

203   *Critique of Pure Reason*, "Transcendental Dialectic," Book II, Ch. 3 section IV

204   "God is dead! God remains dead! And we have killed him!" in *The Gay Science*, 125, "The Madman"

205   The notion of "emblems" is integral to Marcel Granet's characterization of Chinese ideographic script cf. *La Pensée Chinoise*, op.cit., p.24 and p.117

206   *Shi Jing*, book III "Greater Odes to the Kingdom," ch.1 "Decade of *Wen Wang*", section 1 "*Wen Wang*," par. 4 and 5

207   *Ibid*, section 3 "Mian," par.4

208   Cf. *Mote, F. W.. Imperial China: 900–1800.* Cambridge, MA: Harvard University Press, 1999

209   *De l'Esprit des Lois*, XIX, ch. 17, original translation

210   Cf. *supra* II.2

211   Cf. *Les deux Raisons de la pensée chinoise. op.cit.*

212   *Xunzi*, ch. 19 "*Li lun*," par. 5

213   *Analects*, XVII, 19.

214   Book IV: "Sacrificial Odes of Zhou," Ode 288, "Jing Zhi,"

215   *Zhou Yi*, I "*Yi jing*," 1: Qian "䷀乾"

216   *Zhou Yi*, II. *Tuan Zhuan*, par. 1

217   Cf. *supra* IV.5.b

218   *Zhou Yi*, V.I "*Xi Ci*", 5

219   Cf. *supra* IV.5.b

220   Ch. II "Qi Wu Lun," par. 6

221   Cf. *Supra* II.2.b, II.3.d, and IV.5.b

222   Ch. 2 "*Qi Wu Lun*," par. 1; for more details on the influence of the *Zhuangzi* on the translation and diffusion of Buddhism in China cf H. Saussy (2017), *Zhuangzi Inside/Out: Translation as Citation*, op.cit, and J. McCrae (2003), *Seeing through Zen: Encounter, Genealogy, and Transformation in Chinese Chan Buddhism, op.cit.*

223   Such was indeed the impetus of the various "Neo-Confucian" moments that have peppered Chinese history since the arrival of Buddhism at the turn of the Common Era, nearly 500 years after its development in India. François Jullien's 1989 study on Wang Fuzhi (*Procès ou creation: une introduction à la pensée des lettrés Chinois*) illustrates how the philosophical tenets of Buddhism were still vividly criticized within literati circles, centuries after its establishment in the China.

224   Cf. *Infra* IX.2.b and IX.4.a-b for detailed commentary and analysis of the Zen koan or gong'an tradition in the context of François Jullien's *intercultural philosophy of living.*

225   Cf Giovannetti-Singh, G. Rethinking the Rites Controversy, *art.cit.*

226   J. Derrida (1993), *Sauf le Nom*, Paris, editions Galilée. For a reason that I ignore, the English translation of this text published at Stanford University Press entirely erases the word play at the heart of Derrida's title and argument by translating it as "On the Name;" *Sauf le nom* means both "except the name" and "safe the name," certainly not "on the name" which would be "*Du nom*" or

"sur le nom."

227   Cf *supra* I.2b

Chapter VIII

228   *Metaphysics* A, 3, 984 a 7.

229   As in Plato's *Theaetetus* 155b-d and Aristotle's Metaphysics 982b

230   Cf. Annex I

231   Cf J. Needham, *Science and Civilization in China, op.cit.*

232   Ch. 6 "Da Zong Shi" par. 6, trans. AC Graham, *op.cit.*, p. 54

233   Ch. 33 "Tian Xia" section 6, translation by François Jullien; A.C. Graham translation at *op.cit.* p.254-255

234   Cf. *supra* I.2

235   For an extensive discussion (in French) of the status of the Death Drive in contemporary psychoanalysis cf David-Ménard, Monique, et Beatriz Santos. *Pulsion de mort. Destruction et créations.* Paris, ed. Hermann, 2023

236   *Gesammelte Werke XIII*, p.268, original translation.

237   *Les Fleurs du Mal*, "Spleen et Idéal," XXXVI, "Le Balcon."

238   Levinas, E [1961] 1969. *Totality and infinity: An essay on exteriority*, tr by A Lingis. The Hague: Martinus Nijhoff Publishers. p.55

239   Lucretius, *De Rerum Natura*, III, 830 and 847-851

Camus in the *Myth of Sissyphus* and Sartre in Being and Nothingness.

240   Cf. *infra* IX.2 for a more detailed analysis of Adorno's *Minima Moralia* as they relate to the question of living.

241   In Book VI of Plato's *Republic* (509b-c) Socrates' interlocutor Glaucon laughingly states that the philosophical hypothesis of a super-natural essence of the Good which lies "beyond essence itself (*ep-eikeina tes ousias*)" constitutes a "daimonic hyperbole (*daimonia hyperbolè*)."

242   M. Proust, *A la Recherche du Temps Perdu I: Du côté de chez Swann* [Swann's Way], original translation, passage consultable online at https://alarecherchedutempsperdu.org/marcel-proust/ par. 56

243   *Poetics*, 1457b

244   P. Ricoeur (1975) *The Rule of Metaphor: The Creation of Meaning in Language*, Routledge, London

245   Cf. *On truth and lie in an extra-moral sense*, summer 1873, W. Kauffman translation consultable online at https://jpcatholic.edu/NCUpdf/Nietzsche.pdf

246   The following article provides an excellent scholarly overview of the significance of Shitao's treatise on painting in sinological studies https://www.shanshuiprojects.net/the-philosophy-of-life-in-the-philosophy-of-art-in-shi-taos-huayulu/

Chapter IX

247   175e-177c

248   *A Season in Hell*, "Deliriums I: Mad Virgin, Crazed Husband."

249   Original translation, in *Minima Moralia*, trans. E.F.N. Jephcott, London: Verso Books, 2005, p.19 and p.39

250   145d-e, trans. Harold Fowler with modifications in italics.

251   The expression « beginner's mind » was coined by the Japanese Zen teacher Shunryu Suzuki who played an important role in the transmission of Zen in the United States in the 1960s cf. *Zen Mind, Beginner's Mind: 50th anniversary edition*, Boulder, CO: Shambala Press, 2020

252   *A la Recherche du Temps Perdu vol. 7: Le Temps Retrouvé*, online edition p.463, original translation, highlights and inserts are mine.

253   Cf. J. McRae, *Seeing through Zen, op.cit.*, p.131

254   For a thorough analysis of the important role of poetry in Song dynasty Ch'an cf. Hsieh, D. (2010). Poetry and Chan "Gong'an": From Xuedou Chongxian (980—1052) to Wumen Huikai (1183—1260). *Journal of Song-Yuan Studies, 40*, 39–70. For additional commentary on the *Shijing* cf. *supra* ch. VII.4.c

255   "Spiritual bypassing" refers to an individual's capacity to use spirituality to repress and deny difficult emotions in himself or in others cf. Picciotto, G., Fox, J., & Neto, F. (2018). A phenomenology of spiritual bypass: Causes, consequences, and implications. *Journal of Spirituality in Mental Health, 20*(4), 333–354.

256   "Overturning Platonism, then, means denying the primacy of original over copy, of model over image; glorifying the reign of simulacra and reflections." G. Deleuze, *Difference and Repetition*, p.66. trans. Paul Patton, Columbia University Press, 1994.

257   Cf. *infra* I.2.b for the definition of the dia-logical.

258   "The logic of the double-bind is the paradoxical conjunction of both structure (binding, restriction) and the transgression of structure (expenditure, dissipation) in a given system." C. Johnson, *System and Writing in the Philosophy of Jacques Derrida*, p. 131, Cambridge University Press, 1993

259   *Poem*, I.25

260   The Western term of "enlightenment" is commonly used to translate the character 悟 (*wu* in Chinese, *satori* in Japanese), which was itself used to translate the Pali notion of "bodhi." Whereas the term "englightenment" suggest sa kind of metaphysical illumination, it is interesting to note that the character 悟 was already used in Classical Chinese literature to denote a prosaic and "down to earth" notion of "realization" (cf. *Zhuangzi* ch. 31 "The old Fisherman" par. 4). Once again, we see how foreign ideas about "supernaturality" were demystified as Buddhist texts were translated into Classical Chinese (cf. *supra* VII.6)

261   Such is the case of Robert Aitken's *op.cit.* translation of Ding-Hwa Hsieh's translation *art.cit.* The most sober translation with the deepest commentary can be found in Zenkei Shibayama (1974) *The Gateless Barrier: Zen comments on the Mumonkan*, Boston, MA Shambhala Press: p.42-48. I would like to thank Dr. Naoki Tsukasaki for point,ing me in the direction of this profound take on a story that has long puzzled me.

262   *Zen comments on the Mumonkan*, op.cit., p.46, emphasis in italics is mine.

263   *Ibid*, p.48

264   Pierre Soulages was indeed quite familiar with Zen: the French painter enjoyed long and fruitful dialog with the Japanese poet Itsuji Yoshikawa who introduced him to Zen when he first visited Kyoto in 1958 cf. Itsuji Yoshikawa , *Poèmes*-詩, bilingual edition, Montpellier, FR: Éditions Méridiane, 2022, p.35

Chapter X

265   For an interesting and critical take on the "positive psychology" movement founded by Martin Seligman cf Wong, P. T. P., & Roy, S. (2018). Critique of positive psychology and positive interventions. In N. J. L. Brown, T. Lomas, & F. J. Eiroa-Orosa (Eds.), *The Routledge international handbook of critical positive psychology* (pp. 142–160). Routledge/Taylor & Francis Group.

266   This analysis primarily draws from the exceptional work of the French paleoanthropologist André Leroi-Gourhan who continues to bear significant influence in this domain cf. A. Leroi-Gourhan (1964/1993/2018), *Gesture and Speech*, trans. Anna Bostock Berger, Cambridge, MA: MIT Press

267   Cf. Jacques Franck, « *L'invenzione dello sfumato* », in P. Galluzzi,

La Mente di Leonardo. Nel laboratorio del Genio Universale, Florence, Uffizi, 2006-2007, p. 338-357)

268   The French phenomenologist Jean-Luc Marion offers perhaps clearest perspective on the radicality of Descartes de-coincidence in the history of philosophy cf. J.L. Marion *On Descartes' Passive Thought: The Myth of Cartesian Dualism*, trans. Christina M. Geschwandtner, University of Chicago Press, 2018

269   For a recent take on Galileo's de-coincidence within the history of science and the influence of Alexander Koyré in Galileo studies cf. Jorland, G. (2018). The Posterity of Alexandre Koyré's *Galileo Studies*. In: Pisano, R., Agassi, J., Drozdova, D. (eds) Hypotheses and Perspectives in the History and Philosophy of Science. Springer, Cham. https://doi.org/10.1007/978-3-319-61712-1_12

270   Richard Rorty's concept of the "ironist" in a sense pre-figures the concept of the "de-coincider" cf. *Contingency, Solidarity, and Irony*, Cambridge University Press, 1989, *Quaestiones de Veritate,* section I.3

271   *Quaestiones de Veritate,* section I.3

272   *The Visible and the Invisible* (1964), section I.1, "Reflection and Interrogation," original translation, p.26 of online edition available at http://classiques.uqac.ca/classiques/merleau_ponty_maurice/visible_et_invisible/Le_visible_et_l_invisible.pdf

Annex 1

273   For an excellent in depth-analysis of the critical and influential Sartrean concept of the "singular universal" developed in his 1964 lectures on Kierkegaard at UNESCO cf. Crittenden, Paul (1998) The Singular Universal in Jean-Paul Sartre. *Literature & Aesthetics 8*:29-42.

274   The French philosopher and historian of philosophy Etienne Gilson (1884-1978) remains a foundational reference for understanding Medieval Christian "scholastic" philosophy, a rich and often neglected segment of Western philosophy's history. His works have been widely translated in English and are easily accessible both digitally and in print.

275   The Greek adjective *"holos"* which refers to the idea of "entirety" is a cognate with the English "whole;" the popular adjective "holistic" which is often assigned to ancient Chinese medicinal traditions therefore clearly brings them right back to an Aristotelian understanding of reality, which is of course foreign to them!

276   This scholastic formulation is derived from a commentary of the following passage of Aristotle's *On the soul* 417b23: "what actual sensations apprehends is individuals, while what knowledge (*episteme*) apprehends is universals (*ton katholou*)" (Trans. J.A. Smith)

277   It should be noted that in this regard Ancient China offers us a refreshing counter-point where epistemological, technical, and literary discourse do not stand in such stark opposition cf. P. Unschuld *Huangdi Nei Jing Su Wen: Nature, Knowledge and Imagery in an Ancient Chinese Medical* Text, op. cit. and Kaptchuk, T. J. (1983). *The web that has no weaver: Understanding Chinese medicine.* New York: Congdon & Weed, 1983

278   While the methodologies and postulates of intercultural philosophy have very little to do with Badiou's brilliant albeit theatrical "axiomatic" approach to philosophizing, his remarkably clear and concise book on Paul remains a foundational reference when it comes to developing a historicized and yet philosophical understanding of the concept of the universal cf. *Saint Paul: The Foundation of Universalism*, Trans. Ray Brassier, Stanford University Press, 2003

279   Readers interested in furthering their understanding of the bonds tying together Christianity, Hegelianism and Marxism can refer themselves to the provocative and yet dense take on popular philosopher Slavoj Zizek's own troubled relationship with the Christian legacy of the lacano-communist worldview that he relentlessly professes to the world cf. Chiesa, L. (2012). Christianity or Communism? Žižek's Marxian Hegelianism and Hegelian Marxism. *Revue internationale de philosophie*, 261, 399-420.

280   Two years after writing *The Critique of Pure Reason*, Kant famously stated: "I freely confess: it was the objection of David Hume which first, many years ago, interrupted my dogmatic slumber" (4:260) in *Prolegomena to Any Future Metaphysics*. Ed. Gary Hatfield, Cambridge University Press, 2003. A recent scholarly book is exclusively devoted to the analyses of the critical significance of this famous sentence within the architecture of Kant's universalist philosophical project cf. A. Anderson, *Kant, Hume, and the Interruption of Dogmatic Slumber*, Oxford University Press, 2020

281   Linus Hagström, Astrid H M Nordin (2020) China's "Politics of Harmony" and the Quest for Soft Power in International Politics, *International Studies Review*, Volume 22, Issue 3, Pages 507–525

282   Cf. Steinberger, P. J. (2008). Hobbes, Rousseau and the Modern Conception of the State. *The Journal of Politics*, 70(3), 595–611.

283   Julia Kristeva's *Powers of Horrors: An Essay on Abjection* (trans. Leon Boudiez, Columbia University Press, 1982) remains the definitive work when it comes to a universalizing understanding the phenomenological and psy-

choanalytic approach to this topic.

284   *Lian hui wang* I.7

285   *Mengzi* 2A.6 (*Gong sun Chou I*).

Annex II

286   *The Standard Edition* translates *Das Unhemlich* as "The Uncanny" to evoke the troubling dimension of the literary effect that Freud is trying to bring to light; the literal translation of *unheimlich* "unhomely" and by extension "unhomeliness," is perhaps less evocative but more relevant in an intercultural reflection where the question of what feels "homely" and what doesn't is central.

287   The term « paradigm » should be understood here as a broad reference to cultural and epistemological systems of *representation*. In this sense, François Jullien's intercultural philosophy very much inscribes itself in the continuity of the project articulated by Michel Foucault in *The Order of Things* and in the *Archeology of Knowledge*: to reflect upon the *conditions of possibility* which led to the (dis)appearance and (non)emergence of topics, modes of knowing and modes of governing across cultural spaces and eras.

288   The tune *Liu Shui* or "Flowing Water(s)" fully inscribes itself in the Shan Shui esthetic paradigm: Classical Chinese musicological treatises associate it with another ancient tune, Gao Shan (高山)or "High Mountain(s)." According to the traditional narrative, the song expresses the grief of the literati Bo Ya mourning the death of his friend the farmer Zi Qi. Readers who wish to listen to the song and obtain further historical details can consult the excellent online resource Silkqin.com: http://www.silkqin.com/02qnpu/07sqmp/sq06ls.htm

289   An early example of such a governmental ideology of Harmony can be found in the canonical *Book of Rites* or *Liji*: "In olden times, behavioral norms determined the Way, music harmonized the voices, government unified conduct, and punishment prevented villainy" (故禮以道其志，樂以和其聲，政以一其行，刑以防其奸) ch. 18 "Yue Ji" or "treatise on music" par. 2

290   Cf. Laplanche, Jean; Pontalis, Jean-Bertrand (1988). "Attention, (Evenly) Suspended or Poised". *The Language of Psychoanalysis*. Karnac Books. pp. 43–44

291   M. David-Ménard, *Deleuze and psychoanalysis*, Paris, PUF, 2005, p. 84, p. 87-88

292   For more information on this melody (the current form is of recent invention) cf. http://www.silkqin.com/02qnpu/07sqmp/sq14szsy.htm